Regionalism and World Order

Regionalism and World Order

Edited by

Andrew Gamble

and

Anthony Payne

St. Martin's Press
New York

REGIONALISM AND WORLD ORDER
Selection, editorial matter, and Chapters 1 and 8 copyright © 1996 by
Andrew Gamble and Anthony Payne
Individual chapters (in order) copyright © 1996 by Stephen George,
Ian Kearns, Anthony Payne, Jean Grugel, Glenn Hook, Ngai-Ling Sum

St. Martin's Press, Scholarly and Reference Division,
175 Fifth Avenue, New York, N.Y. 10010

First published in the United States of America in 1996

Printed in Malaysia

ISBN 0–312–15987–0 (cloth)
ISBN 0–312–15988–9 (paper)

Library of Congress Cataloging-in-Publication Data applied for

Contents

v

List of Abbreviations

AFL-CIO	American Federation of Labor–Congress of Industrial Organizations
AFTA	American Free Trade Area
APEC	Asia-Pacific Economic Co-operation
ARF	ASEAN Regional Forum
ASEAN	Association of Southeast Asian Nations
CACM	Central American Common Market
CARICOM	Caribbean Community
CBI	Caribbean Basin Initiative
CFE	Conventional Forces in Europe
CFSP	Common Foreign and Security Policy
CMEA	Council for Mutual Economic Assistance
CSCAP	Council for Security and Co-operation in the Asia-Pacific
CSCE	Conference on Security and Co-operation in Europe
EAEC	East Asia Economic Council
EAEC	East Asian Economic Caucus
EAI	Enterprise for the Americas Initiative
EBRD	European Bank for Reconstruction and Development
ECAFE	Economic Commission for Asia and the Far East
ECLA	Economic Commission for Latin America
ECSC	European Coal and Steel Community
EEC	European Economic Community
EMS	European Monetary System
EPC	European Political Co-operation
EPG	Eminent Persons Group (of APEC)
ERM	Exchange Rate Mechanism
ESCAP	Economic and Social Commission for Asia and the Pacific

EU	European Union
Euratom	European Atomic Energy Community
FDI	foreign direct investment
FTA	free-trade agreement
G7	Group of Seven
GATT	General Agreement on Tariffs and Trade
GDP	Gross Domestic Product
GSP	Generalised System of Preferences
IEA	International Energy Agency
IMF	International Monetary Fund
IPE	international political economy
ISI	import-substitution industrialisation
JCP	Japan Communist Party
JSP	Japan Socialist Party
LAC	Latin America(n) and Caribbean
LAFTA	Latin American Free Trade Association
LDP	Liberal Democratic Party (of Japan)
MERCOSUR	El Mercado Común del Sur
MFN	Most Favoured Nation
MITI	Ministry of International Trade and Industry (of Japan)
NAFTA	North American Free Trade Agreement
NATO	North Atlantic Treaty Organisation
NIC	Newly Industrialising Country
OAS	Organisation of American States
OECD	Organisation for Economic Co-operation and Development
OEM	Original Equipment Manufacturing
OPEC	Organisation of Petroleum Exporting Countries
PAFTAD	Pacific Trade and Development
PAFTA	Pacific Free Trade Area
PBEC	Pacific-Basin Economic Council
PECC	Pacific Economic Co-operation Conference
PFP	Partnership for Peace
PHARE	Poland and Hungary: Aid for Economic Reconstruction
PMC	Post-Ministerial Conference (of ASEAN)
PRC	People's Republic of China
PRI	Partido Revolucionario Institucional (of Mexico)
ROK	Republic of Korea

SAFTA	South American Free Trade Area
SDF	Self Defence Forces (of Japan)
SEA	Single European Act
SEATO	South-East Asian Treaty Organisation
TEU	Treaty on European Union
UPD	Unidad para la Promoción de la Democracia (of the OAS)
WEU	Western European Union
WTO	Warsaw Treaty Organisation
WTO	World Trading Organisation

Preface

This book constitutes the first output of one of several new research groups set up under the auspices of the Political Economy Research Centre (PERC) of the University of Sheffield in late 1993. PERC itself was created in the belief that the perspectives of the past cannot address the problems posed by the world-wide economic and political transformation of the last decade. Its mission is thus to explore the new issues in political economy from an interdisciplinary standpoint. The research group which we jointly convened sought to tackle the most basic implications of this transformation by focusing directly upon the concept of world order. It subsequently decided to enter this debate by examining the contemporary trend towards regionalism. We have met many times amongst ourselves and with other colleagues and research students who have therefore also contributed indirectly to the book. In addition, we owe a particular debt to the Nissho Iwai Foundation and the Chubu Electric Power Company which jointly helped fund our work on regionalism. Thanks to their support we were able to benefit from the views of a number of Japanese academic colleagues and friends. The editors are also grateful to Dominic Kelly for preparing the index.

Sheffield   ANDREW GAMBLE
                                               ANTHONY PAYNE

Notes on the Contributors

Andrew Gamble is Professor of Politics at the University of Sheffield.

Anthony Payne is Professor of Politics at the University of Sheffield.

Stephen George is Jean Monnet Professor of Politics at the University of Sheffield.

Jean Grugel is Lecturer in Politics at the University of Sheffield.

Glenn Hook is Professor of Japanese Studies at the University of Sheffield.

Ian Kearns is Lecturer in Politics at the University of Sheffield.

Ngai-Ling Sum is Alex Horsley Research Fellow in the Political Economy Research Centre at the University of Sheffield.

1 Introduction: The Political Economy of Regionalism and World Order

ANTHONY PAYNE and ANDREW GAMBLE

This book seeks to assess the origins, significance and likely evolution of the trend towards regionalism within the world order of the 1990s. Many observers have seen this development as threatening, warning that the world may presently be in the process of becoming dangerously divided between three broad regions – Europe, the Americas and Asia-Pacific. They focus on the so-called 'fortress' dimension of the 1992 project in the European Union (EU), offer an alarmist reading of the defensive impulse supposedly lying behind the negotiation of the North American Free Trade Agreement (NAFTA) and do all they can to write up the salience of initiatives such as Asia-Pacific Economic Co-operation (APEC). These diverse initiatives are then quickly constructed into a 'regional bloc scenario' which is used to stoke fears of 'trade wars' between the blocs leading to 'real wars'. All of this, it might be added, is usually accompanied by casual reference to the supposed lessons of the 1930s and the inexorable descent into world war which followed the unfortunate regionalist tendencies of that decade.

The problem with this line of interpretation – which has become something of a conventional wisdom, especially in journalistic circles – is that it is grounded intellectually in a particular body of international theory which is itself fundamentally flawed. The so-called 'hegemonic stability thesis' does indeed argue that, in the absence of an effective hegemon to

1

keep order, the world will degenerate into conflict which in the present era is most likely to be manifested between regional blocs of states. The authors of this book reject this assumption. They take regionalism seriously and are prepared to relate the growth of regionalism to the question of hegemony, but they do not proceed on the basis of the normative considerations which underpin mainstream notions of hegemonic stability. Instead, they adopt an approach which focuses upon the issue of state strategy and conceives of regionalism as a state-led or states-led project designed to reorganise a particular regional space along defined economic and political lines. However, they also seek to set their analyses of regionalist developments in Europe, the Americas and Asia-Pacific against a specific background. This highlights the economic and political pressures which increasingly make for globalisation and notes that the world is actually becoming more unified as barriers to trade and financial and cultural flows continue to be dismantled. This thesis must be taken on board, although it can easily be exaggerated and should certainly not be presented, as is sometimes the case, as the diametric opposite of the regional bloc scenario. Another more sensible claim is that the relationship between these two apparently competing tendencies in the contemporary world political economy – regionalism as a statist project and globalisation as a social process – appears still to be in the balance and indeed that there is no reason to assume that one must necessarily triumph over the other. It should also be noted at this point that the reverse concepts, namely globalism defined as a state-led political project conceived at the global level and regionalisation defined as a social process manifest at the regional level, cannot be excluded from the framework of analysis.

This first chapter reviews the main strands of the theoretical literature which can be used to illuminate such an enquiry. It begins by developing the argument, already briefly stated, that mainstream theories of international political economy (IPE), essentially those of neo-realism and neo-liberalism in ever closer conjunction, do not constitute a satisfactory basis on which to embark upon an enquiry into contemporary regionalism. It goes on to set out the essential elements of the 'new IPE' which a small, but growing, number of critical theorists deploy as their

way into these kinds of debates. It then uses some of these
ideas to offer an alternative, although necessarily abbreviated,
account of the development of the 'world orders' of the modern era, focusing on the problems of transition generated by
the hegemonic decline of the United States over the last two
decades. Finally, it raises the key research questions about the
construction of state-led regionalist projects in the contemporary era to which the chapters of the book respond.

Mainstream theories of international political economy

As is well-known, mainstream IPE has been built over the last
two decades around dominant neo-realist and neo-liberal or-
thodoxies. As it initially developed as a separate field of study
within North American international relations scholarship in
the 1970s, the debate between these paradigms was genuine
and lively. Keohane and Nye set the pace with their studies of
transnational and transgovernmental relations and coined the
term 'complex interdependence' to encapsulate what they saw
as the new web of linkages across trade, finance and resource
issues within which states were increasingly caught.[1] Although
they were building on earlier liberal arguments developed by
the functionalists and neo-functionalists, their ideas nevertheless proved unable to withstand the counter-attack mounted
by the new neo-realist school. Its distinctiveness was the combination of the classical realist insistence upon the primacy of
the state in international relations with the rational choice
assumption of neo-classical economics that states were best
understood as utility maximisers. The work of Krasner was
particularly influential[2] and served to inspire a burgeoning neo-
realist orthodoxy in the literature which 'bolted tight the doors'
against 'arguments that were most likely to deliver the "social
depth" to the analysis of international power that the idea of
complex interdependence invited'.[3]

Yet defeat and triumph are not the best metaphors by which
to characterise the theoretical evolution of mainstream IPE.
Crane and Amawi's recent review points instead to a gradual
process of cross-fertilisation, and ultimately convergence, between the neo-liberal and neo-realist strands of the emergent

sub-discipline since these early disputes. They argue that thinking has lately come to cohere around three focal points – rational action theories of the state, the theory of hegemonic stability, and regime theory.[4] In other words, IPE, simply put, has become a discourse constructed around a particular view of the hegemonic state. The extent of the literature generated in this vein of analysis has been enormous. Kindleberger and Gilpin dominated the debate about the need for a stabiliser to manage the world economy but did not actually use the term hegemony.[5] As a result, the most-cited definition has been provided by Keohane himself who described hegemony as a 'preponderance of material resources'.[6] For him, the elements of hegemonic power, as they relate to the world economy, were comprised of control over raw materials, markets and capital as well as 'competitive advantages in the production of highly valued goods . . . involving the use of complex or new technology'.[7] These material resources then provided the means by which the hegemon could both make and enforce the rules of the world political economy. Power is thus conceived in traditional resource terms and hegemony is deployed as force. It is perhaps worth noting here that world-systems theorists like Wallerstein, although operating generally from a different theoretical perspective to that of the neo-realists, converge in offering a definition of hegemony as primarily economic in origin.[8] Wallerstein adds only the suggestion that hegemony is gained and lost in a particular sequence of preponderance (production, commerce, finance) and that it only exists when advantage is simultaneously held in all three spheres of economic activity.

This conception of hegemony has set up a number of specific debates. One has disputed the normative manner in which hegemonic power is exercised, positions ranging from the vision of hegemony as the provision of international public goods (Kindleberger) to the imposition of 'self-regarding' actions designed to shape the system to particular advantage (Gilpin). Snidal has usefully reviewed this strand of the literature, distinguishing overall between benign hegemony exercised by persuasion, benign hegemony exercised by coercion, and exploitative hegemony.[9] Another prolific debate has concerned the impact of the loss of US hegemony, which is nearly always presumed, on the viability of the various post-war 'regimes' designed to improve international economic co-operation. Krasner himself has been the key figure here, defining a regime as a set of 'principles, norms, rules and decision making procedures around which actor expectations converge in a given area of international relations'.[10] The substantive issue at stake in the debate relates to the autonomy of regimes once their hegemonic creator begins to decline.[11] A third, and logically prior, debate has addressed the very matter of whether the United States has indeed lost its hegemonic position. This aspect of the IPE debate moved from the academic to the political and media worlds in the US in the late 1980s. 'Declinists' vied with 'revivalists' in studios and *op.ed.* columns as well as in the journals, although without advancing the theoretical clarity of the concept of hegemony to any significant degree or ever resolving the matter of whether or not the US was in decline.[12] A final, and still current, debate couched in these same broad terms disputes how best to explain international economic co-operation. The neo-realists emphasise the importance of relative gains in conditions of international anarchy and consider that this inhibits co-operation; the neo-liberals assume that states are more concerned with absolute welfare maximisation and are thus more inclined to believe that co-operation can be learned.[13]

The theoretical underpinnings of this whole approach are marked by a number of biases which render many of the attendant arguments deficient.[14] The definition of the core concept of hegemony was based upon a limited range of variables, largely drawn from a selective reading of the US post-war experience minimally qualified by reference to nineteenth-century Britain. Geopolitical power, rather oddly, was usually omitted, Keohane providing only a partial exception by talking about security as a 'prestige good'.[15] Other questions were also excluded from consideration, notably the matter of why some states came to accept and others resist the rule of the hegemon. Additionally, the vital issue – for an approach which believed in the measurement of power – of exactly how much power was needed to engender hegemony was never satisfactorily resolved. One could go on. In the end, Ikenberry was right to suggest that 'the texture of hegemonic power has not been captured' in the major American texts of the IPE literature.[16] In fact, the criticism can be widened to embrace the whole thrust of mainstream IPE theory. Leaver concludes his survey of recent neo-realist and neo-liberal theorising by suggesting that Crane and Amawi's process of convergence, which he accepts has occurred, is 'evidence of involution rather than evolution'.[17] Higgott notes that mainstream theory is 'no longer a self-evident way of enframing the study of power in IPE'.[18] Strange is typically the most robust of all in her call for a clearing of the decks. In an essay published at the beginning of 1995 she called unequivocally for the abandonment of both neo-realism in the study of international relations and liberalism and neo-classical notions of equilibrium in the study of economics. For IPE, she said, they were 'culs-de-sac, *strade senza uscita*, no through roads'.[19]

New international political economy

Underpinning all these critiques of mainstream IPE, but not always articulated, was an important philosophical point. It was made most effectively by Murphy and Tooze in a volume which first advanced the call for a 'new' (or heterodox or critical or counter-hegemonic) IPE.[20] They argued that, beneath the surface impression of a field where many voices were heard, there existed a methodological orthodoxy which shaped much of the substantive output of mainstream IPE. This orthodoxy was characterised by a largely unquestioning positivism and overrode the apparent contest between the respective concepts and theoretical constructs of realism, liberalism and neo-Marxism, the conventional competing paradigms of the IPE field.[21] In other words, Murphy and Tooze identified the IPE mainstream not so much by its preoccupation with, or privileging of, certain issues (although that was certainly part of their critique) but rather by its commitment to a mode of production of knowledge dependent upon the belief that the separation of subject and object and fact and value are unproblematic.

A different approach is developed by Robert Cox, who argues that 'theory is always *for* someone and *for* some purpose'.[22] This claim appeared in a remarkable piece of theoretical writing

first published in the journal *Millennium* in 1981 and entitled
'Social Forces, States, and World Orders: Beyond International
Relations Theory'. This article is really the founding document
of new IPE and, as such, deserves considerable attention in
this preliminary review of the IPE field. Cox made his comment
about the bias of theory in the course of drawing a distinction
between problem-solving theory and critical theory. The former
took the world as it found it, concentrating its attention on
making the existing relationships and institutions work more
smoothly. It was grounded in a positivist political economy and
was typified by most US neo-realist and neo-liberal scholarship
from the 1970s onwards. The latter, by contrast, was 'critical
in the sense that it stands apart from the prevailing order of
the world and asks how that order came about'.[23] It was a theory
of history concerned not just with the past but with a continuing process of change; it was directed to the social and political complex as a whole rather than to its separate parts; and it
contained within its brief the possibility of identifying the outlines of alternative distributions of power from those prevailing at any particular time. In short, from this moment onwards,
new IPE was hitched to a different epistemology from the
mainstream. It favoured a reflectivist position which stressed
the relationship of subject and object rather than the conventional position which insisted upon their separation.

On this basis Cox proceeded to set out his version of a critical theory appropriate to the study of international political
economy. He proposed a method of historical structures, defined as configurations of forces (material capabilities, ideas
and institutions) which do not determine actions but nevertheless create opportunities and impose constraints. There is
presumed 'no one-way determinism'[24] between the three forces,
the question of which way the lines of influence run always
being conceived as a research question. It is also important to
stress that in this view people are not just bearers of structures; they create them. For Cox historical structures mean no
more, but no less, than persistent social practices, made by
collective human activity and transformed through collective
human activity. Within IPE, interaction between material capabilities, ideas and institutions is seen to take place across three
interrelated levels: the social forces engendered by different

and changing production processes; the varying forms of state/
society complexes (not just states); and types of world order.
This last concept is an important one in Cox's lexicon. He
acknowledged world-systems theory as a valuable radical alternative to conventional international relations theory, but argued
that the notion of world order was preferable to that of world-
system because it indicated a structure which may only have a
limited duration in time and which does not have the inevitable
equilibrium connotation of system. Order, it should be noted,
'is used in the sense of the way things usually happen'; it does
not imply 'orderliness' or lack of turbulence in international
affairs.[25]

What is particularly appealing about Cox's formulation of a
critical theory for IPE is the way he has consciously sought to
draw upon the best insights of other preceding perspectives.
He thus argues in broadly conventional terms that the varying
forms of state which derive from different state/society complexes still remain the crucial level of analysis. But, in addition, he also incorporates into his thinking the wide reach of
world-systems theory, the traditional historical materialist concern with social forces, and the particular Gramscian preoccupation with ideas and ideologies as sources of power. This last
aspect of the package, which was developed more fully by Cox
in another later article which served to introduce Gramsci's
ideas to the international relations community, was especially
important because, as we have seen, mainstream IPE has always
been very much preoccupied with materialist definitions of power.
Yet, as Cox himself has put it, 'ideas and material conditions
are always bound together, mutually influencing one another,
and not reducible one to the other'.[26] The insertion of an idealist
dimension into the standard framework of analysis was thus
another novel feature distinguishing new IPE from the
mainstream.

The greater richness of such a perspective can be demonstrated most effectively by counterposing the Coxian, or neo-
Gramscian, account of hegemony with that offered by neo-realist
and neo-liberal IPE for which, it will be remembered, it constitutes the core concept. For Cox hegemony means 'more than
the dominance of a single world power'. Instead, it is understood as 'dominance of a particular kind where the dominant

state creates an order based ideologically on a broad measure
of consent, functioning according to general principles that in
fact ensure the continuing supremacy of the leading state or
states and leading social classes but at the same time offer some
measure or prospect of satisfaction to the less powerful'.[27] Thus
'there can be dominance without hegemony; hegemony is one
possible form dominance may take'.[28] Crucially, hegemony is
seen as bringing together both coercive *and* consensual elements
of power. It is important to emphasise this. Although the novelty
of this approach *compared* to most of the mainstream lies in
the attention it gives to the role of ideology in establishing
and maintaining a hegemonic world order, it does also theorise
the objective elements of power which lead to the capacity for
the exercise, ultimately, of coercion. Power is conceived, famously,
as a centaur, part man, part beast, with different elements deployed in different situations. Broadly, the stronger the position of the ruling group or state, the less the need for the use
of force. In sum, it is not difficult to see that Coxian theory is
substantially more nuanced than mainstream approaches and
enables analysts to catch more of the essence of hegemony.

There are some problems with Cox's account of hegemony,
notably a failure fully to separate out all the various elements
which constitute hegemony across different structures of power.[29]
He has also rightly been taken to task for consistently stressing
the importance of ideas in his theoretical work and yet falling
back on more straightforward class analysis in his empirical
work.[30] Even so, his innovativeness has been crucial in opening up the field of new IPE. He has served to inspire and legitimise both a wider and a deeper range of thinking than was
previously possible. New IPE presently constitutes a loose col-
lege of scholars and a diverse range of approaches. One would
include within its ambit, *inter alia*, the work of the neo-struc-
turalists,[31] some of the more sensitive refinements now being
made to early world-systems theory,[32] institutionalist economics,[33]
the French regulation school,[34] and many of the accounts of
political economy deriving from scholars from the developing
world,[35] as well as the neo-Gramscian and Gramscian schools
that have flowed directly from Cox's lead.[36] What they all have
in common and, most importantly, what differentiates them
from the mainstream is, firstly, a commitment to give due weight

to both structure *and* agency in their explanations, and, secondly, an awareness that globalisation, although still uneven
and incomplete, is nevertheless sufficiently developed to have
established a new context within which IPE has to be rethought.

The development of modern world orders

As already indicated, new IPE approaches possess a commitment to historical analysis and seek habitually to analyse the
dilemmas of the present and the possibilities for the future by
reference to the limitations of the past. A prior task before
turning to the detailed explication of the contemporary era is
therefore to give a brief contextual account of the development of world order in the modern period. The objective here
is not to bring forward new evidence but rather to retell familiar events by reference to the Coxian view of hegemony.

From this perspective, the obvious starting point is the emergence of a liberal world order spanning broadly the period from
1789 to the 1870s. The liberal state was initially forged in Britain and it was British power and prestige which transmitted
the norms of liberal economics and politics to much of the
rest of the world during the nineteenth century. The *Pax
Britannica* was characterised by an open trading world, free
movement of capital and persons and a real indifference as to
whether or not peripheral countries were formally independent (for example, Argentina) or under the control of a colonial power (for example, Canada). What mattered was that
the rules of the international economy were observed and, where
necessary, policed. The latter was a relatively rare requirement
since most states were only too glad to have access to British
capital and technology, but when and where it was needed British
naval power was the crucial enforcer. In this period of hegemony,
which reached its apogee in the 1850s and 1860s, there were
no formal international institutions of world order: for the most
part the City of London was capable of administering and regu-
lating the liberal order on its own.

This world order began to be undermined in the last decades of the nineteenth century. The liberal form of state was
challenged as the incorporation of the new industrial labour

forces of capitalism necessitated an extension of the range of
state action in the direction of economic intervention and the
embrace of welfare policy. This fed in turn a politics of protectionism and an expansionary search for new overseas markets and colonies. In the process Britain found its supremacy
overtaken by the rise of Germany and then the United States.
Nascent international institutions came into being after the First
World War but could not be sustained in the absence of an
accepted hegemon possessed of a universalistic ideology. Following their collapse the world order degenerated into an era
characterised by the rivalry of regional power blocs. As well as
having visible trade and military dimensions, this rivalry had
an ideological significance since it could also be construed as
reflecting a contest between welfare, Fascist and Marxist–Leninist
forms of state. The world order was in the end only rescued
from the destructive implications of this era by the US triumph
in the Second World War.

Against such a background, the 'golden years' of the post-
war *Pax Americana* were marked by the remarkably successful
combination of two processes – the reassertion of liberal economic ideas and values across western Europe and their espousal
within the vast majority of the new emerging states of the Third
World, on the one hand, and the containment of the major
alternative world order which had emerged after 1917 under
the leadership of the Soviet Union and was legitimised by
reference to the appeal of a Marxist–Leninist form of socialism, on the other. The steady, if uneven, reconstruction of a
liberal international economic order, characterised by the freeing
of trade between national economies and the eventual
convertibility of other major Western currencies with the US
dollar, thus went hand in hand with the development of national
security states in the West, characterised by the acquisition of
nuclear arsenals, a readiness to fight localised wars in the Third
World and the deployment of intelligence operatives for
subversive purposes. In this sense, the Truman Doctrine was
the other side of the coin to the Marshall Plan, the destabilisation
of radical Third-World regimes the counterpoint to the many
programmes of development aid. The rhetoric of the Cold War,
extolling 'freedom' over 'repression', was the ideological cement
which bound the whole system together, although it should be

noted that the actual form of capitalism which mostly prevailed
in this early post-war period was an 'embedded liberal' variant
committed to a measure of state economic intervention and
welfare provision.[37]

This order was managed by the US with growing confidence
until the late 1960s and early 1970s. The key event which marked
the onset of crisis was the Vietnam War, the most ambitious
expression of US post-war containment strategy. The long boom
of the Bretton Woods era, which ran through the 1950s and
into the 1960s restoring western Europe and Japan to prosperity and buoying up the early developmental aspirations of
many Third-World countries, had been largely funded by the
willingness of the US to export liquidity to the rest of the Western
world via official loans, corporate investment and military
expenditure. This 'dollar overhang', as the jargon dubbed the
gap between US foreign-exchange reserves and the extent of
its financial liabilities overseas, was already considerable as involvement in Vietnam began to deepen.[38] The dollar's status
as the core currency of the system could not in the end survive the combination of enormous US expenditure on the war
in south-east Asia and the unwillingness of US politicians to
tax their people sufficiently to cover the costs of the global
operations of the US state. President Nixon's devaluation of
the dollar in August 1971 and the suspension of its convertibility into gold has thus to be understood as the moment which
signalled the end of an era.

Because the post-war world order was a *Pax Americana*, these
problems were problems for the whole of the West. The inability of the US to manage the world economy in a financially
responsible way served to transmit inflation internationally. This
stimulated further cost pressures and falls in profit levels in
the advanced Western countries, which in turn generated fiscal
crises imperilling the welfare commitments of the post-war period.
It also created pressures to push up raw material prices in
peripheral economies, as effected most dramatically of all by
the OPEC countries in 1973 and as subsequently articulated in
Third-World demands for the negotiation of a 'New International
Economic Order'. In the US, unlike other developed capitalist
states, Presidents Nixon, Ford and Carter were still able to
counter recessionary conditions by stimulating the economy

towards full employment, but only by continuing to run a deficit and thus in effect forcing devalued dollars on US allies in exchange for the maintenance of its defence guarantee of the West. In so doing, the dollar slipped from 'top-currency' to 'negotiated-currency' status.[39] The overall impact was to bring about a diffusion of power within the global political economy, with labour gaining *vis-à-vis* capital and western Europe, Japan and parts of the Third World gaining *vis-à-vis* the US.

The reaction came in the form of an attempt by the US to reassert control of the system during the course of the 1980s by means of the political economy of Reaganism. Feeding upon a popular emotional rejection of the new realities of US power, or 'weaknesses', which Jimmy Carter had asked the US people to confront, President Reagan offered the twin prospectus of 'militarism' and 'monetarism'. The former involved a major re-arming of the US military machine designed to allow the US once again to 'walk tall' on the world stage. More specifically, its purposes were to defeat Third-World nationalism, which was wrongly but deliberately interpreted as the advance of Communism, and also to force the Soviet Union into what proved to be a final decisive arms race which would divert resources from its attempts to shore up its increasingly stagnant economy. The latter was premised upon increasing profit margins, weakening trade unions, eliminating inflation through the adoption of monetarist macro-economic management and boosting growth by means of supply-side economics. It also sought to impose the same neo-liberal economic doctrine within the multilateral financial institutions in which the US voice was still critical. In other words, the thinking behind this strategy sought to re-create behind the rhetoric of the 'Second Cold War' a new mixture of consent and coercion comparable in effect to that which had characterised the establishment of the *Pax Americana* after 1945.

It only partly worked. It succeeded to the extent that the economic ideas of the neo-liberals spread widely, whether adopted enthusiastically by allies of the US or forced upon reluctant reformist Third-World regimes in the name of 'structural adjustment' by the combined pressures of the IMF, the World Bank and the US Agency for International Development. Under Reagan, the US also demonstrated again its willingness to intervene, by force if necessary, in intimidating regimes, such as those in Nicaragua and Libya, which stood out against its interests and its world view. In 1985, in an even more dramatic shift, the Soviet Union embarked upon the process of *perestroika*, a restructuring of its own internal economic and political arrangements deliberately intended by the new leadership under Gorbachev to open up Soviet society to outside influence from the West. And yet, in the final analysis, the US under Reagan was not able to reconstitute its control of the world order. In part, the failure was a consequence of the administration's unwillingness, like that of its predecessors in the 1960s and 1970s, to tackle the problem of the endemic trading and expenditure deficits of the US economy. It also obviously reflected the continuing growth in strength of the economies of Japan and western Europe, the latter increasingly enmeshed and protected by the structures of the European Community, as well as the emergence of other successful export-oriented economies in the so-called Newly Industrialising Countries (NICs) of east Asia.

As regards the US, this account of the post-war world order implies that 'hegemony has given way to domination'.[40] Within a non-hegemonic world order, the power of the US unquestionably remains preponderant – certainly in the military sphere given the demise of the Soviet Union, substantially too in the ideological domain given its continuing leadership of old and new organs of international management such as the IMF and the Group of Seven (G7) summits, and also, not least, to a very considerable degree still in economic matters. The size and technological vigour of the US economy, the origins of much international capitalist enterprise in the US, and the continuing centrality of the US dollar as an international currency are all factors which continue to make the US the most formidable single national player in the world economy. What is different is that the US is no longer powerful enough to shape on its own the rules of a consensual hegemonic order. It has not been willing or able to initiate a new Bretton Woods; it has not even sought consistently to use the G7 process to shape the economic policies of the leading Western states; and although it did succeed in putting together a powerful coalition to fight the Gulf War in 1991 it had to rely upon German,

Japanese and Arab funds to pay for its military effort. In short, the US no longer possesses that self-reinforcing and largely unchallenged primacy across *all* the necessary constituent elements of hegemonic power. Without this, it is reduced to mortal status, increasingly likely to behave in the same fashion and be constrained in the same way as other leading states in the world.

The contours of the contemporary world order

Viewed in this way, the contemporary world order is immediately rendered a quite different phenomenon from the post-1945 period with which, relatively speaking, we have become so familiar. It may be too that there are no historical precedents which can routinely illuminate present and future prospects. An important argument deriving from an awareness of the extent of globalisation in fact suggests that, during the crisis of US global hegemony in the 1970s and its attempted reconstitution in the 1980s, control of the world order slipped beyond the capacity of any single state and perhaps even any group of states. Moving into the vacuum left by the vagaries of US financial policy after 1971 and then both inspiring and drawing sustenance from the ascendancy of neo-liberal ideas during the Reagan years, a 'transnational managerial class' or 'an international business civilisation' has come to the fore, based in the major private banks and global corporations.[41] Under its auspices a genuine *global* economy, grounded in production and finance, has been created, replacing the former Bretton Woods *international* economy premised upon exchange relations between national economies. This change contains within it other technological and organisational features, such as robotisation, the dematerialisation of production and post-Fordism, which are much discussed in the literatures. Nevertheless, the formative aspect of the new global political economy is seen to be the structural power of internationally mobile capital.[42] States now have to recognise the power not only of other states and inter-state organisations, on which international relations analysis has traditionally focused, but also of international capital, the banks and the foreign exchange markets, all of which constantly scrutinise what states are doing and have the means, by either bestowing or withdrawing their favour, to force them to adopt economic policies appropriate to capitalist interests.

This argument, even in its weaker forms, changes the way we have to think about the behaviour of states. The process has been described within new IPE as the internationalisation or transnationalisation of the state, by which is meant, simply put, the adjustment of national political practices to the exigencies of the global economy.[43] In other words, all states – the strong and the weak, the ex-hegemon as well as the would-be developer – now have to react to the pressures of global production, choosing broadly between an offensive strategy which takes on the challenge and usually gives some support to the competitive thrust of national industries, and a defensive strategy which enshrines protection and seeks to effect at least a partial withdrawal from world competition in some sectors. In practice, during the course of the 1980s and early 1990s the choice has been increasingly resolved in the former direction. Nearly all states now seek, as it were, to ride two tigers simultaneously: they have to respond to the structural power of international capital, which demands the continuing openness of the world economy, *and* to the continuing pull of national interests of various sorts, which requires that they compete for relative advantage in the global economy as effectively as possible.

Once more Cox, writing in 1987, detected more clearly than most what may be the implications of these changes for the future of the world order. In his view, they did not imply that the world was moving towards a system of self-contained economic-strategic blocs similar to the trend of the 1930s. The world order was, however, likely to be characterised more and more by 'an aggressively competitive trading pattern in which negotiating power ... determines outcomes', albeit in a way 'which tends to encourage an emulative uniformity in the way problems are confronted and solved rather than withdrawal into isolated spheres within which distinctive solutions can be attempted'.[44] In sum, Cox suggested that regionalist and globalising tendencies would coexist in the next post-hegemonic phase of the world order. What was understandably left unexplored at that time was the precise nature of this coexistence. This is the area of analysis which this book seeks to develop.

Its central research questions can be expressed as follows: first, to what extent have states been responding to the end of US hegemony by seeking either to build or join regionalist projects, and, second, to the degree that they have, what sort of regionalist projects are coming into being? Furthermore, the method of enquiry explicitly draws attention to the ideological aspects of region definition and region building and certainly does not presume the existence of natural or immutable regions. Regionalism is seen as something that is being constructed, and constantly reconstructed, by collective human action. Accordingly, all the chapters not only consider the economic and security policies that have lately been pursued by key states within the region in question but also discuss whether or not ideological power has been or is being used to define, shape, or give identity to that region. The regions are also explored in each case by reference to the differing roles of the putative 'core' state (or states), on the one hand, and likely 'peripheral' states, on the other.

A range of specific questions are inevitably raised by such a study. They include the following. Why has a regionalist project been going on in western Europe for so much longer than anywhere else? To what extent did the 1992 project of the EU reflect an attempt to reposition itself within the world order? Are there social and political forces within the EU likely to promote a 'Fortress Europe' type of development in the future? Do the states of newly liberated eastern Europe feel that they must get 'inside' the EU? If so, why, and will they succeed, and what are the implications of either entry or rejection? What has motivated the US launch of its so-called Enterprise for the Americas and its subsequent negotiation of NAFTA? What kind of a regionalist project is in the process of being built in 'North America'? Why did Mexico press so hard to bring about NAFTA and will other Latin American and Caribbean states eventually seek, and be allowed, to join? Is Asia-Pacific in any way following suit in creating its own regionalist project, or is the dynamic here quite different? What has been the position and policy of the Japanese state? Is it seeking regional leadership? What has been the response of the other NICs in East Asia to Japanese and other forms of regional identity creation? How should APEC and other regional fora be understood? The core chapters of the book seek to provide the best answers that can presently be given to these various questions. Collectively, of course, they also raise very important general issues about hegemony and world order and the deeper significance of the new regionalism and the conclusion will indicate the nature of the debate that needs to be instigated on these matters.

Notes

1. R. O. Keohane and J. S. Nye, *Power and Interdependence: World Politics in Transition* (Boston: Little, Brown, 1977).
2. S. D. Krasner, *Defending the National Interest: Raw Materials Investments and U.S. Foreign Policy* (Princeton: Princeton University Press, 1978).
3. R. Leaver, 'International Political Economy and the Changing World Order: Evolution or Involution?', in R. Stubbs and G. R. D. Underhill (eds.), *Political Economy and the Changing Global Order* (London: Macmillan, 1994) p. 133.
4. G. T. Crane and A. Amawi (eds.), *The Theoretical Evolution of International Political Economy: A Reader* (New York: Oxford University Press, 1991), Introduction.
5. C. P. Kindleberger, *The World in Depression 1929–39* (Berkeley: University of California Press, 1973) and R. Gilpin, *U.S. Power and the Multinational Corporations: The Political Economy of U.S. Foreign Direct Investment* (New York: Basic Books, 1975).
6. R. O. Keohane, *After Hegemony: Cooperation and Discord in the World Political Economy* (Princeton: Princeton University Press, 1984) p. 32.
7. Ibid., p. 33.
8. See I. Wallerstein, *The Politics of the World-Economy* (Cambridge: Cambridge University Press, 1984) pp. 38–9.
9. D. Snidal, 'The Limits of Hegemonic Stability Theory', *International Organization*, 39 (1985) 579–614.
10. S. D. Krasner, 'Structural Causes and Regime Consequences: Regimes as Intervening Variables', in S. D. Krasner (ed.), *International Regimes* (Ithaca: Cornell University Press, 1983) p. 2.
11. The debate launched by the Krasner volume was subsequently reviewed in S. Haggard and B. Simmons, 'Theories of International Regimes', *International Organization*, 41 (1987) 491–517.
12. The references that could be assembled here are enormous. For a taste of this literature, see S. P. Huntington, 'The U.S. – Decline or Renewal?', *Foreign Affairs*, 67 (1988/9) 76–96; J. S. Nye, 'Understating U.S. Strength', *Foreign Policy*, 72 (1988) 105–29; and many other articles in these same two journals around this

period. The text that received the most media attention was P. Kennedy, *The Rise and Fall of the Great Powers* (London: Unwin Hyman, 1988).

13. For contending positions, see J. Grieco, 'Anarchy and the Limits of Cooperation: A Realist Critique of the Newest Liberal Institutionalism', *International Organization*, 42 (1988) 485–508, and R. Axelrod and R. O. Keohane, 'Achieving Cooperation under Anarchy: Strategies and Institutions', in K. Oye (ed.), *Cooperation under Anarchy* (Princeton: Princeton University Press, 1985) pp. 226–54. A good, recent review of this debate is D. Baldwin (ed.), *Neorealism and Neoliberalism: The Contemporary Debate* (New York: Columbia University Press, 1993).

14. A particularly sharp critical review is provided in R. Leaver, 'Restructuring in the Global Economy: From the Pax Americana to Pax Nipponica?', *Alternatives*, 14 (1989) 439–41.

15. Keohane, *After Hegemony*, pp. 32ff.

16. G. J. Ikenberry, 'Rethinking the Origins of American Hegemony', *Political Science Quarterly*, 104 (1989) 379.

17. Leaver, 'International Political Economy and the Changing World Order', p. 139.

18. R. Higgott, 'International Political Economy', in A. J. R. Groom and M. Light (eds.), *Contemporary International Relations: A Guide to Theory* (London: Pinter Publishers, 1994), p. 161.

19. S. Strange, 'Political Economy and International Relations', in K. Booth and S. Smith (eds.), *International Relations Theory Today* (Cambridge: Polity Press, 1995), p. 171.

20. C. N. Murphy and R. Tooze (eds.), *The New International Political Economy* (Boulder: Lynne Rienner Publishers, and London: Macmillan, 1991).

21. See, in particular, C. N. Murphy and R. Tooze, 'Getting beyond the "Common Sense" of the IPE Orthodoxy', in ibid., pp. 11–31.

22. R. W. Cox, 'Social Forces, States and World Orders: Beyond International Relations Theory', *Millennium: Journal of International Studies*, 10 (1981) 128. Cox's emphasis.

23. Ibid., 129.

24. Ibid., 136.

25. Ibid., 152.

26. R. W. Cox, 'Gramsci, Hegemony and International Relations: An Essay in Method', *Millennium: Journal of International Studies*, 12 (1983) 168.

27. R. W. Cox, *Production, Power and World Order: Social Forces in the Making of History* (New York: Columbia University Press, 1987), p. 7.

28. Cox, 'Social Forces, States and World Orders', 153.

29. This can be alleviated by conceiving of hegemony as possessing separable but interrelated elements of power located in the security, production, financial and ideological structures of the global political economy identified by Susan Strange in her 'eclectic

approach' to IPE. See S. Strange, 'An Eclectic Approach', in Murphy and Tooze (eds.), *The New International Political Economy*, pp. 33–49.

30. See M. Laffey, 'Ideology and the Limits of Gramscian Theory in International Relations', paper presented to the International Studies Association annual convention, Atlanta, 1–4 April 1992, cited in S. Whitworth, 'Theory as Exclusion: Gender and International Political Economy', in Stubbs and Underhill (eds.), *Political Economy and the Changing Global Order*, p. 126.

31. B. Gills and R. Palan (eds.), *Transcending the State-Global Divide: A Neo-structuralist Agenda in International Relations* (London: Lynne Rienner, 1994).

32. C. Chase-Dunn, *Global Formation: Structures of the World-Economy* (Oxford: Blackwell, 1989).

33. G. Hodgson, *Economics and Institutions* (Cambridge: Polity Press, 1988).

34. A. Lipietz, *Mirages and Miracles: The Crises of Global Fordism* (London: Verso Books, 1987).

35. For just one example, see W. Ofatuey-Kodjoe, 'African International Political Economy: An Assessment of the Current Literature', in Murphy and Tooze (eds.), *The New International Political Economy*, pp. 171–89.

36. S. Gill (ed.), *Gramsci, Historical Materialism and International Relations* (Cambridge: Cambridge University Press, 1993).

37. J. G. Ruggie, 'International Regimes, Transactions and Change: Embedded Liberalism in the Postwar Economic Order', *International Organization*, 36 (1982) 379–415.

38. See R. Triffin, *Gold and the Dollar Crisis* (New Haven: Yale University Press, 1961).

39. S. Strange, *Sterling and British Policy* (London: Oxford University Press, 1971).

40. Cox, *Production, Power and World Order*, p. 299.

41. The former phrase is used by Cox in R. W. Cox, 'Structural Issues of Global Governance: Implications for Europe', in Gill (ed.), *Gramsci, Historical Materialism and International Relations*, p. 261; the latter phrase is used by Strange in S. Strange, 'The Name of the Game', in N. X. Rizopoulos (ed.), *Sea-Changes: American Foreign Policy in a World Transformed* (New York: Council on Foreign Relations, 1990), p. 260.

42. S. Gill and D. Law, 'Global Hegemony and the Structural Power of Capital', *International Studies Quarterly*, 33 (1989) 475–99.

43. These positions are set out in Cox, 'Social Forces, States and World Orders', 144–6, and S. Gill, 'American Hegemony: Its Limits and Prospects in the Reagan Era', *Millennium: Journal of International Studies*, 15 (1986) 311–36.

44. Cox, *Production, Power and World Order*, pp. 298–9.

2 The European Union, 1992 and the Fear of 'Fortress Europe'

STEPHEN GEORGE

Regionalism is probably better established in western Europe than in any of the other areas surveyed in this book; and in recent years moves towards the strengthening of regional structures in both the economic and security spheres have gathered pace. Yet to view this regional enterprise as inimical to the existence of a world order is to perceive the issue falsely. The stark alternatives of regionalism or globalism are formulated within the terms of a US discourse about international relations. There is no voice in the debate on European union that advocates an exclusive regionalism. The debate has always been more subtle, nuanced, and European than that.

It is true that one loud voice, associated with Margaret Thatcher, the Bruges Group, and elements within the British Conservative party, has consistently maintained that the debate *is* about globalism versus regional exclusivity; but to present the issue in these terms is to misunderstand what the other voices in the debate are saying.

European integration 1945–85

Throughout the late 1940s the states of western Europe struggled to recover from the effects of the Second World War and to reconstruct their economies. In France this process was guided by the *Commissariat au Plan*, headed by the experienced civil servant Jean Monnet, who put the modernisation of the French steel industry at the centre of the plan. The decision in 1949

21

to create an independent sovereign West German state created problems for France. The most fundamental was that France had been invaded by Germany three times within one generation (1870, 1914, and 1939). French statesmen strongly opposed the creation of the Federal Republic of Germany but, unable to prevail against the United States and Britain, they had to turn their minds to the problem of how to guarantee that the new Germany would not pose a threat to France. A second problem was that the return of the Ruhr to sovereign German control meant that the French steel industry could no longer rely on guaranteed supplies of coking coal for its furnaces.

Monnet responded to these problems with a plan for France and West Germany to pool their supplies of coal and steel under a supranational high authority which would make decisions on production and distribution of the two commodities. This would have the immediate effect of ensuring that the French steel industry was not left with insufficient coal; and it would also make war between France and the new West German state almost inconceivable, since coal and steel were so central to any war effort. This idea was taken up by the French Foreign Minister, Robert Schuman, and became known as the Schuman Plan. It led directly to the formation of the European Coal and Steel Community (ECSC) by the Treaty of Paris of 1951. Italy, Belgium, Luxembourg and the Netherlands chose to join the ECSC, but Britain, although invited, declined the offer.

So successful was the ECSC in resolving the problems of the European coal and steel industries that the same six states went on to form a European Atomic Energy Community (Euratom) and a European Economic Community (EEC) by the Treaties of Rome in 1957. By this time the motivation had moved beyond economic recovery to ensuring economic prosperity, strengthening western European unity against the threat from Communism, and, at least in the eyes of some of the advocates of further integration, making a positive European response to what, in a famous book, Jean-Jacques Servan-Schreiber described as 'the American challenge'.[1]

The basis of this challenge was the technological and financial dominance of US companies, which were penetrating the European market. Servan-Schreiber argued that no one European state could provide a sufficiently large home base for companies that would be able to compete with the Americans, and that a larger domestic market, on a European scale, was necessary. He also advocated the development of European industrial and research policies to help European companies to match the technological base of their US competitors. This concern was particularly felt in France, and was widely shared across the French political spectrum.

A related concern was the inability of France to play a role in world affairs. Resentment of US hegemony in the era of the Cold War was not a theme that appeared in French politics for the first time in 1958 with the Fifth Republic and President de Gaulle. It was a persistent theme of the coalition governments of the Fourth Republic too. Indeed, the nuclear force (the *force de frappe*) that de Gaulle employed with such symbolic effect was developed under the Fourth Republic. It was partly for this reason that French support for the EEC was dependent on West German support for Euratom; the latter, although concerned with the development of nuclear energy for peaceful purposes, offered the prospect to France of a West German subsidy for its nuclear-research programme, with military as well as civilian application.

Other member states were less concerned with the challenge of US hegemony in the security sphere, although they were concerned about US competition in the economic sphere. As part of a nation divided by the Cold War, West German governments were strongly supportive of US military involvement in the defence of Europe. At the same time, one of the motives for West German involvement in the EEC was the advantage that membership of a preferential trading bloc would give to its industries over their American competitors. Similar considerations applied to the Italians, whose northern industrialists needed access to a wider market for their developing automobile and consumer durables industries, but whose centre–right governments were strongly Atlanticist on security issues. However, the staunchest European ally of the United States on security issues was Britain.

Initially British governments declined to join the EEC, doubting whether it would be successful and seeing Britain as having a world role in partnership with the United States, which might be jeopardised by involvement in a regionalist project. However, by 1961 the British Conservative government had changed its position on membership. This was primarily because of alarm in both London and Washington at the prospect that de Gaulle might succeed in asserting French leadership over the six, and turn the EEC into a political third force between the United States and the Soviet Union. Prime Minister Harold Macmillan was urged by President Kennedy to join in order to offset the 'eccentricities' of policy in Paris and Bonn, and to take over the running of the EEC on behalf of joint Anglo–American interests.[2]

From this point of view, de Gaulle was perfectly justified in vetoing British membership in 1962, and again in 1966 when the Labour government of Harold Wilson renewed the application. By this time, it had become the norm to refer to the ECSC, Euratom and the EEC collectively as the European Community (EC). De Gaulle still believed that Britain had not accepted a European vocation, and would act as the American Trojan Horse in the EC. Given the French view of the purposes of the European enterprise, he was probably correct, although it is only fair to Wilson to note that his government was committed to the creation of a European technological community for very similar reasons to those put forward by Servan-Schreiber.[3] Nevertheless, it was only after the resignation of de Gaulle in 1969 that France came round to taking a more sympathetic view of British membership. By the time that Britain joined, in January 1973, the golden years of EC economic growth were over. The capitalist world had already been shaken by the ending of the convertibility of the dollar in 1971, and was about to enter a period of recession triggered by the OPEC price rises of December 1973.

Following the collapse of the Bretton Woods system in 1971, the EEC member states tried to tie their currencies together as a way of avoiding chaos in their economic transactions. The ultimate aim was to have a single currency, which would consolidate the single market. In the background there was always the idea that if the United States could not maintain monetary stability, one of the primary tasks of a hegemonic power, then the Europeans must do it for themselves, and perhaps in the process provide a rock of monetary stability on which a new international monetary regime could be built. Interestingly, the British Conservative government of Edward Heath backed these moves, although the enthusiasm seems to have come from the prime minister's political commitment to European integration, and was not shared by the Treasury, which viewed the matter in purely economic terms.

However, economic crisis led to economic divergence in Europe. West Germany and a few other strong economies, not all of which were members of the EC, weathered the storms well; most of the others, including Britain and France, did not. Plans for moving from a general common market to a monetary union collapsed in the face of fierce speculative pressure that tore apart the system of fixed exchange rates. Indeed, over the next decade there was even some retreat on the degree of economic integration already achieved. Tariffs had been abolished by the end of the 1960s, but during the 1970s and into the 1980s a whole range of non-tariff barriers to trade grew up as governments, in the face of recession, attempted to reserve domestic markets for domestic producers.

Surprisingly, given the unfavourable economic conditions, the project of tying together national exchange rates was successfully relaunched in 1978, by an alliance of West German Chancellor Helmut Schmidt, French President Valery Giscard d'Estaing, and European Commission President Roy Jenkins. This was the European Monetary System (EMS), the central instrument of which was the Exchange Rate Mechanism (ERM). It was seen as a means of establishing a zone of monetary stability in Europe at a time of international monetary instability, which had not been helped by the policies of successive US administrations to drive the value of the dollar first up and then down in order to benefit the US economy. It was only later that the ERM came to be seen as a step towards monetary union.[4]

On the political front, there were some achievements in the period from 1973 to 1985 in the forging of a common policy on external relations, although the united front tended to split apart in a crisis, usually over the question of how far the EC should follow US leadership. Nevertheless, in key areas of the world where the economic interests of the Europeans conflicted with those of the United States, such as the Middle East and eastern Europe, the basis for a separate European policy did emerge through the mechanism known as European Political Co-operation (EPC). However, the political influence of the EC was vitally dependent on its economic power and, as the years of stagnation dragged on into the 1980s, few observers saw it as a potential rival for core status within the world system. This all changed very rapidly after 1985.

Project 1992

In January 1985 Jacques Delors became President of the European Commission. Within a matter of months the new Commission had produced a White Paper on the freeing of the internal market, which was adopted by the European Council with a target date for completion of the end of 1992.[5] The project involved dismantling the non-tariff barriers to trade in industrial goods that had grown up during the 1970s, freeing the market for services, ending the practice of awarding public contracts only to national companies, finding ways of facilitating the free movement of labour throughout the EC, and removing controls on the movement of capital. Each of these measures involved risks for some vested interests in some member states, but in 1986 the governments indicated that they were in earnest about achieving the project when they signed the Single European Act (SEA), which instituted qualified majority voting in the Council of Ministers for almost all measures concerned with the freeing of the internal market, replacing the previous system of unanimity, which had allowed each member state a veto over proposals. The SEA also contained a separate section on EPC, which remained explicitly intergovernmental rather than being brought under the rules of the EC, but which was nevertheless thereby incorporated into a formal treaty commitment for the first time.

In launching the 1992 project, the opinions of experts were mobilised behind the idea to convince governments and industrialists that it was necessary. The Commission produced a report from a group of European economists on 'the costs of non-Europe' which promised great benefits.[6] Other economists criticised the methodology and conclusions of the report, but the propaganda effect was to put greater momentum behind the freeing of the market. Once major European industrialists were convinced that the governments were in earnest, they began a programme of mergers and investments in anticipation of the appearance of the single market. This ensured that the leading industrial concerns, organised in the European Round Table of Industrialists, would keep the pressure on governments not to retreat from their commitments. It also meant that the economies of the EC member states flourished in the approach to 1992.

All this activity, and the propaganda for the 1992 project, led to suspicion from the governments of other countries, particularly the United States, which feared the emergence of a 'Fortress Europe' from which their own companies would be excluded. However, such fears were allayed somewhat after the settlement of a dispute over a proposed banking regulation which arose in 1989. The United States administration was very critical of the draft regulation, which offered equal rights in the European market to banks from third countries provided that European banks were given reciprocal rights in the home country of the foreign bank. The United States at first saw this as an attempt to exclude US banks, since the United States did not have a nationally-regulated banking system and therefore could not offer European banks the same rights as would be available to US banks in Europe. However, after it was clarified that the EC would only demand the same rights for its banks in the United States as US banks enjoyed there, the immediate fear of 'Fortress Europe' lessened.

The single-market programme made rapid progress after this. By the end of 1992, the target date, 260 out of the consolidated list of 280 measures that had been identified in the White Paper had been agreed in the Council of Ministers, a staggering 95 per cent success rate.[7] In the meantime the EC had also moved on to a further revision of the founding treaties, marking another step in the consolidation of the regional commitment. Throughout 1991 intergovernmental conferences met to agree on further steps towards monetary union and political union, culminating in the signing of the Treaty on European Union (TEU) in Maastricht, the Netherlands, in December 1991. The TEU created a new international organisation called the European Union (EU), which contained within

it the existing EC, together with two other 'pillars', one covering intergovernmental co-operation on justice and home affairs,
the other covering intergovernmental arrangements for a
common foreign and security policy (CFSP). The main feature
of the EC pillar was a commitment to achieve a full monetary
union by 1999 at the latest.

Although in some ways the TEU had more intergovernmental than supranational elements, it ran into problems during
the ratification process, particularly in Britain, Denmark and
France, because it was perceived as a decisive step away from
national sovereignty and towards the government of Europe
from Brussels. The strength of the public reaction against the
TEU led to a crisis of confidence in the central institutions of
the EC, particularly the Commission; it also led to a currency
crisis in the autumn of 1992 that precipitated the effective
collapse of the ERM. Although the system was rescued by
expanding the permitted bands of fluctuation in the values of
the currencies from 2.5 per cent to 15 per cent either side of
parity, the prospects for the achievement of monetary union
by the target date of 1999, except by a very small group of
states, were seriously damaged.

The TEU itself was saved only by allowing both Britain and
Denmark to reserve the right to opt out of any future monetary union, and Britain to opt out of the process of harmonis-
ing social policy by majority voting. This left a large number
of questions hanging over the new European Union, which were
made more acute by its impotence in the face of the crisis in
the former Yugoslavia. Nevertheless, the EC/EU had come a
long way from the 'Eurosclerosis' and 'Europessimism' of the
start of the 1980s. The regional commitment of the governments
of the member states had been reaffirmed, although the precise
form that this regional organisation would take remained unclear.
It is to this matter that we now turn.

Ideology and interests

An early and influential theoretical analysis of the process of
European integration, known as neo-functionalism, stressed the
extent to which the process, once launched, would become

self-sustaining, partly because of the logic of sectoral integration in an interdependent economy, and partly because of the
role of interest groups.[8] Even the neo-functionalist writers,
however, accepted that interest groups did not play a significant role in the setting up of the EC. Governments took that
step, following strategies determined by their perceptions of
the practical problems facing them, and often against the
opposition of vested interests.

There has been considerable academic debate about how far
the 1992 programme was driven by pressures from interest
groups, but at least one influential case has been made for the
argument that once again the initiative came from the governments of the member states.[9] Perhaps, though, the question is
presented here in too general a fashion. Different governments
have different degrees of autonomy from vested interests. The
West German government has rarely managed to pursue a
consistent and coherent view of the national interest without
being driven by the claims of interest groups, either from the
private or the public sector.[10] On the other hand, successive
French governments, while not immune from pressure groups,
have shown a reasonably consistent view of the nature and
purpose of the EEC. The only other national governmental
view that has displayed a similar consistency has been that of
Britain. This has meant that the debate about the future of
the EC/EU has been conducted essentially between the French
and British views, with an independent German voice only
coming strongly to the fore in the 1990s.

While German policy towards European integration has been
generally marked by a concern to liberalise trade, which reflects the country's high level of trading interdependence with
the rest of Europe, this concern has not come through consistently in policy in every sector, because:

> The main characteristic of Germany's European 'policy-
> style' . . . is precisely that there is no single pattern of policy-
> making . . . The array of discrete policy networks is merely a
> reflection of the situation in German domestic politics.[11]

This fragmentation of policy must also be viewed in the light
of German reluctance over the early post-war years to play a

strong assertive political role in Europe, so as not to revive old fears amongst its neighbours. To some extent this tendency was overcome in the 1970s when Helmut Schmidt was chancellor, although he always tried to act in concert with the French President, Valery Giscard d'Estaing. This meant that measures such as the EMS were presented as joint Franco-German initiatives, and were justified in a terminology that drew upon a French discourse about the nature of European integration. All in all, no separate German perspective emerged until the 1990s, after the unification of Germany, when Chancellor Helmut Kohl became the loudest voice advocating further integration, and adopted a more thoroughly federalist terminology than had conventionally been used even in France. Until this late stage, though, the German position was voluntarily subordinated to that of France.

The French view has shown some variation across changes in government, but its essential elements can be clearly seen in Servan-Schreiber's book from the 1960s. As noted above, this book identified a challenge to Europe from the penetration of American capital. Servan-Schreiber compared this situation to the relationship between Europe and Africa in the nineteenth and early twentieth centuries.

> It is a historical rule that politically and economically powerful countries make direct investments (and gain control) in less-developed countries. Thus, European capital used to flow into Africa – not for simple investment, but to gain economic power and exploit local resources. Economically weak countries, suffering from the reverse side of the same classic law, see their savings seep away to the stronger countries in the form of investments. This is precisely what is happening today in the underdeveloped countries of Africa, where the property-owning classes invest their savings in Europe.[12]

Servan-Schreiber feared that if Europe did not meet the American challenge it would never be able to recover its autonomy; its economic fortunes would be dependent on decisions made by US-based multinationals in their headquarters in New York, Detroit, and other US cities. They would owe no allegiance to any European government, and would be able to switch their investments to any part of the common market to evade national controls that they did not like.[13] This fear was widely shared in French political circles, and avoiding such dependence became a consistent theme of French thinking on the purposes of the EC.

Servan-Schreiber went further: he pointed to the dominance of American companies in the strategic sector of electronics. This was not just any industry: it was the basis for a second industrial revolution in which Europe threatened to become technologically dependent on the United States.

> A country which has to buy most of its electronic equipment abroad will be in a condition of inferiority similar to that of nations in the last century which were incapable of industrializing. Despite their brilliant past, these nations remained outside of the mainstream of civilization. If Europe continues to lag behind in electronics, she could cease to be included among the advanced areas of civilization within a single generation.[14]

This structural analysis of the world economy became almost common ground in France. It is important to note here that Servan-Schreiber was not a member of a left-wing party, but of the centre–right Radicals. It is also significant that the thrust of his argument was not for defensive protection against the rest of the world. He was quite clear that this was no solution, and would only result in technological backwardness.

> Restricting or prohibiting investments is no answer, since this would only slow down our own development.[15]

> ... a flow of manufactured products would replace the flow of capital, and even more easily since most tariff barriers were lowered by the Kennedy Round [of the GATT negotiations]. After having raised walls against American capital, should we then build new ones against American products? This would merely assure our own underdevelopment.[16]

The answer to the American challenge was to develop a clear strategy for promoting European champions which could rival

US corporations both on the European market and as world players. This in turn involved having an active industrial policy, including a policy on research and development; and these should be developed at the European level because the resources of any one state were insufficient to provide either the size of market or the public-sector funding necessary to bring about the emergence of companies that could meet the challenges being posed from within the US.

On the need for an interventionist EC industrial policy, the thinking of French supporters of the EC, right through to Jacques Delors, has centred on the importance of Europe keeping control over its own destiny. Indeed, this has been the most persistent theme in French writing on economic planning. Delors, who worked at the Commissariat for over seven years in the 1960s, wrote that the plan was necessary to act as a 'support, correction, or substitute for the market'; it could 'embody the will of a society to master its future'.[17] The French view of the EC is of the national plan writ large. Within this perspective, a fundamental aspect of being in charge of one's own future was being able to have some influence over the pattern of investment in the economy. This was difficult in a capitalist economy, where there was private ownership of the means of production, but it was possible to work in partnership with the capitalist enterprises to provide a structured framework for investment decisions, which was to the advantage of everybody because it reduced the associated risks. The task became impossible, however, if investment decisions were in the hands of corporations that were headquartered outside of the geographical territory within which the planning authority had jurisdiction. Hence the link to Servan-Schreiber's arguments about decisions that were made in New York, except that in the 1980s the challenge came not only from the United States, but also from Japan. The aim nevertheless remained to avoid becoming a dependent part of the world economy.

This view of the purpose of the EC, which later would become known as a 'strategic trade' view, was the only coherent vision that existed in its early years. It was not an analysis that was fully shared by the governments of other states, but the discourse on the EC was increasingly conducted in terms derived from this French concept in the absence of any coherently formulated and articulated alternative. It was not until British membership in 1973 that an alternative discourse was on offer.

There has been a remarkable consistency in the way in which British politicians have viewed the EC. Both supporters and opponents of membership initially saw it as potentially an inward-looking club of rich states in contrast with the outward-looking perspective of Britain, which was concerned with the management of the world system as a whole, and the development of the Third World in particular. Opponents, on both left and right, tended to argue that the EC was irredeemably regionalist and protectionist in outlook.[18] Supporters of membership argued that with British leadership it could be weaned away from its narrow outlook and made into a vehicle for the more effective pursuit of traditional British liberal, or 'free trade', policies of global management. All British governments since the war can be classified as liberal in their orientation to the international political economy. Although there have been differences over the role of the state in domestic affairs, marking the distinction between what McKinlay and Little call 'pure liberalism' and 'compensatory liberalism',[19] they have all been committed to an open world economy, and have been keenly aware of the dangers of a regional grouping becoming not a step towards a single world economy, but a regional super-state.

The difference between the British and French views became particularly marked after 1979 and the long period of Conservative governments committed to a 'pure liberal' view as opposed to the 'compensatory liberal' view that prevailed under previous Labour and Conservative governments. The compensatory liberals marked out a larger role for the state in domestic economic management and looked for a more active promotional role in managing the world system from states and from international organisations. By the 1980s the pure liberal stress on the role of the market had acquired a new ascendancy in international affairs and in the management of the internal affairs of capitalist states because of its acceptance in the United States; but within the EC this ideological offensive was to some extent repelled by the continuing dominance of the French view of the organisation and its purposes. British governments always appeared to be awkward partners in the EC because they conducted the defence of their views in a language that did not mesh with the dominant discourse, and this tendency increased after 1979.

The British view was also committed to the necessity of hegemonic leadership in the world system. Despite frequent assertions to the contrary, there was no illusion amongst the British élite that Britain remained the strongest power in the world, no 'illusion of grandeur'. There was, though, a recognition that as a legacy of its imperial past, Britain had worldwide interests. British companies operated in every part of the world, and it was a legitimate role of government to protect their interests. However, the dominant British view was that international order could only be achieved if the most powerful capitalist state took responsibility for it, and that state in the post-war era was the United States. Britain was prepared to offer itself as the loyal ally of the United States, as a guide and mentor even, and there was consistent British suspicion of attempts to move away from the order imposed by hegemony to establish rival regional centres of power for fear this would destabilise the system.

The partial exception to this generalisation was the Heath government of 1970–4. Led by a prime minister who was personally convinced of the merits of European integration, it also faced a situation in which the US administration of Richard Nixon was no longer able to play the hegemonic role. Nixon appeared to put US interests before the maintenance of stable international regimes in the spheres of trade, monetary stability, and security. In response, the Heath government tried to mobilise the EC, which it only joined in January 1973, as an alternative vehicle for maintaining certain aspects of the hegemonic system. However, this meant marking out for the EC an international role very different from that envisaged by France, and involved the British 'stepping with heavy feet' within the EC, a factor which contributed towards Britain's reputation for awkwardness.[20]

Subsequent British governments returned to a more conventional Atlanticist orientation. Both Wilson and Callaghan were instinctive Atlanticists, and Callaghan saw it as his role to mediate between the antagonistic Chancellor Schmidt and President Carter. The strength of the Atlantic orientation, though, was considerably stronger under Margaret Thatcher. Although she did have her differences with President Reagan, the personal *rapport* between the two added to an ideological meeting of minds. Many of Thatcher's objections to the wider aspects of the 1992 project can be traced to her belief in the importance of US leadership. It was in this context that she came to be at odds with the Bush administration. Bush inherited massive budget and trade deficits from Reagan, and in response began to emphasise the importance of the EC taking a bigger responsibility for ensuring the maintenance of world order. Thatcher found herself fighting a rearguard action against the United States itself, trying to deflect the Bush administration from encouraging closer unity within a more independent EC.[21]

Although not all differences between Britain and France can be explained by their different perspectives on international political economy, much of the debate about the regionalist project in western Europe has centred around this fundamental ideological divide. However, ideas alone do not determine behaviour. These different perspectives have interacted with pressures bearing on goverments that derive both from shifts in the world system and the changing balance of forces domestically. This interaction is examined below first for economic affairs, and then for security issues.

Economic affairs

The single-market programme

Why did the governments of the member states agree to such a far-reaching programme as that proposed by the Commission in its 1985 White Paper? The brokerage skills of the new Commission were important in getting agreement; but what opened up the window of opportunity for Delors and his team was the international situation that faced the European states. In the aftermath of the 1979 oil crisis even the West German economy had been weakened. While the EC as a whole continued to suffer from lack of investment and high levels of unemployment, the economies of the United States and Japan made a remarkably strong recovery from recession. Not only were Europe's global rivals performing much better economically;

their recovery was based on the development of new technologies in the fields of computers, robotics, laser technology, and information technology, threatening Europe with technological obsolescence.[22] Unless European companies were able to get into the technology race, they would lose out heavily in global markets to US and Japanese companies. Europe was in danger of returning to the position of the 1950s when its industries were dependent on US technology, the American challenge that the EC had helped to combat. This time, however, Europe would not just be behind the US; it would be third behind Japan.[23]

The European Commission first addressed this technological challenge in the early 1980s, producing the ESPRIT programme to promote collaborative pre-competitive research between large European electronics companies and European universities.[24] But given the concern of all governments to control public expenditure, it was clear that European industry would have to provide the bulk of the funding for the research. To do so the large corporations needed to generate bigger profits, which they insisted that they could only do in a European context if there was a single large European market rather than the fragmented national markets that faced them in the early 1980s. The arguments of the Commission were accompanied by a determined campaign by Wisse Dekker, the president both of Philips and of the European Round Table of Industrialists, to promote the idea of the large internal market.[25] Beyond industrial production, there was also a concern to see European financial institutions that could be global competitors in what was expected to be the growth sector of the future for the advanced economies. Hence the moves to free the markets in banking and insurance.

Despite US concerns about a 'Fortress Europe', there is no evidence that this was ever the intention. The pressure for the single market came from the largest industrial concerns in Europe, which were not only European but global players. Such companies were unlikely to advocate regional protectionism because retaliation would have damaged them. In fact, Pelkmans argues that the 1992 project resulted in an opening of the EC market to third countries. This was not predominantly because of a switch in direction following the 'Fortress Europe' campaign by the United States, although that may have had some effect in sectors where reciprocity rules were needed because there were no GATT rules. Mainly, though, it was because most sectors did not easily tolerate differences between internal and external measures. Pelkmans quotes as examples the removal of technical barriers; the abolition of national quotas for imports of cars, footwear, textiles, and clothing; financial capital; the market for telecommunications terminal equipment; and reciprocity in financial services.[26]

Subsequently the EC exported its 1992 principles to the GATT negotiations on services, public procurement, and technical barriers, 'thereby embarrassing the United States with its more circumspect positions in these areas'.[27]

The GATT negotiations

In the public perception of the Uruguay Round of GATT negotiations the sticking point for an agreement was agriculture, and the EC was the cause of the problem. This is only partially true. At the same time as there were real difficulties over the agricultural package, there were also serious problems in other sectors, including services, where the recalcitrant party was the United States.

Initially it was the United States that campaigned for services to be included in the Uruguay Round. The EC at first was cool; but the combined influence of France and Britain, both of whom had a comparative advantage in services, led to a change of attitude, and the inclusion of services in the 1992 programme converted the EC into the leading advocate of liberalisation of services across the board. The United States, on the other hand, negotiated for a more partial liberalisation. The US Treasury opposed the inclusion of financial services because it wished to retain domestic regulatory control, and the US air-transport and sea-transport industries, which had successfully resisted their inclusion in the US–Canada Free Trade Area, campaigned for exclusion from GATT also.[28]

Late in 1990, the United States demanded that the Most Favoured Nation (MFN) principle not be applied in the services sector. This move was in response to lobbying of the Bush administration by powerful actors such as the telecommunications giant ATT, which wanted the United States to use access to the large US market as a bilateral bargaining counter to force other states to open their markets. The move reflected a widespread lack of confidence in the United States in the efficacy of GATT to achieve genuine liberalisation. Since MFN is central to the whole concept of GATT, the US demand threw a considerable spanner into the works.[29]

It is true that right at the end of the negotiations, in December 1993, the EC was responsible for another crisis in the services sector when it adopted French demands that films and television programmes be excluded from the agreement, because of the cultural implications of the possible destruction of the European film and television-programme industries by efficient US competitors. To secure a deal, the sector had to be omitted. This was a clear example of the French view on the limits to free trade being backed by other member states. It was not as important a derogation from the deal, though, as the exclusion of financial services, on which the United States would not compromise. However, the problems caused by US demands in the services sector were overshadowed by the difficulties over agriculture, where the EC was presented as the cause of the problem.

In the agricultural sector the EC did find it difficult to reach an agreement that it could accept, but this was not because of any regional protectionist tendencies at élite level. It was more because of the political influence of farmers in France, who were already alarmed by reforms to the Common Agricultural Policy from which they had always benefited. It was less a case of regional protectionism than of national vested interests preventing one government from agreeing to a deal that would damage them. France stood to benefit tremendously from an agreement under GATT in other sectors, but cultural factors meant that farmers had considerable public sympathy and, with elections approaching, neither the socialist president nor the conservative prime minister wanted to be seen to be damaging the interests of French agriculture. The intervention of Jacques Delors to try to prevent Commissioner Ray MacSharry from accepting a deal that Delors did not think would be acceptable in France may have owed something to Delors' own political ambitions to be the next president of France (as Washington claimed), but it may also have been (as his aides maintained) because he shared the French sympathy for farmers.[30]

In the end an agreement was reached against which French farmers protested, but which was ultimately accepted by their government following intense pressure from its EC partners, particularly its closest ally, Germany. Although the farmers made a noise, and although both the government and the president gave sympathetic nods in response, in the end the deal was accepted with only minor modifications, although it had to wait until after the parliamentary elections. The eventual outcome clearly indicated the limits on the influence of public opinion in the face of powerful pressures in the opposite direction. These came from the industrial and service sectors in France, which stood to gain from the GATT deal. More importantly, the strategy of the French government for the French economy demanded that it listen to the dynamic sectors of the economy and not to the farmers, however much political sympathy the farmers might have. This applied both to the outgoing socialist and the incoming conservative govern-ments. The requirements of successful management of a modern capitalist economy are often not compatible with the pressures of democracy.

Social policy

Although capitalist modernisation and democracy are often difficult to reconcile, governments still have to be able to carry enough of the population with them to implement their policies. An important aspect of this is the social settlement that is negotiated between capital and labour. Without the co-operation of the work-force, change can be frustrated. The fact is that after the Second World War both West Germany and France put in place a more successful accommodation between capital and labour than did Britain.

In West Germany an elaborate system of consultation of workers through two-tier boards of directors was devised at the end of the war, designed to prevent a repetition of the support for extreme right-wing movements that German industry had given to the Nazis before the war. So successful was this system in ensuring social harmony that the West German economy soon outstripped all its competitors and became the strongest in Europe. In France such a system took longer to put in place.

For a decade after the war the relationship of capital and labour was chaotic, and this acted as a serious constraint on the ability of French governments to carry through their ambitious national economic plans. However, after 1969 the pieces of a similar accommodation of labour and capital began to be put in place by conservative governments during the presidencies of Pompidou and Giscard d'Estaing. The initial successes were achieved by the reforming government of Jacques Chaban Delmas (1969–72), and the architect was his adviser on social affairs, Jacques Delors. It is little wonder that Delors retained a strong attachment to the idea of social dialogue when he became President of the Commission, since his first great practical success in government was the negotiation of the *Contrats de Progrès* which achieved a period of industrial harmony in France. The same policies were retained by the socialists when they came into office, and one reason for Mitterrand and Delors turning to Europe was to maintain this system of social protection. They were not prepared to allow it to be undermined by the opening of the French economy to the single market, hence their insistence on the need for a social dimension to 1992.

In Britain, by contrast, attempts to incorporate labour into a national effort for economic prosperity never fully succeeded, and finally collapsed in a wave of strikes in the winter of 1978–9, bringing defeat for Callaghan's Labour government and the arrival in office of Thatcher. The Conservatives chose not to try to reach a settlement with the labour movement, but to weaken it through a combination of legal restrictions on trade unions and high unemployment. It is little wonder that Thatcher retained a strong hostility to the idea of social dialogue at the European level, since her great success in government had been to dispense with it in Britain.

However, the dispute over the social dimension also connected with the opposing British and French perspectives on international political economy. In her infamous Bruges speech in 1988 Thatcher said, 'we certainly do not need new regulations which raise the cost of employment and make Europe's labour market less flexible and less competitive with overseas suppliers'.[31] The logic of this argument was that proposals such as the harmonisation of social security benefits and the introduction of workers' rights to information on the investment plans of companies would make European industry uncompetitive with companies in other parts of the world which did not have to pay the taxes necessary to sustain high social benefits, did not have to bear the direct burden of paying employees during periods of pregnancy and child rearing, did not have maximum working weeks imposed on them, and did not have to reduce their managerial flexibility by consulting their employees on their corporate plans. The resulting lack of competitiveness would feed demands for protection against the products of countries that did not have the same social costs.

Monetary union

As well as the social dimension, Margaret Thatcher disagreed with France, and with Jacques Delors, on the need for the single market to be completed by a monetary union. The French supported monetary union because the ERM meant that monetary policy throughout Europe was effectively decided by the German Bundesbank. Because the deutschmark was the strongest currency in the system, all other members had to maintain a premium above German interest rates to encourage fund managers to keep their assets in anything other than the German currency. This meant that when the Germans put up their interest rates, everyone else had to follow suit. Effective monetary sovereignty had been lost. The surrender of formal sovereignty by accepting a single currency meant that French representatives on the European central bank, which would control monetary policy, would at least have a say in the level of interest rates. The same arguments applied to most of the other states in the system. Significantly, Britain remained outside of the ERM until October 1990. Sterling floated, and although account had to be taken of German interest rates, the relationship was not so close as that experienced by currencies inside the system.

Thatcher's opposition to a single European currency was expressed in terms of loss of national sovereignty. However, a subtext of her position was that she consistently supported US leadership in international affairs, and the emergence of a rival to the dollar as the basis of the international monetary system was inconsistent with this position. As in trade matters, Thatcher may have suspected the French and Germans of wanting to displace the Americans as the leaders of the capitalist world system. But her Atlanticist position took no account of the fact that the United States was no longer in a position to play the hegemonic role. As Sandholtz and Zysman made clear as early as 1989:

> The dollar remains the financial core of the world system, but because of America's huge and growing debt, the dollar remains the basis of the system by the choice of others, not so much by American decisions. Japan's export boom has put immense financial resources under Japanese control . . . For Europeans, decisions in Tokyo will have as much or more impact on monetary conditions as decisions taken in Washington or New York. Perhaps the European Monetary System (EMS) will soon need to be conceived as a mark zone moving in relation to the yen. The dollar is no longer the obvious sole choice for the world's reserve currency.[32]

So, Thatcher argued against a European currency partly because she did not want to undermine the hegemony of the United States in monetary affairs, but that hegemony had already effectively dissolved. A similar problem undermined her arguments against a more autonomous European security structure.

Security issues

The Treaty on European Union makes provision for a common foreign and security policy (CFSP) for the EU. Article J.4 says that the CFSP 'should include *all* questions related to the security of the Union, including the eventual framing of a common defence policy, which might in time lead to a common defence'. This could be interpreted as a move towards regionalism in the sphere of security and defence policy, although the mechanisms are intergovernmental rather than supranational.

In fact, there was never a commitment to supranational policy making in these sectors. Although the six original member states said in their Messina declaration[33] that eventual political unity was their objective, the areas of high politics, which impinged most directly on the sovereignty of member states, were deliberately excluded from the remit of the EC. The Treaty of Rome drew a clear distinction between international economic affairs, including trade, where the Commission had a role as the negotiator of agreements on behalf of the EC as a whole, and political and military aspects of external relations, which after 1973 were dealt with through the intergovernmental mechanisms of EPC. However, the distinction was a difficult one to maintain, and it started to break down in the 1970s with the opening of the Euro–Arab dialogue.

European Political Co-operation

The Arab states were important to the Europeans because of their control over the oil supplies of the EC; but they were intent on using the lever provided by the oil resource to gain support from the Europeans in their struggle with Israel, in which the United States invariably took the Israeli side. The dialogue, which the Arabs instigated, ran into serious difficulties because of this linkage, but it was in the interests of the Europeans to pursue it, and to do so they had to treat economic and political issues together.[34] Indeed, throughout the 1970s, which in the sphere of economic integration were (with the exception of the creation of the ERM) years of little achievement, EPC made steady advances. The EC member states increasingly acted together as a bloc in the United Nations, responding to the prevalence of bloc diplomacy in the General Assembly. They also formed a common front in pressing the United States to support the opening of a Conference on Security and Co-operation in Europe (CSCE) in Helsinki in 1975. Throughout the CSCE the EC states worked together to get agreement, and the outcome can be interpreted as a major success for EPC.

These two instances show two reasons for the extension of EPC. First, despite its internal problems, the EC was already the world's largest single trading bloc, and other states and groups of states expected to be able to deal with it as an entity rather than with its constituent parts. Second, even the large member states were in a stronger position if they could pursue their objectives through joint diplomacy rather than individually. Of course, interests did not always coincide, but increasingly the EC states came to realise that they had more interests in common with each other than they had with states from outside, and especially with the United States.

Differences with the United States

Although they needed the US security umbrella in the context of the Cold War, the EC states were nevertheless commercial rivals of the United States, and had different attitudes to some areas of the world for geographical, historical, and cultural reasons. This manifested itself particularly in differences over relations with the Arab states and with the Communist bloc.

Differences over relations with the Arab states went back to the 1970s. In response to the December 1973 increase in the price of oil, the United States took a more confrontational stance towards the oil producers than the Europeans were inclined to do. Membership of the International Energy Agency (IEA), which the United States administration formed as a consumers' cartel to counter the OPEC producers' cartel, split the EC, France refusing to join. Problems increased considerably in the 1980s. The confrontational stance of the Reagan administration towards Arab states which the United States accused of supporting terrorism was fully backed only by the British government. In 1986 the United States accused Libya of involvement in the bombing of a discothèque in West Berlin in which a US serviceman was killed. The US administration said there was indisputable evidence of Libyan involvement, but would not show the evidence to the Europeans. When a bombing raid was launched against Tripoli, only Britain was prepared to allow NATO bases on its soil to be used to launch the attack; France and Spain refused the US jets permission to fly over their air space.

Italy, the former colonial power in Libya, continued to receive a high proportion of its oil from that source, and had practical as well as ideological objections to the aggressive approach of the Americans. France, with former colonies in north Africa and a large Muslim population which originated in those states, and Spain, another Mediterranean state with historic links with the Arabs, both considered the US action to be insensitive and ultimately unhelpful. Greece, which again had strong cultural links with the Arab world, condemned the Libyan bombing, and subsequently refused to support economic sanctions that the United States demanded against Syria on the basis that Syria had been behind an attempt to plant a terrorist bomb on an Israeli airliner at London airport. Even the northern European states of the EC had qualms about the insensitivity and aggressiveness of US actions in the Arab world.

In the case of the Communist bloc, the Europeans were more strongly and consistently supportive of the opening of trade links than was the United States. During periods of *détente*, the commercial benefits tended to accrue to European companies. With the exception of US sales of wheat to the Soviet Union, US companies secured few of the contracts that were concluded between eastern Europe and the West. This gave the Europeans a bigger stake in the continuation of *détente*, and so made them less inclined to take a hard-line attitude to what the United States interpreted as infringements of the rules.

A prime example of how differing commercial interests led to a rupture between the EC states and the United States was the Siberian gas pipeline issue which arose in 1982. The Reagan administration unilaterally decided that the construction of the pipeline would damage the interests of the Western alliance, because it would give the Soviet Union a guaranteed source of hard-currency income which it could use to head off the problems that were caused to its economy by trying to keep up with the United States in the armaments race. The US administration also argued that the pipeline would lead to west European dependence on the Soviet Union for energy. Finally, having access to the technology that was involved in the construction of the pipeline was held to be advantageous to the Soviet Union. When Reagan eventually imposed an embargo on the supply of equipment for the pipeline, applying it to European companies that were producing equipment under licence from US companies, he ran into opposition even from his staunchest ally, Margaret Thatcher, and eventually had to back down.

This was not the only example of a rift between Thatcher

and Reagan. In common with other European leaders, Thatcher was shocked when Reagan appeared to come near to agreeing a package of reductions in nuclear weapons with President Gorbachev at the Reykjavik summit in October 1986, without consulting the NATO allies of the United States. The issue of closer EC collaboration on defence moved up the European agenda as a direct consequence of Reykjavik.

A Common Foreign and Security Policy

By the late 1980s there were even more circumstances pushing the EC states to consider extending EPC. The rapid collapse of Communism in eastern Europe and the Soviet Union produced a new and unstable political situation in Europe, accompanied by increasingly strong signals from the Bush administration that the United States could not afford to continue to carry the burden of European defence, and that once the Cold War was ended the Europeans would have to look after their own backyard. Also, the reunification of Germany revived latent fears of domination of the continent by the Germans, not least in France. Taken together, these circumstances contributed to the decision at the Dublin European Council in April 1990 to call an intergovernmental conference on political union.[35]

Adding to concern was the divided European response to the crisis in the Gulf region in 1990–1. EPC was always better at getting co-ordinated positions on routine matters than in crisis situations.[36] The Gulf crisis underlined this. Britain immediately supported US leadership of the coalition against Iraq, and committed substantial naval, air and ground forces. France also made a significant military commitment, but initially not under US command, and until the very last moment tried independently to negotiate a settlement; although once war broke out French troops and aircraft played a full and important role in the conflict. Germany pleaded that its constitution did not allow it to take part, although it did contribute money to the cost of the US war effort; while Belgium even refused to sell the British ammunition for their weapons for fear of terrorist reprisals.[37] It is interesting to note that this display of disunity led to diametrically opposed conclusions by Jacques Delors and the British Foreign Secretary, Douglas Hurd. Delors argued that the failure to reach an agreed position indicated the need for EPC to proceed in future on the basis of majority voting, while Hurd argued that the lack of a common view indicated that there was no basis for majority voting, which requires a broad underlying consensus.[38]

A similar lack of common ground was demonstrated over the crisis in Yugoslavia. When Croatia and Slovenia declared independence in June 1991 the German government argued in favour of their recognition; Britain and France argued for the agreed EC policy of supporting the integrity of the Yugoslav federation. After unsuccessful attempts to negotiate an agreement with the contending parties in Yugoslavia, the German government, under intense pressure from public opinion in Germany, insisted that either the EC recognise Croatia and Slovenia or it would do so unilaterally. The French and British governments, which realised that they would have to commit troops should peace-keeping prove necessary, backed the argument of the EC-appointed peace envoy, Lord Carrington, that any acceptance of the break-up of Yugoslavia would lead to civil war spreading into Bosnia and Macedonia. To preserve the appearance of unity, France and Britain eventually backed down in the face of German intransigence, but insisted on guarantees from the new states of protection of minority rights. Even then, the Germans broke ranks and recognised the republics independently without the agreed guarantees. As with the Gulf War, the EC failure in Yugoslavia led to different conclusions – on much the same basis – about the implications for CFSP.

Western European Union

Another subject of differences over regional security arrangements was the role of the Western European Union (WEU). This organisation, formed in 1954, had never really emerged from the shadow of NATO. However, it came increasingly to be seen as a potential vehicle to carry the security aspects of the EC in the face of US demands that the Europeans take more responsibility. It had the advantage that its membership included France, which although a member of NATO had withdrawn from the joint command structure in 1966; but that it did not include Ireland, Greece or Denmark, the states that had the biggest problems in being involved with any common security effort. Eventually WEU was incorporated in the TEU as an integral part of the European Union, and a bridge between the EU and NATO.

This did not resolve the question of how independent of the United States the European security structure should be. Britain and Italy were still committed to keeping the United States tied into the defence of Europe; France took the line that a more independent position was necessary; Germany appeared to want it both ways, so as to maintain its position as privileged partner of France while developing a special relationship with the United States that would displace British influence.

The Euro-corps

In addition to revealing differences between the member states of the EC, the Gulf crisis exposed the inadequacy of French forces to engage in such an exercise without assistance from the United States in the areas of intelligence and airlift capacity. Following the war the French began to advocate the creation of a European rapid-deployment force, under either EC or WEU control, which would have its own command structure, reconnaissance satellites and transport aircraft.[39] This initiative, combined with French concern about the threat of a resurgent Germany, led to the creation of a joint Franco-German brigade, which was seen as the basis for such a rapid-response force. Britain and the United States asked France and Germany to reconsider whether such a brigade was necessary given that NATO had just created a similar rapid-response force under British command, but other member states subsequently joined what became the 'Euro-corps', seeing it as a better alternative to an eventual German force that otherwise might prove inevitable.

The Treaty on European Union and beyond

The question of the relationship between the EC, WEU, and NATO took up a lot of the time of the 1991 intergovernmental conference on political union. In the end the TEU 'tilted more towards the Europeanists than the Atlanticists'.[40] The WEU was recognised as 'an integral part of the development of the European Union', and a declaration attached to the Treaty indicated that the member states intended to 'build up WEU in stages as the defence component of the Union'. At the same time, the declaration said that the future development of WEU was seen 'as a means to strengthen the European pillar of the Atlantic alliance'.

This ambiguous phrasing smacked of compromise and diplomacy. However, the issues that lay behind the declaration would have to be resolved in 1996 when the whole TEU was due to be reviewed, not least because the WEU itself expired in 1998. This promises to be a difficult issue to resolve, as the gap between the Europeanists and the Atlanticists shows no signs of closing. On the contrary, the removal of Russian troops from German soil might have inclined the German government to side more clearly with the Europeanists in the debate. As with monetary union, this threatened to become an issue on which a smaller group of countries than the full membership of the EU might decide to pursue a greater degree of unity than other members would be happy with.

The issue of military technology further complicates the situation. France and Britain remain the two largest military powers within the EU. However, whereas Britain is prepared to equip its armed forces with purchases from the United States where these are better value for money, the French insist on developing their own technology in this field, as in others. Their argument is the familiar one, dating back to Servan-Schreiber, about avoiding technological dependence. But the costs of R&D in this sector are escalating rapidly, and are increasingly proving to be beyond the capabilities of any one state to carry alone. European co-operation is indicated in this field as in others; the logic is to link arms-procurement policies to the existence of, if not a European army, then at least a closely integrated group of national armies. As in all these debates, the French position points to a greater degree of regionalism than the British.

Conclusion

Until the end of the 1980s moves towards regional integration
in western Europe revolved around a debate between two clear
views of the nature of the process: a French 'strategic trade'
view that stressed the need for the European states to organise
themselves to regain their autonomy in the economic sphere;
and a British 'free trade' view that saw regional integration as
no more than a contribution to a wider project to ensure that
the conditions existed for a global expansion of capitalism. In
the 1980s both voices in the debate supported the 1992 project
to free the internal market, although there were considerable
differences between France and Britain over the extent to which
the freeing of the market needed to be accompanied by monetary union and harmonisation of social provisions, with Germany and most of the other member states apparently siding
with France. Important Anglo-French differences also existed
over the extent to which Europe should develop an independent security identity. Britain was consistently more attached than
France to following the leadership of the United States, but
this became an untenable position as the United States itself
retreated from the hegemonic role and stressed the need for
partnership with Europe and a sharing of the burden. The
disagreement then extended to the issue of just how independent
the European position should be. Also, new security issues
appeared on the agenda, as the single market raised the question of how to combat cross-border criminal activity, and the
collapse of Communism in eastern Europe opened up the possibility of large-scale migration into the EU.

However, in the 1990s a newly powerful voice came to be
heard in the debate. It would not be accurate to call this the
voice of Germany, because the signals coming out of Germany
continued to be diverse. It was more accurately described as
the voice of Chancellor Helmut Kohl, who gained a new confidence and determination following reunification. Although
he had often appeared indecisive prior to the fall of the Berlin Wall, Kohl subsequently acted quickly and positively to ensure
the absorption of the East German Länder into the Federal
Republic. Having secured his place in history as the man who
reunified his country, Kohl became concerned to 'tie down'

the new Germany by binding it into closer European unity. He did not want to be remembered as a Frankenstein who created a monster that ran amok. This meant that he adopted many of the most federalist schemes for the future of the EU. From 1990 on it was the German chancellor who kept up the momentum for closer European integration, while the French government, in the face of the problems it encountered in getting the TEU ratified, retreated somewhat from these more advanced positions.

This left the prospects for a regional bloc in Europe somewhat unclear. Although Kohl supported closer European integration, it was not necessarily the case that the rest of Germany did. In particular, neither the Bundesbank nor the majority of the German people were in favour of monetary union, which Kohl advocated strongly. However, whether the argument went in favour of Kohl or of the other voices in Germany, the indications were that there would be no full-scale resort to protectionism. As Stephen Gill has pointed out, German industry and commercial banks were aware that the German economic position had to be both Europeanised and globalised if they were to prosper, and it is difficult to argue with his conclusion that 'the power of these interests will prevent any substantially inward-looking mercantilism, or economic nationalism, on the part of the new German state'.[41] The same analysis would suggest that Germany would not be a voice for regional protectionism within the EU.

This did not mean that there would be no attempt to protect certain industrial sectors. In trade terms, the momentum of the 1992 programme began more and more to run into problems as governments, including the German government, recoiled from the politically damaging effects of opening their markets. Derogations from the rules became more common in a number of fields. On the other hand, the opening of new markets in essential fields such as telecommunications showed that the pressure from large business interests had not abated.

In security terms, difficulties remained over the extent of military co-operation; but progress was made on internal co-ordination of rules on asylum, refugees, and the granting of visas. However, the common rules that were agreed were so restrictive that they opened up another meaning of the term

'Fortress Europe': an EU barricading itself against a possible influx of non-citizens. Again the agenda here was driven forward by German demands, Germany being the country that attracted by far the largest number of asylum applications.

Germany's new assertiveness caused strains in the Franco-German alliance in the 1990s, while the domestic problems of the British government over Europe weakened its ability to exploit these divisions and to bring its own view of the nature of the integration project to dominate within the debate in the EU. With clear signs emerging of public disillusionment with the whole project, the prospects for the emergence of a regional bloc were very difficult to define as the 1996 review of the TEU approached. The key issues were whether the EU would emerge as a more unified actor on the world stage, or whether Germany would emerge as the new dominant power in Europe, rather than whether Europe would try to disentangle itself from wider world affairs.

Notes

1. J.-J. Servan-Schreiber, *The American Challenge* translated by Ronald Steel (New York: Athenaeum, 1979).
2. A. Sampson, *Macmillan: A Study in Ambiguity* (London: Penguin 1967) p. 224.
3. Servan-Schreiber, *The American Challenge*, p. 47.
4. S. George, *Politics and Policy in the European Community* (Oxford: Oxford University Press, 2nd edn., 1991) pp. 173–8.
5. Commission of the European Communities, *Completing the Internal Market* 14 June 1985, COM(85) p. 310.
6. P. Cecchini, *The European Challenge, 1992: The Benefits of a Single Market* (Aldershot: Gower, 1988).
7. J. Pelkmans, 'The Significance of EC-1992', in P-H. Laurent (ed.), *The European Community: To Maastricht and Beyond*, special edition of *The Annals of the American Academy of Political and Social Science*, 531 (1994) 103.
8. For a detailed explanation of how these processes were supposed to operate, see George, *Politics and Policy in the European Community*, pp. 20–4.
9. A. Moravcsik, 'Negotiating the Single European Act: National Interests and Conventional Statecraft in the European Community', *International Organization*, 45 (1991) 19–56.
10. S. Bulmer and W. Paterson, *The Federal Republic of Germany and the European Community* (London: Allen & Unwin, 1987).

11. Ibid., p. 19.
12. Servan-Schreiber, *The American Challenge,* p. 41.
13. Ibid., p. 43.
14. Ibid., p. 42.
15. Ibid., p. 45.
16. Ibid., p. 51.
17. C. Grant, *Delors: Inside the House that Jacques Built* (London: Nicholas Brealey, 1994) p. 26.
18. M. Holmes, *Mrs Thatcher, Labour and the EEC* (London: Bruges Group, 1991).
19. R. D. McKinlay and R. Little, *Global Problems and World Order* (London: Pinter, 1986).
20. S. George, *An Awkward Partner: Britain in the European Community* (Oxford: Oxford University Press, 2nd edn., 1994) pp. 60–70.
21. Ibid., pp. 223–4.
22. S. George, 'The European Community: A Structuralist Perspective', *Sheffield Papers in International Studies,* No. 5 (Sheffield: Department of Politics, University of Sheffield, 1990).
23. W. Sandholtz and J. Zysman, '1992: Recasting the European Bargain', *World Politics,* 42 (1989) 95–128.
24. J. Peterson, 'Technology Policy in Europe: Explaining the Framework Programme and Eureka in Theory and Practice', *Journal of Common Market Studies,* 29 (1991) 269–90; M. Sharp and C. Shearman, *European Technological Collaboration* (London: Routledge & Kegan Paul, 1987); M. Sharp, 'The Community and the New Technologies', in J. Lodge (ed.), *The European Community and the Challenge of the Future* (London: Pinter, 1989), pp. 202–20; M. Sharp, 'The Single Market and European Policies for Advanced Technologies', in C. Crouch and D. Marquand (eds.), *The Politics of 1992: Beyond the Single European Market* (London: Political Quarterly Publishing Co., 1990) pp. 100–20.
25. Pelkmans, 'The Significance of EC-1992', 97.
26. Ibid., 98–9.
27. Ibid., 111.
28. S. Woolcock, 'The Uruguay Round: Issues for the European Community and the United States', *RIIA Discussion Papers, 31* (London: Royal Institute of International Affairs, 1990) p. 23.
29. C. Barclay, 'The Uruguay Round of GATT Negotiations', *House of Commons Background Paper No. 226* (London: House of Commons Library Research Division, 1991) pp. 6–7.
30. Grant, *Delors,* p. 176.
31. M. Thatcher, *Britain and Europe. Text of the Speech delivered in Bruges by the Prime Minister on 20th September 1988* (London: Conservative Political Centre, 1988) p. 7.
32. Sandholtz and Zysman, '1992: Recasting the European Bargain', 105.
33. In 1955 the foreign ministers of the six member states of the ECSC met at Messina in Italy and agreed to 'a fresh advance

towards the building of Europe' and to create a common market 'free from all customs duties and all quantitative restriction.' D. W. Urwin, *The Community of Europe: A History of European Integration since 1945* (London: Longman, 1991) p. 74.

34. E. Regelsberger, 'The Euro-Arab Dialogue: Procedurally Innovative, Substantially Weak', in G. Edwards and E. Regelsberger (eds.), *Europe's Global Links: The European Community and Inter-Regional Co-operation* (London: Pinter, 1990) pp. 57–65.

35. S. George, 'The European Community in the New Europe', in C. Crouch and D. Marquand (eds.), *Towards Greater Europe? A Continent Without an Iron Curtain* (Oxford: Blackwell, 1992), pp. 52–63.

36. C. Hill, 'EPC's Performance in Crises', in R. Rummel (ed.), *Toward Political Union: Planning a Common Foreign and Security Policy in the European Community* (Oxford: Westview Press, 1992) pp. 135–46.

37. S. Anderson, 'Western Europe and the Gulf War', in ibid., pp. 147–60.

38. J. Delors, 'European Integration and Security', Alastair Buchan Memorial Lecture, London, 7 March 1991; D. Hurd, The Churchill Memorial Lecture, Luxembourg, 19 February 1991.

39. Anderson, 'Western Europe and the Gulf War', p. 158.

40. D. Dinan, *Ever Closer Union? An Introduction to the European Community* (London: Macmillan, 1994) p. 472.

41. S. Gill, 'The Emerging World Order and European Change: The Political Economy of European Union', *Socialist Register*, 1992, p. 183.

3 Eastern Europe in Transition into the New Europe

IAN KEARNS

The collapse of Communism in 1989 symbolised, perhaps more effectively than anything else, the ending of the post-war era in world politics. In a few short months state élites in eastern Europe – in some cases supported by mass public pressure, though not in all – seized the opportunity afforded by Soviet weakness and relocated their countries within the nascent global order.[1] Theirs was a move to, or even in the eyes of some a 'return' to, the West and all it stood for in economic, political and ideological terms.[2] This move to the West, and in particular the establishment of a new pattern of relationships between the former-Communist countries of eastern Europe and the European Union (EU) and North Atlantic Treaty Organisation (NATO), was also accompanied by, and indeed partly caused by, an ongoing process of restructuring in the world economy and a renewed interest in region building in western Europe and elsewhere.[3]

The unfortunate effect of this, from an eastern European point of view, has been to complicate and confuse the already monumental task of post-Communist transformation. For it is clear that that which eastern Europe has sought to copy and, in an institutional sense become attached to, has itself been undergoing a dynamic process of change. This climate of change has in its turn led Western governments to respond to advances from the east with a mixture of vigour and caution. They have been vigorous in deploying the full force of Western ideology and economic power in order to open up eastern European markets and cautious in restricting the nature of emerging

55

institutional links between eastern Europe and the EU and NATO. For the post-Communist eastern European states, this has meant a frustrating relationship with the West, characterised by abundant rhetoric but little substance. Nevertheless, both caution and frustration are predictable in such periods of historic change and the possible enlargement of western European economic and security institutions to include eastern European states is, publicly at least, still on the agenda of policy makers in both parts of Europe. It is, consequently, the central purpose of this chapter to examine just how likely such a future enlargement can be said to be.

Clearly, in addressing this question a number of factors, both external and internal to the eastern European region, need attention. Externally, decisions taken in Bonn, Paris and London over the needs of the EU in the global competition with the United States and Japan, and the potential impact of such needs upon cost/benefit analyses of an enlargement of the Union to the east, will be critical. The same is true also of the actions and reactions of an increasingly reassertive Russian foreign policy élite on questions of eastern European international relations. Crucial though these areas may be, however, for reasons of space they are left largely unexplored here. Internally, within eastern Europe, the nature of emerging links to the EU and other bodies will be determined by the unfolding course of economic and political transformation. Successful progress towards capitalism and pluralist democracy is seen in the West as a prerequisite to final acceptance and membership in the western European bloc. Failed transformation, economic collapse and a rising tide of nationalist tensions would almost certainly destroy any such prospects for membership and may, ultimately, lead to a destabilisation of the continent as a whole.

In view of this, and the consequent need to focus upon the transformation process, the main body of the material presented below is organised into three sections. The first explores the nature of the post-1945 eastern European experience with regional co-operation in the form of Soviet hegemony. It is argued that an understanding both of the difficulties and course of post-Communist transformation and of initial post-1989 eastern European attitudes to 'Europe' is impossible without a prior exploration of this period. The second and largest section examines the ideology, strategy and impact of post-Communist transformation and, in particular, focuses upon the themes of liberalisation and democratisation. The analysis of these two interrelated processes then forms the backdrop to the third and final section of the chapter, which reviews the changed nature of relationships between the EU, NATO and eastern Europe and sets out the constraints and patterns of development which will govern their future direction.

A prior task is, however, to clarify what is meant by the term eastern Europe as used in this chapter. Hereafter this term refers to the Visegrad four of Poland, Hungary, and the Czech and Slovak Republics, plus Bulgaria and Romania. Yugoslavia and its former constituent republics, due to the distorting influence of war, are not discussed, other than in terms of the impact which the dissolution of Yugoslavia may have upon transformation in the region more generally. The republics of the former Soviet Union are also excluded, partly again for reasons of space, but also because, in so far as any eastern enlargement of the western European bloc is likely, it will embrace the countries in focus here rather than those further to the east. With this limited geographical focus in mind, it is now possible to turn to an exploration of the nature of post-war Soviet hegemony.

Soviet hegemony 1945–89

The Soviet perspective

> Brezhnev spoke at length about the sacrifices of the Soviet Union in the Second World War: at such a cost, the Soviet Union had gained security, and the guarantee of that security was the postwar division of Europe. . . .'For us,' Brezhnev went on, 'the results of the Second World war are inviolable, and we will defend them even at the cost of risking a new war.' And then he said in so many words that they would have undertaken the military intervention in Czechoslovakia even if such a risk had existed.[4]

During the years of the Cold War, it was fashionable in the West to dismiss Soviet attitudes and policies towards eastern

Europe as clearly motivated by malicious and aggressive intent. As the above quote illustrates, however, the key Soviet priority under all generations of leaders who witnessed the appalling and disproportionate cost to the Soviet state of the Second World War was the achievement of security. It is not possible, therefore, to separate out the massive psychological impact of war upon Soviet citizens and politicians from the institutions and patterns of international relationships which were imposed on eastern Europe in the post-war period. For in Soviet eyes, and indeed over a much longer period of history in the eyes of Imperial Russia and its rulers, the main source of insecurity was to be found coming from, or through, eastern Europe itself. The building of a bloc centred on eastern Europe was, therefore, seen as a justified response to a traumatic history.

The sense and legitimacy of such a post-war security strategy was further reinforced by a number of deeply-held Soviet, or perhaps more properly Russian, cultural predispositions toward eastern Europe. Russian views on Europe since the early nineteenth century may be said to have reflected a debate between 'Westernisers' and 'Slavophiles'.[5] All of those caught under these labels share a common view that Europe is a divided continent between the Latin West and the Slavic East. Whereas Westernisers are in favour of a partial merger between the two via an incorporation of enlightened political institutions and ideas from the West, 'Slavophiles' oppose such moves. Western Europe, in the view of the latter tradition, is like a contagious disease which threatens to infect the morally superior and distinct Slavic civilisation. The 'Slavophile' view received a boost in the context of a widespread failure of European Communist parties in the inter-war period and from the simultaneous rise of Fascist influence in central and eastern Europe. According to Dawisha, the adoption of Stalin's 'Socialism in One Country' as a response marked 'the final ascendancy of Slavophile reflexes *vis-à-vis* Europe.'[6] The subsequent costs of the Second World War only served to magnify this sentiment many times over. It was Europe that had given rise to Fascism and the Soviet Army which had largely buried it. The mental furniture of Soviet policy makers at the end of the war was dominated, therefore, not only by fear of insecurity and the need to do something about it. Despite what were perceived as the dubious roles played by some eastern European countries in the war, it was also endowed with a genuine sense of pan-Slavic identity and a belief that Soviet control of the region would set the eastern Europeans free from their troubled history.

The eastern European response

Although understandable historically, the Soviet perspective was largely unacceptable in eastern Europe in almost every respect. No matter how noble the Soviet sentiment, in eastern European eyes at least Soviet policy still amounted to repression. Rather than being saved from their history, many eastern Europeans felt they were being denied it. Far from feeling a sense of pan-Slavic identity, Soviet dominance reinforced (perhaps only temporarily) a sense of cultural affinity to the West. Far from feeling secure, eastern Europeans felt the cold hand of another dominant power and the absence of both state and individual political rights.

An alternative view of eastern European history and culture, especially within the central European states of Poland, Hungary and Czechoslovakia, has been offered by Kundera.

'What,' he asks, 'does Europe mean to a Hungarian, a Czech, a Pole: for thousands of years their nations have belonged to a part of Europe rooted in Roman Christianity. They have participated in every period of its history. For them the word 'Europe' does not represent a phenomenon of geography but a spiritual notion synonymous with the West. The moment Hungary is no longer European – that is, no longer Western, it is driven from its destiny, beyond its own history: it loses the essence of its identity.[7]

Because of such differing perceptions of history and identity, the Soviet insistence on placing Communist regimes loyal to Moscow in each of the eastern European states post-1945 created a serious potential for conflict. This would not have been a problem had the extent of support for Communist parties in the eastern European countries been higher. In most cases, though, as is well-known, these parties either came to power as a direct result of Soviet interference (as in Poland, the German Democratic Republic, Hungary and Romania) or, where they had come to power with a degree of indigenous support (such as in Czechoslovakia and, to a lesser extent, Bulgaria), later lost legitimacy and relied upon Soviet power for the maintenance of their positions in government.[8] This conflict, in which whole nations and societies were looking to the West but regimes were looking to the Soviet Union, became visible in dramatic fashion time and again over four and a half decades of Soviet domination. Events in Berlin in 1953, Hungary in 1956, Czechoslovakia in 1968, and Poland in 1980–1 were all evidence of crises in regime legitimacy. The sense of political frustration, and of a betrayal of traditions and values, was added to for many eastern Europeans by a perception that their material development was being held back by Soviet influence. This was felt particularly strongly in countries such as Poland and Czechoslovakia where democracy and a degree of capitalist success characterised the inter-war period.[9]

Within the context of this basic tension, the major institutions of the Soviet bloc, namely the Warsaw Treaty Organization (WTO) and the Council for Mutual Economic Assistance (CMEA), need primarily to be seen as attempts to manage eastern European affairs in the Soviet interest, rather than as genuine expressions of a sense of regional identity and collective interest. The Warsaw Pact Treaty, signed in 1955, formalised and attempted to give some legal basis to the continued Soviet military presence in eastern Europe. Its entire structure and operation support the view of an alliance designed, again in Dawisha's words, 'to present a credible military threat to NATO without giving east European armies, individually, or collectively, the ability to defy the Soviet Union'.[10]

Underpinning this security arrangement was a political and economic system developed under Soviet tutelage and clearly reflecting the influence of the Stalinist model developed in the Soviet Union itself. Communist parties, through their internal organisation according to democratic centralist principles and via their position as the leading force in society, were able to keep tight control over their populations. They were assisted in this by the organisation of centrally planned economies and the party-led bureaucracy which staffed and implemented them.

Press, media and all other social activities were also monitored and exposed to rigid ideological indoctrination.[11]

Ultimately, in the event that all of these mechanisms of control failed to deliver the desired outcome, the Soviets relied directly upon the threat, or actual use, of military force in order to maintain or restore order. After the 1968 invasion of Czechoslovakia, this instrument of policy was legitimised in the underlying principles of the Brezhnev Doctrine. These declared, 'the indivisibility of the socialist commonwealth, the primacy of its interests over the sovereignty of an individual socialist country, and the legitimacy of military assistance to a fraternal country where the overt actions of enemies of socialism within the country and beyond its boundaries . . . create a threat to the common interests of the socialist camp.'[12] Given that this doctrine effectively remained in force until 1989, the evidence is clear that eastern European security interests were effectively subordinated to those of the Soviet Union and that the security structure was imposed upon the region, rather than growing out of it.

In economic terms, the bloc was co-ordinated via the CMEA and, in Soviet eyes at least, there is little doubt that this organisation was designed to fulfil a parallel function to that performed by the WTO in the military sphere. However, the evidence of its impact is less clear. The extent to which the CMEA system operated to Soviet or eastern European advantage has been the source of genuine economic debate.[13] Although the eastern European states appear to have been more adept at fighting their corner in the economic field, the central economic consequence of being tied into the Soviet bloc was nevertheless severe trade, and especially energy, dependence on the Soviet Union. Certainly, relative to their trade with the Soviet Union, the eastern Europeans traded little among themselves and even less with states outside the CMEA.[14]

The major changes in Soviet policy toward eastern Europe which were introduced under Mikhail Gorbachev's leadership represented a fundamental Soviet reassessment of interests and benefits associated with the structures outlined above. While not dismissing long-held and legitimate security concerns, Gorbachev clearly downgraded Soviet assessments of the likely threat posed by NATO. In this context, control over eastern Europe was no longer necessary; influence was enough. Furthermore, as the eastern European economies stagnated in the late 1970s and through the 1980s and the legitimacy of Communist rule deteriorated even further, it became clear that relations with the West were suffering and that, paradoxically, Soviet security was being threatened by the continuation of the policies and regimes initially designed to preserve it. For these reasons, Gorbachev effectively allowed the Brezhnev Doctrine to lapse by not intervening to save Communist rule in Poland and Hungary in early 1989 and, by so doing, let it be known that eastern Europe was free to pursue its own course. The result was an attempt by eastern Europe to abandon everything associated with the post-war period and to attach itself firmly to the West.

Post-Communist transformation

Western ideas and institutions in this historical context possessed an almost magical quality in eastern European eyes at the beginning of the post-Communist transformation process. In contrast to the Soviet-imposed system, the West appeared to enjoy a morally superior, more legitimate and more successful system of political and economic life. The theme of 'returning to Europe' became, therefore, an umbrella for the simultaneous attempts to liberalise economies, move to pluralistic political systems and join western European organisations such as NATO and the EU. To understand this ideological affinity with the West, however, and to appreciate its content and impact more fully, it is insufficient simply to draw upon the level of legitimacy which Western systems and institutions appeared to have in the context of freedom from the Communist past. Other factors, including resource dependency and the socialisation of eastern European élites into Western ways of thinking, also played their part.

The ideology of transformation

The receptivity of eastern Europeans to Western ideas was heavily structured by the ideological legacy of the Cold War. Although including a naively optimistic and Utopian view of the West

relative to Communism, this legacy also included a misunder-
standing of the nature of the West itself. The logic of the Cold
War was that only two socio-economic systems existed and that,
as the opposite of the Communist system was 'capitalism',
capitalism itself constituted a single system. As Communist
regimes collapsed, therefore, there did not occur debates over
the varieties of capitalist system available. Nor was democracy,
and the state and non-state institutions required to make it a
reality, discussed as anything more than the implementation
of periodic and relatively free elections. Capitalism and democracy were simply to be viewed as the inversion of what had
previously passed for Marxism.[15]

In conceiving of a more detailed content for their capitalism,
eastern European dissidents and political activists drew dispro-
portionately upon the ideological legacy left by the Thatcher
and Reagan administrations which dominated the West in the
1980s. These Western politicians, above all others, came to
symbolise freedom and democracy in eastern Europe. They were
elevated in status by broadcasts from *Voice of America* and *Radio
Free Europe* and were, then, literally projected into a context in
which east Europeans lacked objective information or the ability
to travel freely outside of the Communist world.

Once the Communists had passed from the scene, eastern
European leaderships hungry for contact with the West were
happy to be socialised further into this view by policy advisers
articulating its central tenets. In particular, the Harvard economist Jeffrey Sachs became the guru of many concerned with
the issues of economic transformation. As the main author of
the 'big bang' or 'shock therapy' approach to the problem
and as adviser to the first Solidarity government in Poland which
later pioneered the transformation process under his guidance,
Sachs's ideas came to reflect and embody a certain orthodoxy.
Essentially, his recommendations were the same as those made
to Latin American governments in the 1980s and involved severe austerity programmes and reductions of state influence
over the economy coupled with a far greater reliance on the
operation of markets to deliver wealth. As applied to eastern
Europe, this involved the reduction of state subsidies to inefficient
enterprises, liberalisation of prices (including food and fuel),
the liberalisation of trade and exchange rates to encourage

foreign investment and competition, and the reform or restructuring of banking and financial-services sectors. Crucially, in
Sachs's view, these measures were needed simultaneously and
quickly since capitalism consisted of an organic whole and attempts to introduce it piecemeal would only destroy the old
centrally-planned system without replacing it with a functioning
new one.[16]

For those in eastern Europe who were less convinced of the
automatic legitimacy of such programmes or who believed,
contrary to the orthodoxy, that this was not the only way to
transform an economy, there has been little room for manoeuvre.
Where ideological persuasion has not proved sufficient to open
an eastern European economy, it, like the old Soviet-dominated
system, has been reinforced by the application, or rather in
this case the withholding, of Western material power. In particular the International Monetary Fund (IMF), which has
developed stand-by agreements with all of the states in the region,
has insisted on close application of the Sachs orthodoxy in
exchange for its stamp of approval and practical financial help.
The same is true also of all other sources of official aid being
offered to the region. Given the compelling influence which
Western ideological and material power has in eastern Europe
and the near impossibility of planning a development strategy
which ignores it, the success in application of the unavoidable
Sachs orthodoxy was clearly vital to a successful post-Communist
transformation of the region. Furthermore, as realisation of
the project of 'returning to Europe' depended upon just such
a successful transformation, economic change was clearly linked
to the prospects for an eastern enlargement of the western
European bloc.

The impact of economic liberalisation

Since early 1990, the orthodox model of economic transformation has broadly guided policies across eastern Europe. Differences between the states with which we are concerned are
differences over speed and detailed application rather than of
substance and direction. The Czech Republic, Hungary, Poland
and Slovakia are, for example, considered to be much further
advanced in the process than are Balkan states such as Bul-

garia and Romania. Within the former group, the Mazowiecki government in Poland led the way with its adoption of 'shock therapy' after September 1989. Polish prices were speedily liberalised, wages were restrained and high real interest rates were maintained in order to encourage savings and discourage consumption. A strategy for severely reducing the budget deficit was introduced which included 'first, a huge reduction in public expenditure (such as in food and energy subsidies and military and internal security spending), and secondly, an increase in revenue through the abolition of numerous tax exemptions, increases in sales tax and more disciplined tax collection'.[17] To facilitate the liberalisation of Poland's international economic relations, exchange rates were freed and the zloty made internally convertible. In addition, quantitative and administrative controls on imports were suppressed and licences abolished while the only measures introduced to replace these protective devices were a low common tariff and some limited subsidies for exporters.

Some of these measures, though introduced primarily for reasons of macro-economic stabilisation, were also counted on to have beneficial effects in terms of micro-economic adjustment. It was, for example, thought that efficiency incentives provided to managers via new hard budget constraints and foreign competition would help to create pressures for enterprise restructuring. However, the main tool of micro-economic adjustment was the strategy for mass and rapid privatisation. Here the Polish government, while maintaining control over some natural monopolies and key industries, swiftly sold off the majority of small enterprises, shops and restaurants. For large-scale privatisation, it adopted a mass programme of voucher distribution to citizens in exchange for small cash payments and in which each voucher could be exchanged for units within a National Wealth Management Fund. Citizens would own fund units which reflected a portfolio of shares and the Fund would invest in, and influence, the restructuring of the enterprises concerned. This strategy was thought to be the fastest and fairest way of redistributing the huge amount of property held in state hands and reflected the dogmatic belief that private ownership of any kind was preferable to state ownership.

Other countries in eastern Europe have since followed Poland's example. All introduced very similar austerity programmes and opened their economies to international competition and many ran, or are intending in future to run, privatisation schemes of a similar nature to the one outlined above. Czechoslovakia, before the Czech and Slovak split at the beginning of January 1993, completed the first of a two-stage process of mass voucher privatisation. In both countries the scheme was popular and in 1995 both will see the beginning of the second phase of the operation. Bulgaria also, despite a much slower beginning, was attempting to proceed with mass privatisation in 1995. Hungary and Romania are the exceptions to this rule, though for different reasons. Hungary, the most liberal state in the region under the Communists, had a head start and has since taken a more gradual approach to privatisation, seeking to sell, rather than give away enterprises.[18] Romania, on the other hand, as perhaps the most tightly controlled of the states in the Communist period, has seen only slow progress in this area (given that the old ruling élite has managed to retain power over the course of two elections on a programme of cautious transformation).[19]

The proponents of the orthodox model of transformation always expected that its implementation would be painful, at least in the short term, but also that in the long term it would lead to sustained growth. Few Western analysts or institutions openly predicted that the effect would be as dramatic or as destructive as it has in fact been. Output in eastern Europe has suffered a spectacular collapse since 1989 and this is clearly reflected in annual percentage changes in real GDP. For eastern Europe as a whole, real GDP declined by approximately 8 per cent in 1990 and by around 11 per cent in both 1991 and 1992. Although the decline for 1993 is estimated to have slowed to only 5.7 per cent and is predicted at around the same for 1994, the IMF did not envisage positive growth for the region until 1995 and even then estimates growth of only 1.4 per cent.[20] Furthermore, if these figures are broken down on a state by state basis it becomes clear that none of the economies under consideration here enjoyed any growth in the three-year period 1990 to 1992, with the exception of Poland which grew by 2.6 per cent in 1992 and by a further 3.8 per cent in 1993. The Czech Republic, the other country most favoured for early membership of the European Union, was expected to have enjoyed growth in 1994 of 2.5 per cent though, if achieved, this would have represented the first growth for four years and would have come on the heels of the very steep declines noted above. To recover the real GDP levels enjoyed at the start of the transformation process in 1989, both of these countries, like the region as a whole, would need to enjoy year-on-year growth for several years into the future and convergence of any kind with western European economies would require growth rates above those either already registered or predicted.

The contraction of the eastern European economies is also clearly reflected in the explosion of unemployment across the region. Unemployment levels in mid-1994 were, in every country other than the Czech Republic, the same or higher than the average EU level of 11 per cent and the painful unemployment generating process of privatisation is only partially complete; the figures will continue to rise. The highest rates of unemployment in eastern Europe could be found in Poland with 17 per cent, followed by the Slovak Republic and Bulgaria on approximately 13 per cent and Hungary and Romania on 11 per cent each.[21] Although the Czech Republic had unemployment of less than 4 per cent at the beginning of 1995, this low figure was not only a reflection of a better economic performance relative to the region as a whole but also derived directly from a reluctance to make inefficient state companies bankrupt. As new bankruptcy laws were implemented more keenly in 1995, the unemployment figure was expected to rise sharply.[22]

To understand this spectacular economic collapse two inter-related factors must be taken into account. First, at the domestic level, it has been far more difficult to lay the foundations of a successful market economy than was anticipated. In particular, the privatisation process has run into serious problems and, even where the process is well-advanced, it is not producing successful enterprises on a scale sufficient to make up for the collapse of the state sector. In many countries the privatisation process was delayed due to the uncertain legal status of much of the property being sold. In Poland, for example, reforms in the early 1980s had, at least legally, given many employees a claim to own the enterprises in which they worked. Before the Polish government could pass a privatisation law, therefore, it was forced to clear up the legal position by re-nationalising property. The result was that a Comprehensive Decree on Privatisation was not passed until July 1990, a full seven months after many other measures of the economic transformation programme were begun.[23] The legal position has also been confused due to compensation and restitution claims from those who had property confiscated by the Communists in the late 1940s.[24]

Furthermore, where such difficulties have been overcome and strategies for privatisation have actually been implemented, a range of other problems have become evident. The adoption of mass privatisation by voucher itself is evidence of this. The alternative of selling enterprises to the highest bidder was deemed politically unacceptable by most governments since, domestically, the only people with money to invest would have been the old *nomenklatura* élite. Similarly foreign investment, while desperately needed, would, if excessive, have symbolised the abandonment of the national economic interest. Pricing enterprises has also proved difficult as accounts were not transparent and the real pattern of former subsidies was unclear to all but a few. Even if such difficulties had not existed the process of privatisation would have been problematic due to the serious shortage of capital in the region. Since 1990 neither the level of domestic capital nor investment from outside has amounted to anything like the sums required to buy the enterprises which needed to be sold. Voucher privatisation, while thought to be politically fair, has then effectively meant the giving away of state assets for very little return in terms of state revenues. What is more, given that it transfers ownership but does not represent an injection of new capital, it does not even provide the resources necessary for the modernisation and growth of the enterprise concerned. The former Polish Minister for Ownership Transformation summarised the situation well. 'Privatisation in Poland,' he said, 'is like selling nobody's property of an unknown value to people who have no money to buy it.'[25]

Where privatisation has been declared as the objective but is still to be operationalised on a large scale, such as in Bulgaria and Romania, the situation is no better. The vacuum created by delay has been filled by corrupt practices which are delegitimising the whole process. So-called 'hidden privatisation' is now occurring in both of these Balkan states. Private companies are formed to supply state enterprises with inputs at high prices and other companies take their subsidised output for selling on at market prices. State-owned companies pile up inter-enterprise debt while a new class of millionaires emerges. Profit is privatised while losses remain the property of the state.[26] In Sofia, the image of gangsterism and rapacious capitalists extracting wealth at the expense of the poor is reinforced by the activities of Serbian sanctions busters, occasional shoot-outs between rival entrepreneurs and periodic car bombings. The decision in late 1994 to withdraw many of the top Bulgarian companies from the mass privatisation scheme before it even started also fuelled suspicions that the governing élite was itself a party to such subversions of the economic transformation programme and sought only to serve its own economic gain.

Quite apart from these difficulties with privatisation, and there-fore with the supposed main engine of new growth in eastern European economies, a second major cause explains the scale of the post-1989 collapse. Liberalisation and geographical reorientation of trade patterns has in many cases exposed eastern European enterprises to a level of competition well beyond their present capacity to respond. Although growing trade figures between eastern Europe and the EU and, more broadly, be-tween eastern Europe and the Organisation for Economic Co-operation and Development (OECD) countries are often interpreted in a positive light as proof of the extent to which the region is reintegrating itself into the world economy, the emergent trading position is best viewed negatively. Between 1989 and mid-1992 most eastern European states registered a surge of exports to the OECD area. For Bulgaria, for example, the increase over the period was 58.1 per cent, for Poland and Hungary around 56 per cent and for Czechoslovakia 40.6 per cent. However, these facts mask a number of important points. For most of the states concerned, the increases in exports to the OECD were more than outweighed by the collapse in trade within the former CMEA itself. This collapse was brought about largely by the decision to switch to trading on a hard currency basis from 1 January 1991. Given that many eastern European states felt they could buy better products outside of the former CMEA area, they effectively stopped trading with each other in favour of trading with the West.

Political factors also played their part in this trade reorientation in that the unification of Germany and the break-up of the Soviet Union destroyed many existing trade deals. Indeed, such was the scale of the collapse in former CMEA members' trade with each other that, despite the increases of exports to the OECD countries noted above, most eastern European states were actually exporting less in absolute terms at the end of 1992 than they had been at the beginning of 1989. Furthermore, the surge of exports to the OECD area was also more than matched by the surge of imports. By the end of 1993, almost all states in central and eastern Europe were running serious trade deficits with the industrialised world.

In addition to changes in the volume and direction of eastern European trade, significant changes in its structure are also evident. Trade with the Soviet Union previously consisted largely of eastern European exports of manufactured goods in exchange for Soviet raw materials and energy. Trade with the Third World also provided opportunities for exports of manufactures since, although the eastern European products were not of the same quality as those produced in the West, they often came with aid and arms packages attached. The combined effect on eastern Europe of the end of the Cold War and trade liberalisation with the West has been, as Haynes has noted, 'a major restructuring of trade which has effectively deindustrialised a significant part of the trade structure'.[27] The eastern European economies are therefore being turned into exporters of low-level manufactures, raw materials and agricultural goods. 'These economies,' Haynes continues, 'are being forced to compete by adjusting downwards into areas where there is both substantial world market competition already and considerable barriers to trade.'[28]

At a far more fundamental level, the changing structure and patterns of economic activity in eastern Europe reflect basic flaws in the assumptions underpinning prevailing orthodoxy on transformation strategy. Capitalism has never been a single system as the diversified models of it found in the US, Japan, Germany and across Scandinavia illustrate.[29] Despite the advice of Western neo-liberal economists and institutions such as the IMF, there is also no single approach of merit which can justifiably claim authoritative knowledge on the way in which capitalist forms should be introduced into the former Communist world. Furthermore, the notion that markets themselves will generate wealth is flawed and bears no relation to the history of capitalist development. With the possible exception of Britain, as the first country to industrialise, modern capitalism has emerged around the world on the basis of massive state intervention. In Imperial Germany, Meiji Japan, Tsarist Russia before the Great War and even the United States, massive state investments and protective devices were used to cultivate and nurture nascent capitalist structures. By focusing attention upon a false choice between states or markets, the current transformation orthodoxy diverts attention away from the real role of the state in capitalist development and, in particular, from the issue of what the correct mix of state and market should be.[30] Unless the current orthodoxy is abandoned, only two paths out of the current crisis can be seen to exist. On the one hand, eastern Europe could receive massive injections of capital in the form of aid, loans and foreign direct investment from the industrialised world to facilitate regeneration or, on the other, policies of even greater austerity could be introduced to help keep each economy afloat internationally but at a low level of *per capita* GDP and at terrible social and perhaps political cost.

All of the indications so far are that the first of these possible outcomes will not happen. Estimates of the amounts required to assist eastern Europe effectively in a successful transformation to capitalism vary. The sums involved in the Marshall Aid programme after the Second World War would, at today's prices, amount to around 300 billion ecu. Although no serious consideration has been given to an aid programme on such a scale, these figures are close to eastern Europe's current needs. It has been estimated that 85–190 billion ecu a year would be necessary to regenerate the physical infrastructure of eastern Europe while the World Bank has calculated that 50 billion ecu would be required over a ten-year period in telecommunications alone.[31] In this context, the recommendation of around 14 billion ecu by former EU Commission President Jacques Delors seems modest in the extreme but even this outweighs the response which has actually been mounted by the West. Figures for official assistance from all Western sources including the EU, the rest of the Group of Twenty-four and institutions

such as the IMF, World Bank and European Bank for Reconstruction and Development (EBRD), indicate that between January 1990 and June 1992 a total of only 38 billion ecu was
transferred to eastern Europe as a whole. Of this, almost half
went to Poland alone as a reward for its good behaviour as the
'shock therapy' initiator.

In addition to official flows of assistance, some foreign investment has occurred, notably in Hungary which has claimed
approaching half of the total. The amounts, however, are not
significant considering the scale of the problem. In late 1994,
the *Economist* magazine noted that: 'Between 1990 and 1993,
the associated countries (of the EU) got less than 10 billion
ecu in foreign direct investment, compared with 15 billion ecu
to Singapore alone.'[32] Clearly, then, the capital inflows to eastern Europe, from all sources, amount to nothing like the sums
required to mount a successful economic transformation. When
debt repayments from the region are added to the equation,
the catastrophic lack of Western assistance comes into full view.
Debt service payments (that is, the actual interest payments
made) between 1991 and 1993 for eastern Europe as a whole
amounted to 33 billion ecu and for 1994 alone were expected
to rise to over 21 billion ecu.[33]

The conclusion must therefore be that the eastern European
transition from the era of the centrally-planned economy, while
certainly integrating eastern Europe into the structures of world
capitalism, will not be a transition producing increased wealth
for most eastern Europeans. The problem is not one of short-
term costs of transition but of fundamental structural weakness. To view the picture positively, one needs either an excess
of economic optimism or an almost biblical faith in the institution of the market. As this author has neither, the argument
proceeds on the assumption that the first great criterion for
membership of the West, namely a successful economic transformation, has not been, and will not be, fulfilled.

Democratisation: trends and prospects

If we turn our attention to the political situation, it can be
said that, at a superficial level, much progress has been made
in the democratisation of eastern Europe. One-party rule has

been replaced by multi-party political systems and the introduction of new constitutions that not only guarantee new parties the right to exist but also give real powers to elected parliaments. In addition, there has been a great proliferation in the number of political parties which appears to suggest an outpouring of political activity and a healthy diversity of views. This situation has prompted some to conclude that, whereas one might have expected an ideological vacuum to have emerged in the post-1989 period, in practice the opposite has been the case. To the extent that a political transformation problem still exists, analysts such as Judy Batt believe it to be one of 'forging a manageable and acceptable pluralistic framework to cope with the surge of fragmented and unstructured interests and values now jostling for a place on the public stage'.[34] This positive picture of change is reinforced by the partial freeing of press and media activity and by evidence of change in the attitudes of the population at large. According to research undertaken in late 1993 and early 1994 by the Paul Lazarsfeld Society in Vienna, the vast majority of eastern Europeans now feel freer than under the former Communist regimes across a whole range of areas. More than 80 per cent of people feel that they have greater freedom of speech and are more at liberty to join the organisations of their choice. Clear majorities also expressed a feeling of greater freedom to travel and the absence of fear of arrest.[35]

Despite these trends and opinion-survey results, however, only the naive or unwary will accept this as a full and accurate reflection of the situation. Eastern Europe faces a number of severe obstacles to a successful process of democratisation and to understand these it is necessary first to correct some widely perpetuated myths about eastern European history and political culture. Over many centuries and long before the recent period of Soviet hegemony, the states of eastern Europe have been dominated and controlled by the major powers of Europe. Almost until the outbreak of World War One, they were subsumed within the Ottoman and Austro–Hungarian Empires and, only when those empires collapsed at the end of the war, did the region as a whole enjoy a degree of political independence. Even then, the course of eastern European development in the inter-war years was gravely distorted by Western ideological influence.

The victorious powers in 1918 created new states and redrew the boundaries of others. They introduced political systems which reflected the essential American model of strong legislatures and weak executives and integrated eastern Europe more fully into the structures of world capitalism than had ever before been the case. In a region of great ethnic diversity and complexity and in which populations were largely illiterate and had no tradition of popular participation in politics, the result was a legacy of states and interstate boundaries which lacked legitimacy and became the focus for many nationalist disputes. Intolerance of the difficult and messy compromises associated with democracy also quickly combined with the economic chaos of the Great Depression to consign to failure this first attempt to democratise the region and, in less than 20 years after 1918, all eastern European democracies, with the exception of Czechoslovakia, had given way to right-wing authoritarianism and Fascism.[36] While it may be legitimate to argue, therefore, that the post-1945 period of Soviet domination divorced eastern Europe from its real history, it is equally if not more legitimate to argue that the history from which it was separated was one of autocracy, authoritarianism and ethnic nationalist strife. The notion of a 'return to Europe' in the political sense is, therefore, best seen as a myth perpetuated only by those who see political advantage in it in terms of setting the new post-Communist course of development. Furthermore, although there is no automatic reason to assume that the future will be like the past, there are sufficient parallels to be drawn between the contemporary period and the tragedy of the inter-war years to make the comparison worthwhile. In particular, it is important to note that the period of Communist rule did not eradicate many of the earlier barriers to a successful democratisation. Indeed, in many cases, the post-1945 period actually saw not only the survival, but also a reinforcement, of some of the earlier traditions and attitudes to politics.

To understand these earlier attitudes, and to contrast them with those in the West, it is necessary in very broad terms to return to the differences between 'western' and 'eastern' variants of Christianity and to the areas forming the borders between the two. George Schöpflin has pointed out that, in the west, secular political systems characterised by popular sovereignty and an autonomous judiciary derive from particular elements of the western variant of the religion. Western Christianity, he notes, has 'tended to emphasise the role of the individual conscience over the collectivity . . . provided space for the working out of individual rather than collective salvation and allowed for a degree of reciprocity and mutual obligation. When translated into politics, this gave saliency to a two-way relationship between rulers and ruled that avoided the most extreme forms of absolutism found outside Europe.'[37]

Crucially, in central and eastern Europe, western Christianity was not able to play this same role. Partly because it was in competition with the eastern variant and partly because it faced pagan challenges, the church was less able to exert its authority over that of the secular rulers. In political terms this meant much less reciprocity between rulers and ruled and laid a foundation for a much stronger role for the state in society. However, through its refusal to allow the cultural and institutional development of society itself, early state forms in central Europe were weakened in their external relations to the point where they easily fell under external domination. Both lack of democracy and lack of national self-determination, therefore, characterised the region. This had two important consequences. First, it meant that civic and ethnic political programmes and collective and individual freedom emerged onto the agenda at the same time and have been confused in the region ever since. Second, it produced political systems in which societies were dominated by states and managed by small élites while the exercise of state power and the exclusion of the mass of people from it was legitimised by reference to nationalism. If anything, this situation was even more pronounced in the Balkans where the dominance of the eastern variant of Christianity stressed external control by community and tradition over individual conscience. In these areas, more than in central Europe, the strength of the state and the weakness of society is still evident today.

Eastern Europe's history and culture is, therefore, clearly distinct from that of the West. In contemporary political practice, this throws up significant problems which the current attempt at political transformation must face and overcome. Across the region, there is an all-pervading sense of suspicion towards politics and politicians and a tendency to compensate for this by the generation of historical myths. Furthermore, as Batt has pointed out, there is a widespread belief that politics is a technical business carried out by a separate class of experts who, in accordance with the various models at their disposal, simply 'do' politics to the people. The notion of a popular participatory role is still to take hold, as witnessed by the generally low turn-outs in elections since 1989.[38] A deep distrust of political parties is also evident. This distrust of the party form and its association with corrupt attempts to accumulate power at the expense of the people explains the popularity of large movement parties which characterised the region immediately after 1989. Solidarity in Poland, Civic Forum in the Czech Republic and People Against Violence in Slovakia were all clear illustrations of this phenomenon. Since the break-up of these movements, the proliferation of parties has come with a volatility in the support attached to them. Consequently, the general condition of the region has been summarised by Vaclav Havel who noted the 'need for the rehabilitation of politics'.[39]

At the level of ideology, the picture is no more comforting. Although Judy Batt is right to note the absence of a post-Communist ideological vacuum, it cannot be concluded from this that the stilted dogma of the Communists has been replaced by a lively debate over possible future political systems and directions. Rather, the combination of élites attracted by the West and the exercise of Western material power in support of its transformation ideology initially swamped any attempts inside or outside eastern Europe to map out a different direction. The alternatives which were emerging by late 1994, therefore, consisted not of serious original thinking on the needs of transformation, but rested primarily upon the mobilisation of pre-existing nationalist sentiment. On the one hand, traditional pre-Communist era political parties have re-formed. Prominent among these are the Greater Romania Party, the Smallholders in Hungary and the Peasant Party in Poland. Elements within these parties effectively reject the West, reject modernisation, and resent urbanisation while seeking to blame eastern Europe's dire condition upon the outside world. On the other hand, and perhaps more prominently, the phenomenon of 'chauvino-communism' has emerged. This term is used to refer to those former Communists who have effectively and opportunistically switched to an espousal of nationalism in order to preserve their political power. According to Schöpflin, this phenomenon 'is very marked in Slovakia, Bulgaria, Romania and, of course, in the country where it was effectively invented and practised with the greatest success, Serbia'.[40] Election results and government changes in Slovakia and Romania in 1994 have also illustrated the potential for traditionalists and chauvino-communists to work together to the detriment of other more progressive political movements. The new government headed by Vladimir Meciar in Slovakia in particular appears at first sight to be a curious combination of the political left and right until the essential unity of purpose provided by nationalism and heavy doses of anti-Hungarian rhetoric is taken into account.

Meanwhile, external constraints imposed by the IMF, when coupled to the negative legacy of the Communist past, are preventing the formation of any serious political centre, or left of centre, response to the economic crisis. Election victories by former Communist parties in 1994 in Poland, Hungary and Bulgaria all illustrate the desire for relief from the economic collapse, but all also illustrate the extent to which these parties are now merely searching for respectability and have no real alternative economic programme to offer. This disorientation of the eastern European political left in the face of economic collapse makes the continued growth of nationalist and populist politics both far more likely and more worrying.

Another cause for concern, but one directly concerned with the above, is the extent to which media and press are still being manipulated. The governments of former Yugoslav Republics such as Serbia and Croatia have already shown how destructive nationalist leaderships can be when in control of the supply of information to their respective populations. The problem, however, is far more widespread than that and in all eastern European states press and media are being openly manipulated and controlled by political élites.

While eastern Europe clearly, then, is freer today than under the Communists, the extent to which this is true is often exaggerated by those in the West who do not want to look too closely. The evidence also is that, in many cases, eastern Europeans are using, and indeed are being encouraged to use, their new relative freedoms to express hatred and suspicion rather than friendship toward one another. Five years into the process of post-Communist transformation, therefore, it is difficult to sustain any optimism in either a political or economic sense. Transformation has caused economic hardship and released often aggressive and mutually exclusive national ideologies and disputes. The criteria for membership of a western European bloc and its institutions are clearly not being fulfilled and the poor record on transformation will continue to act as a constraint on the course of future developments in this area. In return, however, it must also be said that the inadequate response of the EU and NATO to change in eastern Europe has also acted as a constraint upon progress in the transformation itself.

Relations with the West since 1989

Links with the European Union

The European Union's relationship to eastern Europe has passed through two main stages of development since 1989 and has been largely centred on questions of trade and aid. The first stage of development consisted of the signing of a string of bilateral Trade and Co-operation Agreements between the EU and each of the eastern states such that, by October 1990, agreements were in existence with all of the former European member states of the CMEA. These agreements covered three main areas. First, in terms of the trade regime, they contained a degree of liberalisation and, rhetorically at least, were intended to provide eastern Europeans both with additional hard-currency export markets and a variety of imports which would aid general economic reconstruction. Second, they contained clauses designed to stimulate economic co-operation through the promotion of joint ventures, licensing agreements, scientific and technical co-operation and the exchange of information and personnel at seminars and trade fairs. The implementation and monitoring of these developments was facilitated by the third area, namely the establishment of a committee structure to allow co-ordination of activity by key officials.

Welcome though such closer relations were to the eastern European states, the limitations of these agreements were betrayed by the aspects of the trade relationship which were not significantly liberalised. The Agreements excepted 'products covered by the Treaty establishing the European Coal and Steel Community, provisions of the existing Agreements concerning trade in textile products, and specific agreements or arrangements covering agricultural products'.[41] In short, in the sectors in which a liberalisation of trade relations with the EU would have benefited eastern European exporters the most, the EU kept up a protectionist guard to placate vested interests within the Union itself.

Nevertheless, and despite this basic economic flaw from the eastern European perspective, the framework of the Trade and Co-operation Agreements formed the basis for the wider and deeper links said to be inherent in the second phase of increased co-operation, the so-called Europe Agreements. Negotiations for Europe Agreements were protracted as eastern European governments fought, unsuccessfully, to gain significantly greater access to the most sensitive EU markets of agriculture, textiles, and coal and steel. Furthermore, in the case of Bulgaria and Romania, which negotiated their Europe Agreements after those completed with the Visegrad countries, even the limited concessions offered to the Visegrad group were further reduced by the EU. Certain lobbies in Spain (steel) and France (agriculture), angered by the first Europe Agreements, mobilised to prevent any further access to EU markets being granted. Despite difficulties in the negotiations, however, Europe Agreements have now been signed by Poland, Hungary, the Czech Republic, Slovakia, Bulgaria and Romania and thus form the centre-pieces of the EU–eastern European relationship. They are seen, from an EU perspective, as stamps of approval for developments in the east and are explicitly political. As Pinder has pointed out, 'they were for those countries giving practical evidence of the commitment to economic and political reforms: economic liberalization in order to create market economies; politically the rule of law, human rights, multi-party systems and fair elections'.[42]

Although based on the Trade and Co-operation Agreement framework, the Europe Agreements go much further in elaborating a comprehensive relationship and even, in their preambles, explicitly concede the possibility of future EU membership for the signatory states. Six areas of co-operation are explicitly identified: political dialogue; movements of goods, persons, capital and services; economic co-operation; approximation of law; financial co-operation; and cultural co-operation.[43] Political dialogue is to be facilitated by joint summits and structures to allow meetings at ministerial, civil service and parliamentary levels. The notion of economic co-operation has also been broadened to include the energy, environmental and infrastructure areas. The four freedoms of movement are laid down only as long-term objectives and depend for effective implementation upon an approximation of eastern European legal regulations to those in the EU.

Running parallel to the Europe Agreements and important to their success has been EU aid policy. The aid strategy of the Union developed in response to the process of what Garton-Ash has termed 'refolution' which was under way in Poland and Hungary throughout late 1988 and early 1989.[44] The Commission of the EU was, in this political context, invited by the G24 group of leading industrialised countries to co-ordinate their aid actions via the Poland and Hungary: Aid for Economic Reconstruction (PHARE) Programme. As with the other EU-led responses, PHARE was to be an aid programme tied explicitly to the political and economic reform agenda. Poland and Hungary had been chosen initially as the two countries most advanced along this path, but as Communist regimes began to collapse right across eastern Europe, the programme was rapidly extended in scope and expanded in size. Despite this, PHARE has struggled to have a major impact for three main reasons. The first and most important is that the resources devoted to PHARE are simply too small. Although between 1990 and 1992 the annual financial support behind PHARE increased from 500 million ecu to 1 billion ecu, this figure is dwarfed by the tens of billions of ecus which eastern Europe needs. Secondly, many of the projects to be paid for under PHARE require 50 per cent funding from the non-EU members of the G24 and they are not always forthcoming with the finance to operationalise aid plans. Third, but not least in terms of importance, despite the urgency of the need for aid, the decision-

making procedures for outlining and approving PHARE programmes can take anything up to 18 months. Needless to say,
the delay is highly frustrating and, from the eastern European
perspective, difficult to understand.[45]

As a consequence of these various weaknesses, the positive
effect on eastern Europe of the changed nature of relations
with the EU since 1989 is open to question. Countries thought
to be the most advanced in terms of reform, such as Hungary
and Poland, were forced to negotiate Europe Agreements which
came into effect on 1 February 1994 knowing that free trade
in industrial goods would not be available until 1995, in steel
until 1996 and in textiles until 1997.[46] Effectively, EU protection of its most sensitive markets, while running alongside the
continued emphasis on opening up the eastern economies in
return for aid, is underpinning a growing trade surplus for
the Union which indicates that, in the short term, it is the EU
and not the eastern European states which is enjoying the greater
economic benefits from the new Europe Agreements. A late-
1994 *Economist* Survey on the European Union makes the point
very clearly: 'In 1989 the Union had a deficit with its poor
eastern neighbours of 600 million ecus; by last year the deficit
had turned into a surplus for the EU of 5.6 billion ecus including, thanks to the subsidised exports of the common agricultural policy, 433 million ecus in farm products.'[47]

Consequently, continued eastern European interest in membership of the EU can only really be explained (in the short
term) by the political benefits perceived by eastern European
leaderships. Payment of a short-term economic price is being
made in exchange both for the immediate prestige and legiti-
mation associated with EU agreements and for the long-term
'guarantee' of democracy and wealth which possible eventual
membership of the Union might bring. In this context, it is
not surprising that, almost before the Europe Agreements had
had time to begin operating, Poland and Hungary became the
first eastern European states to apply formally for membership
of the EU in April 1994. President Havel and Prime Minister
Vaclav Klaus of the Czech Republic also disagreed in public in
early 1995 over the timing of the Czech application though
the issue was only one of when, and not if, an application should
be made. Similarly, in late January 1995, in one of his first

addresses to the Slovak Parliament since resuming power, Meciar declared that 'the cabinet's most important strategic goal is European integration'.[48] Slovakia later declared its intention to apply for EU membership by 30 June 1995 at the latest and both Bulgaria and Romania are expected to follow suit at a later stage.

If the analysis in this chapter is correct, however, it is clear that such applications will not lead to membership of the EU in the near, or even long-term, future. The failure of the economic transformation programme in eastern Europe means that no real convergence between eastern and western European economies is likely. This, in turn, indicates that the financial costs to current EU members of an eastern enlargement would be enormous and are estimated by some to be in the region of a 60 per cent increase on current contributions to the EU budget.[49] While it is possible in such a climate to envisage a highly selective enlargement, perhaps starting with the Czech Republic as the smallest and wealthiest of the eastern European states, it is much less likely that the larger countries such as Hungary and, especially, Poland could be incorporated. The prospects for Bulgarian and Romanian membership, furthermore, are so remote as to make the issue for these countries largely irrelevant for the time being.

New security concerns and links with NATO

Given the imposed nature and Soviet-dominated structure of the WTO, it was not surprising that the end of Communist rule in eastern Europe should quickly spell the end of that organisation. As the WTO was dissolved each eastern European state with Soviet troops on its soil negotiated bilaterally for the removal of those troops and for the restoration of full state sovereignty in the security field. This process was largely completed by the end of 1993 and was widely welcomed and celebrated. However, the demise of the WTO brought with it not only direct eastern European control over security policy for the first time for a generation but also a whole host of new and complex post-Cold War security concerns in urgent need of attention. East Europeans today commonly conceive of themselves as existing within a 'security vacuum' caused by 'the region's lack of international structure, uncertain democracies, weak economies, ethnic strife, and potentially troublesome neighbours to the east'.[50]

Although this notion of a security vacuum correctly relates security concerns to the underlying political, economic and historical situation of the region, its more immediate origins stem from a traditional military agenda. In particular, the events in former Yugoslavia have fuelled the sense of insecurity. Historically, the Balkan region has been the flashpoint for wider European conflict and the current war in Bosnia-Hercegovina, not to mention the continued tension in Croatia and Macedonia, illustrate that none of that potential has been lost. Furthermore, the danger of spill-over effects from the territories of the former Yugoslavia is only one pressing military concern among many. Almost every state in the eastern and central European region has either a minority or border dispute which has the potential to cause conflict in its own right.[51] The most serious of these in central Europe is the Hungarian problem, involving the rights of Hungarians living in Slovakia, Vojvodina in Yugoslavia, and Transylvania in Romania.[52] Further to the north-east, Poland has concerns over the treatment of the Polish minority in the Baltic states and Slovakia is in dispute with the Ukraine over the territory of the Subcarpathian Rus. On the territory of the former Soviet Union, similar problems exist which could draw in or impact directly upon the eastern European states. Disputes in Abkhazia, the Transdnestr republic, Ingushetia, South Ossetia, Tajikistan, Nagorno-Karabakh and between the Ukraine and Russia over the status of Crimea have, in the words of Geoffrey Hosking, 'the potential to unleash a serious war involving Russia and perhaps other nuclear powers as well'.[53]

Not far from the minds of most eastern Europeans is also a continued and deeply held fear of Russia and of long-term Russian intentions. This surfaced, understandably, during the failed August 1991 coup by Soviet hardliners and has not disappeared since. The break-up of the Soviet state and the coming to power of Boris Yeltsin only briefly suggested a period of healthy Russian democracy and friendly relations with eastern Europe. Subsequently, the pro-Serbian stance of Russia in the Yugoslav War, and pressure from the Russian military on Boris

Yeltsin to exert authority in the Russian 'near abroad', have sustained eastern European apprehension. In addition, several statements by senior Russian officials have created the impression that Russian commitment to the Conventional Forces in Europe (CFE) Treaty may be weakening. Not least of these was the statement in late 1994 by Russian Defence Minister Pavel Grachev that 'the Treaty would have to be revised or violated, otherwise it would be impossible for Russia to enforce regional stability on its flanks'.[54]

Some of the Russian concerns over the CFE are shared by the eastern Europeans themselves. In Poland, for example, there is concern that the force levels in the CFE, signed in 1990, reflect Cold-War thinking and leave the Polish state exposed to both a militarily powerful united Germany and instability in the east. Such concerns are understandable. As Jeffrey Simon has pointed out, 'by the end of 1994 Poland will likely have an unstable eastern frontier with potential problems from four independent states (Lithuania, Russia, Belarus and Ukraine). A German force of 370 000 will exist across from Poland's western border. And yet, confronting these, Poland will have a maximum of 200 000 troops (a decline of over 50 per cent since 1988) and maybe fewer.'[55] In this context, in January 1995, President Lech Walesa made an impassioned plea to the Polish Parliament, the Sejm, not to reduce the size of Poland's military any further.[56]

While such concerns are understandable in the Polish historical context, there is widespread acceptance across the region that unilateral changes in force levels and postures before the CFE Review Conference in 1996, on the part of any signatory, would set a precedent with dangerous destabilising consequences. Indeed, the prevailing view in eastern Europe, given the complexity of the current climate, is that military solutions to security problems must be avoided wherever possible. Consequently, the cutting in size of the Polish military has been repeated elsewhere in the region both due to CFE Treaty obligations and the difficult economic conditions associated with the transformation process. Before the split of the Czech and Slovak Republics at the beginning of 1993, for example, the Czechoslovak military was reduced from 200 000 to 90 000 personnel. Furthermore, these reduced forces were redeployed away from the western border of the state as, in March 1991, the Czechoslovak Federal Assembly adopted a new territorial defence doctrine. The doctrine was said to be one which did not 'identify any specific enemies or allies and one that stipulates an equal distribution of armed forces throughout the country'.[57] The adoption of such doctrines has now become a regional phenomenon with Poland, Hungary and Bulgaria all following suit. Romania had already espoused such a territorial defence doctrine in the Soviet bloc during the maverick years of Ceaucescu's leadership and continues with it today. In addition to redeployment, steps have also been taken in all eastern European states to subordinate each of the military machines to effective civilian control.

Despite these positive and desirable steps, however, most eastern European governments still clearly believe that the security threats they face far outweigh their ability to respond effectively as individual states. Consequently, the search has continued for a collective security organisation to replace the WTO. In this context, the eastern European states have had little room for optimism to date with regard to their changed relationship to NATO. In the immediate post-1989 period, NATO rejected overtures from eastern and central European countries for fear of alienating Soviet policy makers who objected strongly to an eastward expansion of NATO's membership. Disgruntled east Europeans, dissatisfied with the apparent veto power the Soviets enjoyed over their security position, sought temporarily to explore the utility of other potential sources of collective security. In this context, their attention focused upon both the UN and the Conference on Security and Co-operation in Europe (CSCE). Several eastern European states committed personnel to the UN-backed operation against Iraq in the Gulf War and encouraged the deployment of UN peace-keepers in the former Yugoslavia. At the regional level, Czechoslovak officials in particular sought also to give the CSCE a central role in European security affairs. In June 1991, President Havel publicly stated his great hopes that the CSCE would 'be the medium out of which a new security structure and a new system of all European security guarantees would grow'.[58] In addition, at the Moscow Conference of the CSCE in the same year, both the Polish and Czechoslovak foreign ministers attempted to use the CSCE as an instrument for the effective management of the minority rights problem. The Polish government pushed Lithuania to defend the rights of its Polish minority while the Czechoslovak Foreign Minister, Jiri Dienstbier, proposed that the CSCE create a committee of non-governmental ombudsmen to monitor and manage minority disputes in general.

Despite the attention given to both the UN and the CSCE, both of these organisations quickly lost credibility as serious instruments of collective security in eastern European eyes. Although the UN operation in the Gulf was successful, the peace-keeping deployments in former Yugoslavia were late and ineffective and, due to divisions in the international community over how to respond to the crisis, the effect was the dismemberment of an eastern European member state of the UN. Security Council resolutions came and went with no political will being displayed to enforce them. For eastern Europeans, many of these difficulties were caused by the size of the UN and its cumbersome decision-making procedures. Unfortunately, with 35 member states, it was felt that the CSCE shared this basic weakness and, in the absence of agreement over how to respond to security threats in the European and former Soviet theatre, it too was thought to be doomed to be ineffectual.

For a brief period, it was felt that the West European Union (WEU), which was being revamped as part of the EU's Maastricht project and moves toward a common western European foreign and security policy, might offer a further possibility. Again, however, there was little faith in this organisation among eastern Europeans. It lacked both the political will to be a distinctive force from NATO and, without the presence of the US military, it lacked technical equipment, expertise and sheer military clout.

The eastern European governments have been driven, therefore, to the conclusion that the only credible organisation on the European continent which could afford them security was NATO and have thus sought to build upon the modest co-operation that was being offered by the latter. In an attempt to balance eastern European states' demands against Soviet, and later Russian, sensibilities, NATO has offered a whole string of agreements and statements since 1990. These included the Hand of Friendship Agreement of July 1990, the Statement on

Dialogue, Partnership and Co-operation in December 1991 and, most recently and extensively, the January 1994 Partnership for Peace Initiative (PFP). The essence of eastern European disgruntlement with each of these steps is that none of them contains either an effective security guarantee nor a detailed set of criteria or timetable for eventual membership of the organisation. What they do offer is a whole series of opportunities for co-operation, consultation, joint training and even joint exercises between NATO and the military and defence establishments of eastern Europe. The most advanced of the agreements, the PFP, has been joined by the Czech and Slovak Republics, Bulgaria, Romania, Albania, Slovenia, the Baltic states, Moldova, Ukraine and Russia. Its geographical spread and number of participants is clear evidence that the PFP is not intended to be the basis of a collective security guarantee, and it obliges members only to consult with a partner who is under threat, not to come to that partner's aid.

Consequently, the sense of a security vacuum in eastern Europe remains and is only reinforced by the unsettling impact of the economic and political transformation processes already described. As with the EU, there is no sign that the West either plans to accept eastern European states into NATO's membership or that NATO's future role will itself expand further towards the east in order to stabilise the region.

Conclusion

As noted at the outset, the events of 1989 in eastern Europe allowed for a major relocation of the region within the world order. This relocation, in the eyes of those eastern European élites driving it and for the Western élites supporting it, was to consist of a 'return to the West'. In pursuit of this goal, much eastern European history has either been rewritten or forgotten and the ideas of the West have been copied and its institutions courted. Whole societies and economies have been dismantled and restructured according to the advice of Western experts, none of whom have any experience in building capitalism from scratch but many of whom claim authoritative knowledge as to how it must be done.

Five years into the process it is already clear that the project of copying and joining the West is unlikely to succeed. Although those with some understanding of eastern European history and political culture are not greatly surprised, the scale of failure of the present project is both unnecessary and is primarily a product not of history but of contemporary hypocrisy and narrow self-interest in the West. It is not enough to view the response to the collapse of Communism of EU and NATO governments as cautious. The response has been positively subversive to the whole process of post-Communist transformation. While preaching free trade to the east, the EU has been practising protectionism at home. While attaching conditions for aid, the aid itself has been too little and often too late. While demanding the introduction of capitalism, the capitalism actually being projected is a grotesque and dogmatic distortion of a complex economic system. In short, as the West asks for a successful post-Communist transformation as the requirement for membership of its key European economic and security organisations, its influence on the process of transformation is being used to prevent the success it requires.

To note, however, that in these circumstances an eastern enlargement of the EU and NATO is almost impossible, is to tell only a part of the story. The context of economic collapse, security instability and rising nationalist influence in eastern Europe represents not only the failure of post-Communist transformation but also a major threat to the stability of the West. Should it be true that a history not learned is a history destined to be relived, then western Europe, as well as the east, has much to fear from the current treatment of the latter. The crisis in former Yugoslavia may only be indicative of much larger problems ahead.

Although the prospects for each of the eastern European states covered in this chapter differ, and although in some it is possible to be more optimistic than in others, the essential key to saving post-Communist transformation and perhaps the wider stability of Europe now lies outside the region. Better trading arrangements, increased aid, and a far less dogmatic view of what capitalism actually is and must consist of, are now required from the West. Furthermore, such additional measures must also be applied to the former Soviet Union and especially to Russia as the domestic and foreign policy of the latter may yet hold the key to the future direction of the whole of eastern Europe. Of course, all such steps would be politically difficult and economically costly for the West, its leaders and its peoples. They should be taken, nevertheless, for the simple reason that not paying the price now may well mean paying a much higher and more dangerous price later.

Notes

1. T. G. Ash, *We The People* (Cambridge: Granta, 1990). Ash discusses events in 1989 in Poland, Hungary and Czechoslovakia and, in the former two cases, notes that the process of change was as much led from the top as driven from the bottom.
2. See I. Kearns, 'Eastern and Central Europe in the World Political Economy', in R. Stubbs and G. R. D. Underhill (eds.), *Political Economy and the Changing Global Order* (London: Macmillan, 1994) pp. 370-09, and R. Linden, 'The New International Political Economy of Eastern Europe', *Studies in Comparative Communism*, XXV (1992).
3. See S. Strange, 'States, Firms and Diplomacy', *International Affairs*, 68 (1992) 1–17.
4. Taken from Czechoslovak Party Secretary Zdenek Mlynar's eyewitness account of the Moscow meeting of the Soviet and Czechoslovak Politburos following the 1968 invasion of Czechoslovakia and quoted in K. Dawisha, *Eastern Europe, Gorbachev and Reform: The Great Challenge* (Cambridge: Cambridge University Press, 1988), p. 7.
5. Ibid., pp. 7–29.
6. Ibid., p. 14.
7. M. Kundera, 'The Tragedy of Central Europe', *New York Review of Books*, 26 April 1984, p. 33.
8. For a discussion of the pattern of the Communist takeover, see G. Swain and N. Swain, *Eastern Europe Since 1945* (London: Macmillan, 1993).
9. For brief accounts of both countries in the inter-war years, see A. Polonsky, *The Little Dictators* (London: Routledge and Kegan Paul, 1975).
10. See Dawisha, *Eastern Europe, Gorbachev and Reform*, p. 80.
11. For a full account of the nature of these regimes and economic systems, see J. Lovenduski and J. Woodall, *Politics and Society in Eastern Europe* (London: Macmillan, 1987).
12. Ibid., p. 398.
13. See Dawisha, *Eastern Europe, Gorbachev and Reform*, pp. 86–101.

14. For figures on the pattern of Soviet–East European trade, see ibid., p. 140.
15. For a more detailed discussion of the legacy of the Communist years and of the ideology of transformation, see H. Wainwright, *Arguments for a New Left* (Oxford: Blackwell, 1994) and B. Ackerman, *The Future of Liberal Revolution* (New Haven: Yale University Press, 1992).
16. For a short review of Sachs's ideas, see I. Jeffries, *Socialist Economies and the Transition to the Market: A Guide* (London: Routledge, 1993) pp. 333–55.
17. B. Granville, *Comparative Progress in the CSFR and Poland, 1989–91* (London: RIIA, 1992) p. 5.
18. Survey on Hungary, *Financial Times*, 11 November 1994.
19. For an account of the initial Romanian transformation strategy, see Jeffries, *Socialist Economies and the Transition to the Market*, pp. 450–9.
20. International Monetary Fund, *World Economic Outlook* (Washington DC: IMF, 1994).
21. Ibid.
22. Survey on Czech Republic, *Financial Times*, 19 December 1994.
23. See Granville, *Comparative Progress in the CSFR and Poland*.
24. See Ackerman, *The Future of Liberal Revolution*, esp. Chaps. 1, 2 and 7.
25. Granville, *Comparative Progress in the CSFR and Poland*, p. 19.
26. Survey on Bulgaria, *Financial Times*, 13 October 1994.
27. M. Haynes, 'Class and Crisis – The Transition in Eastern Europe', *International Socialism*, Spring (1992) 45–104.
28. Ibid., 75.
29. D. Marquand, *The Unprincipled Society* (London: Jonathan Cape, 1988) pp. 91–114.
30. A. Pickel, 'Jump-starting a Market Economy: A Critique of the Radical Strategy for Economic Reform in Light of the East-German Experience', *Studies in Comparative Communism*, XXV, 2 (1992) 177–191.
31. J. Pinder, *The European Community and Eastern Europe* (London: RIIA, 1991) p. 96.
32. *The Economist*, 5 November 1994.
33. See International Monetary Fund, *World Economic Outlook* (Washington DC: IMF, 1994).
34. J. Batt, *East Central Europe from Reform to Transformation* (London: Pinter Publishers/RIIA, 1991) p. 43.
35. R. Rose, *What is the Chance for Democracy in Central and Eastern Europe? Testing the Churchill Hypothesis* (London: European Policy Forum, 1994) p. 17.
36. For an account of this period, see Polonsky, *The Little Dictators*.
37. G. Schöpflin, 'Culture and Identity in Post-Communist Europe', in S. White, J. Batt and P. G. Lewis (eds.), *Developments in East European Politics* (London: Macmillan, 1993) p. 17.

38. See Appendices in Batt, *East Central Europe from Reform to Transformation*.
39. Vaclav Havel, quoted in ibid., p. 47.
40. Schöpflin, 'Culture and Identity in Post-Communist Europe', p. 32.
41. T. Verheijen, 'The EC and Romania and Bulgaria: Stuck Between Visegrad and Minsk', unpublished paper presented to conference of British International Studies Association, Swansea, 1992.
42. Pinder, *The European Community and Eastern Europe*, p. 59.
43. Verheijen, 'The EC and Romania and Bulgaria'.
44. See Ash, *We The People*.
45. See Pinder, *The European Community and Eastern Europe*.
46. G. Kolankiewicz, 'Consensus and Competition in the Eastern Enlargement of the European Union', *International Affairs*, 70, 3 (1994) 477–95.
47. See *The Economist*, 22 October 1994.
48. *Central Europe Today* , 19 January 1995.
49. Kolankiewicz, *Consensus and Competition in the Eastern Enlargement of the European Union*.
50. H. Frost, 'Eastern Europe's Security Blanket', *Orbis*, 37, 1 (1993) 37.
51. For an account of many of the minorities disputes in the region, see H. Poulton, *The Balkans* (London: Minority Rights Group, 1994).
52. See G. Schopflin, *Hungary and Its Neighbours* (Paris: Institute for Security Studies of Western European Union, 1993).
53. G. Hosking, 'West Must Let Yeltsin Police the East', *The Times*, 6 July 1993.
54. See *The Economist*, 5 November 1994.
55. J. Simon, 'Does Eastern Europe Belong in NATO?', *Orbis*, 37, 1 (1993) 21–35.
56. *OMRI Daily Digest* Part 2, 20 January 1995 (Open Media Research Institute, 1995).
57. Frost, *'Eastern Europe's Security Blanket'*, p. 42.
58. Ibid., 41.

4 The United States and its Enterprise for the Americas

ANTHONY PAYNE

The United States has had to make its own response to the ending of its global hegemony and it too has turned, at least in part, to a form of regionalism. There certainly cannot be any doubt that, since the late 1980s, the US state has re-engaged with its own hemisphere in a new and energetic fashion. These last few years have witnessed a veritable series of initiatives, treaties and summits bearing upon hemispheric matters. Although they have not all emanated from the US, the power and policies of the US have been critical in every case in determining the outcomes. The concept of the Americas has also been dusted down and fashioned anew to give shape to the process.[1] Obviously, in one sense the United States has never left the Americas: it has had to have an interest in Latin American and Caribbean (LAC) affairs throughout its history. This chapter thus begins by considering briefly the phases through which previous US policies towards the Americas have passed, noting in particular the impact of the post-1945 era of global hegemony on these relations. It argues, however, that a new phase in the history of US–LAC relations has begun and develops this thesis by means of an examination of contemporary US economic and security policies towards the Americas in all their various forms. Another section then endeavours to ground this analysis in a discussion of the changing political sociology of the United States itself and the conclusion attempts to assess what kind of a regionalist project the new US enterprise for the Americas presently constitutes.

The US and the Americas 1823–1989

All accounts of US relations with LAC necessarily commence by citing the Monroe Doctrine. Enunciated by President James Monroe in his annual message to Congress in December 1823, the Doctrine was in origin a warning to the European powers of the day that interference in the newly-emerging Latin American republics of the western hemisphere would be considered an unfriendly act towards the United States itself. It had nothing to do with inter-American relations and indeed the US rebuffed early Latin American overtures to convert it into a collective defensive alliance guaranteeing the security of the hemisphere. Yet, as the US itself gradually pushed westwards, annexing large parts of Mexico after 1848, and then began to probe southwards, asserting control over Nicaraguan affairs after 1867, the Monroe Doctrine came to be interpreted in a new light – in the US as an assertion of its growing power and in the Americas as a potential threat to precious autonomy and liberty. By the 1890s the United States was a country on the move: it was expanding hugely in population as European immigrants poured towards its shores; it was already outpacing Europe in the production of steel, coal and iron; and it was possessed of enormous confidence in its 'manifest destiny' as a civilising force throughout the hemisphere. It was in this mood that the US moved in 1898 to 'liberate' Cuba from Spanish control and, in so doing, established a Caribbean empire.

As Lester Langley has expressed it, the vision held by the US was of a Caribbean empire composed, not of colonies (except for Puerto Rico ceded to the US by Spain as part of the spoils of war) but of 'small, politically unstable republics with fragile economies' within which 'the United States, on occasion for genuinely unselfish, and at other times, for blatantly selfish, motives, would impose political order, economic tutelage, and civic morality'.[2] Cuba was emblematic. US troops occupied the island from 1889 to 1902, only leaving after the US had imposed on Cuba the so-called Platt Amendment giving it the right to intervene in Cuban affairs and establish military bases on the island more or less at will. The precise tactics and style of subsequent US interventions varied, ranging from the 'big stick' waved by Theodore Roosevelt, the US hero of the Spanish-American War, in the first decade of the twentieth century, to the 'dollar diplomacy' practised by William Howard Taft in order to safeguard US investments in what were contemptuously referred to as 'banana republics', to the system of protectorates established by Woodrow Wilson. The cumulative outcomes of these policies saw the US entrench its control over Cuban economic and political life; interfere in Panama in a way which enabled it to build a strategically important isthmian canal in that territory; send troops to Nicaragua in 1912 and leave them there until 1925; and occupy both the Dominican Republic and Haiti for long periods of time, the former between 1916 and 1924 and the latter between 1915 and 1934. In a nutshell, the whole of the Caribbean and Central America, with the sole exceptions of the continuing European colonies in the area, came steadily and ever more firmly under US economic and political domination.

It is important to note that the imperial thrust of US policy initiated by Theodore Roosevelt was only ever really applied to the small and weak territories of the Caribbean and Central America. The rest of Latin America felt the growing economic influence of the US and its business corporations, particularly as British investment and trade with these countries generally lessened during the 1920s and 1930s. But most did not experience directly the heavy political hand of the US state. For all that, the reaction of Roosevelt's 'big stick' was enough to weaken, and in the end destroy for a generation, the nascent Pan-Americanism of the mainland Latin American states as expressed at the first Pan-American Conference of 1889 in Washington. Rather than viewing the Monroe Doctrine as a shield of protection against Europe, LAC states instead felt it to be necessary to use Europe, and after 1919 the League of Nations, as a bulwark against potential US interference in their affairs. Four more Pan-American conferences were in fact held between 1889 and 1933 but they only served to bring out the enormous gap with existed between US and LAC views of what might constitute a common inter-American agenda. The US could not and did not ignore the Mexican revolution, which began in 1910, and its diplomats repeatedly sought to intervene in the revolution's different phases. This only made other Latin American leaders even more concerned at least to establish that the Monroe Doctrine had no force south of the Gulf of Mexico.[3]

It was only after Franklin Roosevelt's inauguration of the 'good neighbour' era in 1933 and the accompanying passage of the Reciprocal Trade Agreements Act in 1934, which was his administration's attempt to revive the depressed Latin American economies by breaking down trade barriers in the hemisphere, that another Pan-American regional agenda could even be essayed. This was focused upon the issue of the external threats posed by the Axis powers and bore eventual fruit in the emergent security community created by the Act of Havana of 1940. This declared the neutrality of the Americas (the so-called 'Hemispheric Safety Belt') in the war that had broken out in Europe but at the same time constituted an agreement by all the states of the Americas that an attack on any one of their number should be considered as an act of aggression against them all. This was to have unexpected consequences. When the US was finally drawn into the Second World War on its own account after Pearl Harbor, the smaller Caribbean and Central American states immediately leapt to its side. Mexico and Brazil joined the war in June and August 1942 respectively after they had had ships sunk and both states contributed forces to the allied effort. Of the remaining LAC states, only Colombia entered the conflict whilst the outcome was still in doubt (in November 1943); the others, including Argentina where Colonel Peron was a growing influence in the military government after 1943, remained neutral until it became apparent that Germany had been defeated. Even these states continued to supply the essential raw materials needed for the war effort and, however uneasily and partially, the US can be said in the end to have forged a political and military partnership in the Americas effective enough to contribute to the winning of the world war.

Nevertheless, there was no master-plan in this, imperial or otherwise. The US was doing no more than using LAC to help it cope with events. But it was a beginning and, as is well-known, after 1945 the US moved decisively to put in place a global network to 'contain' the new threat of Communism wherever it arose. In the Americas, this involved the signing of the Inter-American Treaty of Reciprocal Assistance in Rio de Janeiro in

1947, the creation in 1948 of a new regional diplomatic framework in the Organisation of American States (OAS), and the expansion (but selective deployment) of military and economic aid throughout Latin America. Yet, as important as they were, the mere elaboration of these various policy mechanisms does not capture the distinctive and highly important place with LAC came to occupy in the politics of US global hegemony after 1945. What was new and vital about US relations with the Americas in the Cold-War years was the way in which the US perceived its own standing as a hegemonic power and its associated credibility in the eyes of both its enemies and allies in all parts of the world to be dependent in some measure on its capacity to maintain and demonstrate control of its own hemispheric community – its 'backyard'.[4] This mind-set dominated the administrations of a run of US presidents, from Dwight Eisenhower to John Kennedy to Lyndon Johnson to Richard Nixon. It explains why Jacobo Arbenz had to be overthrown in Guatemala in 1954; why the success of the Cuban revolution of 1959 was felt to be such a blow and set in train a series of hostile responses (including the Bay of Pigs invasion of 1961); and why US marines were sent into the Dominican Republic in 1965 to prevent the return to power of a moderate nationalist government. Quite simply, no ideological challenge of any description, however mild, could be allowed to survive in the 'backyard' if US global hegemony was to be sustained.

What is more, in a significant expansion of the boundaries of the critical sphere of influence beyond the limits of the pre-1940 era, the whole of Latin America, not just the Caribbean and Central America, was included within the ambit of US policy. The whole region was in effect treated as an homogeneous zone by Washington. That, in turn, was why in the early 1960s the Alliance for Progress (which was the Kennedy administration's short-lived response to the Cuban revolution) sought to stem the revolutionary tide by giving support to reformist regimes where they existed; why counter-insurgency tactics were taught to the militaries of the whole of Latin America at the US Army School of the Americas in Panama; and why the CIA thought it appropriate to support the coup in Brazil in 1964 which brought down President João Goulart and to destabilise the government of Salvador Allende in Chile in 1973.

The only exception to the hard line adopted right across the hemisphere by Washington in these years was the dispensation given to Mexico allowing its leaders to dissent from US policy. This was tolerated out of deference to Mexico's domestic political need to appease the revolutionary tradition in its own recent history. In general, though, the perceived need to play a global leadership role overtook US policy towards the Americas with a force which could not be broken in the Cold War.[5] The administration of Jimmy Carter tried to introduce a more modulated approach which took note of the different histories, cultures and problems of the various parts of LAC, but it failed to escape the pressure to use the region to demonstrate 'resolve' in the struggle against the Soviet Union and in the end stood charged with having 'lost' Nicaragua and Grenada, both of which experienced socialist revolutions in 1979.[6]

The Ronald Reagan administration coming to office at the beginning of the 1980s saw the Caribbean, and even more Central America, as the most obvious part of the world in which to redress some of the weaknesses in the wider manifestation of US hegemony which had arisen under Carter in the 1970s. It thus refocused US attention on its traditional Caribbean Basin agenda but did so from the familiar globalist perspective of the Cold War. Most analysts have focused on the military aspects of Reagan's policies, highlighting in Central America the arming of conservative forces, in government and opposition respectively, in El Salvador and Nicaragua, and focusing in the Caribbean on the invasion of Grenada in 1983. Amidst the applause and denunciation generated by these highly controversial actions, the cleverness of Reagan's policy was often missed.[7] This derived in part from its sheer rhetorical simplicity but more importantly from its capacity to integrate political, economic and military activities within a single ideological framework. It did not matter, on this reading, that the so-called Caribbean Basin Initiative (CBI), the trade and aid package proposed by Reagan in 1982, always promised more than it could deliver. The point was that it succeeded in attaching the US to the argument that social and economic underdevelopment was at the root of the Caribbean Basin's new political instability. Indeed, it is not too much of an exaggeration to suggest that, under Reagan, the US progressively succeeded in reshaping the agenda of Caribbean Basin politics to the point where, in almost every arena, it was able to lay down the parameters of what could be done and almost what could be thought. Relations with the rest of LAC were not given the same priority, and sometimes proceeded awkwardly. The effect was to give some states greater space within which to pursue a more autonomous foreign policy. On the other hand, the Caribbean and Central America were largely 're-won' for the US during the 1980s. The problem for the Reagan strategy was that this victory was insufficient to restore US global hegemony.

Several different phases can be detected in this history of US policy towards the Americas. Broadly, they reflect a progression in the US position from national consolidation in the nineteenth century; to the assertion of regional power in the Caribbean and Central America in the first 30 years of this century; to a tentative embrace of partnership with the wider Latin America from the mid 1930s to the mid-1940s; to the acquisition after 1945 of a global position with all its attendant symbolic ramifications for the whole of the hemisphere; and finally to the partially successful, partially unsuccessful reassertion of that hegemony in the 1980s. The Cold-War years thus stand not as an exemplar or a norm but merely an episode in the history of US relations with the rest of the Americas. They are important because they are the immediate backdrop to the present, but they are concluded and new considerations now bear upon the making of US policy towards its own hemisphere.

Contemporary US economic policies towards the Americas

The dominant themes in contemporary US policy towards the Americas are economic, although, as we shall see, there is often still a security subtext to apparently economic matters. In retrospect, the beginnings of this shift of orientation towards the region can be traced back to two events in the early 1980s. The first was the eruption of Latin American's debt problem into a crisis directly affecting the US, the second was the US decision to seek to launch another GATT round, an initiative which proved to have many unanticipated ramifications. Separate in origin and different in nature, these strands of policy became intertwined over time and eventually flowered in President Bush's so-called Enterprise for the Americas Initiative (EAI) in 1990. Out of this emerged first the prospect and then the reality of the North American Free Trade Area (NAFTA), as well as the idea, taken up again recently by President Bill Clinton, of developing the concept into a genuinely American Free Trade Area (AFTA) embracing the whole of the hemisphere.

The US and the Latin American debt crisis

Mexico's shock declaration in August 1982 that it no longer had the foreign-exchange reserves to service its debt was not something which the US could treat as an isolated case. Although Mexico was the first country to turn its debt problems into a political crisis, other LAC governments were also in a position where they were unable to negotiate new loans and needed to reschedule their debts. Collectively, these were on a scale which could not but threaten the stability of the international financial system as a whole. The US Federal Reserve was already worried by the weak financial position of many of the major banking institutions in the United States and, following the Mexican announcement, took the lead on behalf of the largest US commercial banks in organising a series of restructuring committees of international bankers whose task was to 'advise' each of the Latin American debtors.[8] 'The actual purpose of the committees,' as Roett has noted, 'was to coordinate the politics of the renegotiations among the commercial banks and to "police" the Latin American and Caribbean debtors to be sure they were tempted neither by a declaration of unilateral default nor the urge to organise a debtors "cartel".'[9]

The immediate strategy worked: the key debtors were offered a variety of emergency packages and bridging loans to help them manage old debts and then gradually drawn into the embrace of the IMF and the World Bank as the price of the provision of new money.[10] The US was still the dominant force within the global financial institutions and saw to it that the whole structural-adjustment package demanded by the neo-liberal agenda was imposed on one LAC state after another during the course of the 1980s. It was a remarkable example of the continuing capacity of the US to use its global position to national advantage. Structural adjustment not only drove home in the harshest of ways the costs of getting into debt, but also served to force the replacement of the old import-substitution model of LAC development, with its statist bias, with a new export-oriented, private sector-led model. With time, and in the face of very limited alternatives, what was initially viewed by most regional élites as an external imposition gradually came to be seen as necessary internal change. Indeed, it was not long before LAC states, and even their attendant intellectuals, were almost competing with each other in the enthusiasm with which they endorsed the market discourse.[11] The import-substitution strategy had undoubtedly run into problems and some regional élites may have been genuinely converted to market liberalism; but, even if so, the extent to which they were initially driven in this direction by the assertion of US economic power should on no account be underestimated.

As regards the debt crisis itself, by the time George Bush assumed the presidency at the beginning of 1989, the US was beginning to realise that the threat to its banking system had in all probability been successfully contained and was ready to offer Latin American governments further inducements to continue the process of economic restructuring. The Brady Plan, introduced by Bush's incoming Secretary of the Treasury, sought to press the banks to negotiate with debtor countries with a view to writing down the value of their loans to them. It took time for the details to be worked out and for the initial resistance of the banks to be overcome.[12] But eventually Mexico, which was always the key, struck the first deal in February 1990 and was followed by Venezuela (March 1990), Costa Rica (March 1990), Uruguay (January 1991) and most of the other major debtors over the following two years. These new arrangements did not mean that Latin America's debt had been reduced, only rescheduled, but from the perspective of the US banks at least they brought the Latin American debt crisis to an end. The bonus for all manner of US interests, both economic and political, was that in the process the overall political economy of LAC had been substantially reorganised in a way that made it even more vulnerable to external penetration than in the past.

Changing US trade policy

At the regular GATT ministerial meeting in 1982 the US representative sought to launch a new multilateral round of trade negotiations centred on new themes such as intellectual property rights and services. The initiative was rebuffed and several observers have suggested that it was after this setback that the US began to turn to a dual-track strategy with regard to trade liberalisation.[13] This consisted of continued pressure within the GATT for a multilateral approach, which eventually led to the inauguration of the Uruguay Round in 1986, and the pursuit of explicit national US economic interests via new forms of protectionism and the initiation of *bilateral* trade liberalisation talks with key economic and political partners such as Israel and Canada. As explained in 1985 by William E. Brock, the then US Trade Representative, 'the reasoning behind these efforts is that additional trade-creating, GATT-consistent liberalization measures should not be postponed while some of the more inward-looking contracting parties contemplate their own economic malaise'.[14] While the primary motive for the free-trade agreement with Israel could be said to be political and the departure from past practice regarding multilateral negotiation on this front therefore something of a special case, the establishment of the US–Canada free-trade area in 1989 – amidst not inconsiderable domestic controversy – signalled the seriousness of purpose underpinning this new dimension of US trade policy. After all, Canada was the main single trading partner of the US, absorbing US$79 billion of US exports in 1989, some 22 per cent of the overall total and almost double the value of US shipments to Japan.[15]

What is more, as political pressure mounted in the US in response to its trade deficit and the growing visibility of Japanese goods and capital and as the Uruguay Round ran into the ground in the face of what was presented in the US as European Community intransigence on the subject of agricultural protection, there was no doubt that the nationalist, rather than the globalist, dimension of the dual-track strategy played the more effectively on the US domestic political scene. For obvious reasons too, the Canadian deal attracted a lot of attention in other parts of the Americas, especially in Mexico which, as we have seen, was undergoing a far-reaching liberal-isation as the price of its response to the debt crisis. Following an unsuccessful tour of EC states in January 1990 in pursuit of new non-American economic links, the Mexican president, Carlos Salinas de Gortari, concluded that the establishment of a free-trade area with the US, as achieved by Canada, was the best means of extending investment opportunities and thus job crea-tion in Mexico. The first contacts on the subject were made with Washington in March 1990, wholly, it should be said, on the initiative of Mexico.[16]

Bush's instant reaction was one of great personal interest and enthusiasm. He had long identified himself as a Texan and the wife of one of his sons was Mexican. In addition, the idea struck an obvious chord with the growing concern in Washington with the preservation of US economic advantage in the face of the difficulties being experienced in moving for-ward the GATT round. The Mexican government argued that, as a result of its liberalisation, US exports to Mexico had al-ready doubled, rising from US$12.4 billion in 1986 to US$25 billion in 1989, and could be expected to increase still further in the future if the huge Mexican market (some 85 million people) became still more dynamic. The same argument ap-plied too of course, although to a more muted degree, to other 'liberalising' LAC economies, all of which sucked in more US imports as they opened up during the 1980s. In the Mexican case, though, it was further claimed that growing Mexican prosperity would also stem the flow of immigrants into the US and serve to 'lock in place' the Salinas reforms. The arguments put to Bush thus addressed security as well as economic issues, feeding cleverly on the uneasiness which has long existed in the US about relations with its nearest southern neighbour with whom it shares a 2000 mile border.[17] Indeed, the political di-mension may have been critical. At any rate, when these ex-ploratory talks leaked to the press Bush and Salinas met openly and jointly admitted their support for the initiation of US–Mexico free trade negotiations.

As already indicated, Bush himself was very much in the van-guard of his own administration on this issue. Buoyed up by the Mexico announcement and also taking heart from the modest achievements of the Brady Plan, he made his EAI speech in late June 1990.[18] It was given little advance publicity, and was certainly not widely discussed between the various relevant government departments before delivery. In fact, it is quite likely that the timing of the speech derived in the main from the President's wish to assure the rest of the hemisphere that Mexico would not be the only country with which the US was prepared to discuss closer economic ties, especially since he was committed to a trip to several leading Latin American countries before the end of the year. The EAI nevertheless became the seminal statement of contemporary US economic policy towards the Americas, asserting the interdependence of debt reduction, trade and investment as policy issues, as well as giving the clearest possible indication of the new importance which LAC was acquiring in at least some official US perceptions of the country's role in international affairs after the Cold War. Put another way, it constituted one of the first major policy responses of the US to its global hegemonic decline and can be interpreted as evidence of a growing realisation in Washington that the US was no longer able to shape on its own the rules of a consensual international economic order.

The EAI and NAFTA

Substantively, the EAI contained three components – the restructuring of some official debt owed to the US by LAC countries, the promotion of increased investment in the hemisphere via the Inter-American Development Bank, and the vision offered of a series of free-trade agreements with different groups of Latin American, Central American and Caribbean countries, leading in time, as Bush himself grandly put it, to a hemispheric-wide free-trade system 'stretching from the port of Anchorage to Tierra del Fuego'.[19] The first two features were useful initiatives but at the same time relatively minor in substance. The Congress was also slow to enact the necessary legislation and the investment thrust of the initiative certainly proved to be even more disappointing in impact than ambition. However, the third feature of the EAI, despite being almost casually thrown up by the US, attracted an enormous amount of interest in the rest of the Americas. Nearly all of it was favourable, reflecting the broad shift from import-substitution to export-oriented strategies of development which had taken place across LAC since the beginning of the 1980s.

Somewhat reluctantly, and for almost wholly defensive reasons, Canada expressed a wish to join the US–Mexico talks which, from February 1991 onwards, thus became trilateral, devoted to the negotiation of a NAFTA intended to eliminate restrictions on the flow of goods, services and investments (but not labour) between the participant countries. In the negotiations the Canadian government clung on to the basic terms of the agreement it had previously signed with the US; the US government sought to open up the Mexican market as much as possible but at the same time defended its domestic producers by insisting on tough rules of origin for incoming Mexican imports; and the Mexican government succeeded in keeping its nationalised, and highly symbolic, oil industry largely outside the NAFTA framework but otherwise did what it had to do to secure the free-trade accord it so badly wanted.[20] A NAFTA treaty was duly signed between the parties in August 1992 and thereafter only required domestic approval in each of the three countries before it could come into being. It promised to embrace over 360 million people and bring together a collective Gross Domestic Product of approximately US$6239 billion.

As regards the rest of the hemisphere, the US signed 'framework agreements' with virtually all other willing partners in LAC. Bolivia, like Mexico, had signed before the EAI announcement; Colombia and Ecuador followed in July 1990; Chile in October; Honduras and Costa Rica in November; Venezuela in April 1991; El Salvador and Peru in May; the MERCOSUR group (Brazil, Argentina, Uruguay and Paraguay), Panama and Nicaragua all in June; the English-speaking Caribbean Community (CARICOM) countries in July; Guatemala before the end of the year; and finally the Dominican Republic in December 1991. These agreements were essentially assertions of principle, reflecting the merits of free trade and liberalisation and served, in effect, as holding operations whilst the US digested NAFTA. The Bush administration never made clear, for example, whether it would be the US or all the NAFTA states which would be the agency which would in time negotiate with the rest of LAC; whether applicants would be treated separately, collectively or in regional groupings; whether a queue would be constructed in accordance with the order in which the 'framework agreements' were signed; or whether alternatively a threshold system would apply whereby talks were initiated first with those countries which had already most fully opened up their economies. All that was revealed by the vacuum which emerged on these matters in the last months of the Bush administration was that it would be the US which would decide whether, when, with whom and on what basis it would eventually enter free-trade talks with other parts of the Americas.

Nevertheless, even in conception, the EAI and NAFTA – which need to be evaluated together – tell us a good deal about the emerging US view of its position *vis-à-vis* the rest of the Americas in the 1990s and beyond. They were designed, as we have seen, in the aftermath of a decade or more of forced structural adjustment of LAC economies and they sought in effect to set out and enforce new economic and political 'rules of the game' in the hemisphere. These rules reflect the triumph of economic liberalism, of faith in export-led growth and of belief in the centrality of the private sector to the development process. They have no truck with anything beyond free trade, openly eschewing any reference to protective and/or social dimensions. For the moment the 'framework agreements' which have been negotiated between the US and its many aspirant free-trade partners in other parts of the hemisphere do no more than restate these core values. The politics of the situation was therefore made very clear: the EAI and NAFTA required that regional countries 'sign up' for this entire ideological regime. The emerging political order of the Americas left no place for political leaders who found it difficult to endorse these nostrums. Behind all this, of course, was the threat of exclusion, of having to pursue export-led development without preferential access to the US market – in short, the punitive consequences of crossing US economic power. In other words, the goal of the US under Bush was nothing less than to bring about the full and final integration of LAC into the new global economy of the 1990s.

Whatever advantages do or do not flow to the developing parts of the hemisphere from such a project, the US itself expects to gain. Peter Hakim, staff director of the Inter-American Dialogue, explicitly emphasised this point in giving testimony to the Congress on the EAI in March 1991:

> I believe that Latin America, with its population of 400 million people, is important to the economic well-being of the United States. Even in the midst of depression, Latin America is a $50 billion a year market for US exporters – larger, for example, than the Japanese market. An economically healthy and growing Latin America could absorb $20 to $30 billion more in US exports each year, an amount equivalent to what we now export to Germany. Of every dollar Latin America spends on imports, 50 cents comes to the United States. There is nowhere else in the world where we enjoy that kind of advantage.[21]

The last comment was the telling one: in a period of intensified economic competition with the EC and Japan the Bush administration and its allies saw Latin America as a part of the world where the US had a greater natural advantage than either of its main trading rivals. It also recognised that parts of the Americas, especially North America, have become increasingly linked at the levels of production and trade over the past decade. Weintraub, for example, has referred to the process of 'silent integration' which has taken place between the US, Canadian and Mexican economies as a consequence of the spreading tentacles of multinational corporations operating across all three countries, and Maingot has shown that the same phenomenon now increasingly embraces the 'offshore Caribbean'.[22] In sum, the Bush administration conceived of the EAI and NAFTA in wholly national interest terms, as devices by which to create an increasingly integrated hemispheric economy which the US could then use as the base from which to export ever more competitively to other, more distant, markets, preferably within the ambit of an extended GATT.

Clinton

Bill Clinton was initially slow to see the significance of either of the two key trade-policy initiatives passed on to him by Bush, GATT and NAFTA. During his presidential campaign he focused on the economy and the issue of national economic revival but he did not clarify in any detail his position on international trade issues, seeking judiciously to distance himself from the protectionist instincts of some of his Democratic Party rivals without embracing liberalisation too enthusiastically. He thus gave support to the GATT round, implying that he could negotiate a better deal than Bush, and endorsed NAFTA whilst expressing some reservations about it in deference to Democratic Party opposition, especially within the labour unions. In office Clinton was true to his candidacy. An early review of his policy noted the emergence of 'an *ad hoc*, even incoherent, trade approach which is characterized by a lack of philosophical underpinning'.[23] On the GATT the administration returned to the negotiating table and endeavoured to unpick some aspects of the arrangements on agriculture which had been provisionally agreed with the EC. ON NAFTA it set in motion the negotiation of two so-called 'side agreements' with Mexico and Canada on environmental and labour issues. But, even when they were agreed, Clinton waited until the final stages of Congressional consideration of the whole NAFTA legislative package before committing his administration to a whole-hearted attempt to see that it was passed. He was successful and NAFTA duly came into being on 1 January 1994.

Even at this moment of triumph, Clinton did not seize on the inauguration of NAFTA as a means to send to the rest of LAC a positive message (à la Bush) about the merits of a free-trade hemisphere. It was not that he was opposed to this vision, for in a meeting with Salinas in late 1992 before actually taking up office he explicitly endorsed the original Bush proposal to extend it southwards as soon as possible. The NAFTA agreement also possessed an access clause, although it was unclear how it might be implemented in practice and interesting, to say the least, that it did not confine future membership to countries within the Americas or indeed any geographical region. Yet, once NAFTA was passed, the other governments of the region found that it was they who had to keep raising the issue with Washington, not the other way round. The US administration seemed to have other priorities and, in general, appeared capable of being able to focus on only a tiny number of issues at any one time. In trade matters GATT naturally

became the focus. It was not therefore until after the text of
the Uruguay Round had finally, and painfully, been agreed
and then approved by Congress, and just before the opening
of a meeting of the heads of government of all the states of
the hemisphere (with the sole exception of Cuba) in Miami in
December 1994 – a gathering which had been promised many
months earlier – that there were any real signs in Washington
of renewed thinking on the matter of trade policy towards the
Americas.

Nevertheless, at this so-called 'Summit of the Americas', the
first such Pan-American conference to have been addressed by
a US president since Franklin Roosevelt went to Lima in 1936
and the first to have been held at all since 1967, Clinton did
finally match Bush's EAI rhetoric. He called for the establishment of an American Free Trade Area and boldly set the year
2005 as the date of its inauguration. 'We can create a new
partnership for prosperity,' he intoned, 'where freedom and
trade and economic opportunity become the common property of the people of the Americas . . . from Alaska to Argentina.'²⁴
His underlying argument was just the same as that deployed
by Bush. Global economic changes made it necessary for the
US to compete and win; exports created jobs; and LAC was a
growing market in which the US could sell. Again, the precise
mechanism by which an AFTA was to be achieved was not spelled
out, beyond the invitation to Chile to open negotiations first,
which was itself merely a reiteration of a promise previously
made by the Bush administration. At a minimum, though,
Clinton can be said at last to have caught up with and taken
on board the far-reaching economic agenda for the Americas
which George Bush set out in his EAI speech in 1990 and given
himself and his successors a decade in which to realise it. How
far and how fast the US will actually travel down the road of
hemispheric economic integration remains of course to be seen.
On past experience there is a case for being sceptical. What
has, however, become evident is that Mexico has now been
drawn so closely into the global economic strategy of the US
that it cannot be let go, come what may. Clinton demonstrated
this for all to see when, within weeks of the Miami summit,
the Mexican currency crashed and the US administration defied
the opposition of Congress to put together a rescue package

of no less than US$20 billion of loan supports. As Clinton said, with notable underemphasis, 'it is in America's economic and strategic interest that Mexico succeeds'.[25]

Contemporary US security policies towards the Americas

The overriding preoccupation with economic issues has not eliminated US security concerns about the Americas but it has placed the security debate in a new light and, to some extent, rendered security policy a derivative of the economic agenda. Most obviously, the traditional US concern of the hegemonic era, defending the hemisphere against Communist incursion, is obsolete. Its new security anxieties are less stark but in many ways more complex: they focus in particular on the creation and preservation of democracies in the Americas; on the containment of the threat posed by illegal drugs trafficking; on the control of migration into the US from LAC; and on the protection of the people and territory of the US from the environmental problems of other parts of the region. It will readily be seen that all of these questions relate, directly or indirectly, to the dominance of the neo-liberal orthodoxy in economic matters.

Democratisation

Under both Presidents Bush and Clinton the US has identified a strong national security interest in the successful democratisation of the Americas. In one sense, this represents nothing new. A number of different academic accounts of recent US foreign policy towards LAC – by Lowenthal, Carothers and Pastor – all highlight US efforts to promote democracy in the region during the Cold-War era. They all also go on to note the many difficulties into which this aspect of policy ran.[26] What has been different for Bush and Clinton, however, is that the ending of the Cold War largely removed the systemic pressure on the US to support authoritarianism in LAC as its best hedge against the rise of revolution. The disappearance of a significant left politics in the region, which has been the other side of the coin of the neo-liberal ideological triumph, has consequently allowed the

US state greater scope to give rein to the democratic tendencies which have always been there within its foreign policy process. Thus, somewhat hesitantly at first under Bush but now with growing rhetorical fervour under Clinton, a positive link between liberalisation and democratisation has been advanced as the guiding credo of what Clinton at the recent Miami summit hailed as a new 'community of nations committed to the values of liberty and the promise of prosperity' currently being forged in the Americas.[27]

On the ground in LAC, the link is nowhere near as firm. Over the last decade democratisation has neither led automatically to liberalisation, nor liberalisation to democratisation. But there is still an important relationship between the two processes in the context of US policy. Put simply, neo-liberalism in LAC *of itself* secures the key contemporary US interest in the region. What its dominance has given the US is the relative luxury to be able to embrace democratisation actively, something it was not prepared to allow itself during the Cold War. It can fairly be said that the official US view of the kind of democracy it wants to see established throughout the Americas is not in the conceptual sense that deep. It is focused on the establishment and maintenance of the traditional freedoms of speech and organisation and on the holding of proper elections, preferably monitored by an external, US-oriented agency. It has also clearly been the case that the US has amply used the stick of democratisation to beat the few remaining undemocratic regimes in LAC, as well as to maintain the pressure on those states and societies in the hemisphere which are deemed still to be less than fulsome in their embrace of democratic forms. Cuba is a public victim of the first strand of policy. Its regime has been repeatedly excoriated by US spokespersons for its illiberal nature and told explicitly that fundamental political change in the direction of democracy must precede any discussion of the ending of the Cold-War embargo on its trade with the US.[28] Mexico itself is the main focus of the second strand of policy which, unsurprisingly given the close political relationship the US now has with Mexico post-NAFTA, has been conducted on a quieter, diplomatic basis. Nevertheless, it has been made clear that both the Bush and Clinton administrations have been keen to see the dominant single-party regime in Mexico effect a fuller political opening than it felt able or inclined to set in train under Salinas. There has also been felt some anxiety about the potentially damaging impact which the Zapatista rising in the Chiapas province of Mexico could have on even the existing level of democracy in the country and a sharp pang of worry when the ruling party's presidential candidate was assassinated at the beginning of the campaign in March 1994.

The Mexican situation certainly contains the possibility that the US may at some stage be hoist by its own democratisation petard in its relations with the Americas. One has only to wonder how US attitudes to NAFTA, and all that it represents, would be influenced by, say, brutal Mexican repression of the Chiapas protest or a ban on opposition politics or a crude attempt to override the popular verdict in a future election. For the moment, it must be admitted that the US has gone further in its response to breaches of democratic behaviour in LAC in the last two or three years than ever would have been conceivable in the Cold-War years. Working with and within the OAS, it sought by various, sometimes tortuous, means to restore President Jean-Bertrand Aristide to his elected position in Haiti following his overthrow by the military in September 1991 and stopped all economic and military aid to Peru following President Alberto Fujimori's suspension of the country's constitution in April 1992.[29] The Haiti saga eventually led in September 1994 to a US-led 'invasion' of the island in the name of reconstructing democracy. Needless to say, the task is formidably difficult and perhaps impossible in the short term. The invasion served also to expose the limits of the Bush/Clinton consensus on the price of democratisation in the hemisphere, with Bush reportedly declaring that Haiti was not worth the life of a single American. It is plausible that Clinton's eventual decision to send troops into Haiti emerged as much from a policy muddle as a policy conviction; either way, it marks a new high-water mark in the willingness of the US to take risks for the cause of LAC democracy.

It is likely that the US would quickly back away from heroic commitments to the principles of democracy if radical challenges to its ascendancy in the region began once more to emerge. As indicated, its commitment to democratisation presumes the victory of liberalisation. What is striking is that it presently feels sufficiently confident of its core security *vis-à-vis* the Americas that it can give this measure of priority to democracy.

Drugs

The US first declared 'war' on drugs in 1982. In so doing, it took the complex set of issues surrounding the economic and social consequences of growing drugs use in the US and simplified them into a national security threat defined as the illegal traffic in drugs largely from LAC countries to the US mainland. This framework of analysis, which in effect alleged that the problem lay on the supply side rather than the demand side of the equation, legitimated the expanded role assigned to the US military in drugs matters, drove the Reagan administration to set up a vast new drugs bureaucracy and caused it to increase hugely its expenditure on drugs interdiction efforts both at home and abroad. Needless to say, the co-operation of LAC governments was required, and was largely if uneasily achieved precisely by raising the problem to the level of a national security threat. Bagley and Tokatlian have in fact commented that there was a historical parallel between the anti-drugs crusade of the 1980s and the tradition of anti-Communism which dominated the US–LAC security agenda throughout most of the post-1945 period. As they described this way of thinking, 'the "enemy" (now drugs rather than communism) has infiltrated the hemisphere. Because "coexistence" is impossible (and immoral), it is essential to act aggressively to curtail the international drug trade; to achieve this end, the governments of the region should accept and internalize the U.S. hard-line approach and implement it voluntarily or they can "justifiably" be compelled to do so involuntarily.'[30]

Although all the evidence available at the end of the Reagan presidency suggested that the US was far from winning its drugs war, the Bush administration largely reaffirmed the supply-side emphasis of existing US policy. Indeed, it sought even broader US military participation in the battle against drugs, readily using the US Navy to assist the Coast Guard with interdiction activities on the high seas, the US National Guard to patrol the Mexican border and the US Air Force to collaborate with Customs in aerial surveillance. Eventually, in December 1989, Bush resorted to direct US military intervention in Panama as a last desperate means of ousting General Noriega, long decried as a key figure in many drugs operations.[31] At the same time, the US under Bush also tried hard to pressure Latin American governments to assign a greater role to their own armed forces in combating drugs trafficking. Substantial additional military aid was thus given to Colombia, Peru and Bolivia and the suggestion repeatedly made that US troops might be sent to these Andean coca-producing countries to help in the battle against drugs. LAC governments opposed this sort of interventionism and were angered by such US actions as the use of surveillance satellites over Mexican territory without the Mexican government's knowledge and, in a particularly controversial case, the deployment of US Navy ships off the Colombian coast in 1990 without the Colombian government's permission. US pressure to extradite alleged drugs criminals was also a frequent source of tension. During the course of his presidency Bush brought regional leaders together in two anti-drugs summits – in Cartagena in 1990 and in San Antonio in 1992 – but he still did not succeed in building a consensus within the Americas around the US definition of the drugs problem.

As a presidential candidate Clinton described the war on drugs as 'phoney', but in office he has in effect allowed much of the momentum of policy to continue unchallenged. As two commentators have recently noted, 'the Clinton anti-drug strategy exists more by default than by design, maintained by institutional inertia and a failure of imagination'.[32] It is true, they concede, that the moralising and militaristic rhetoric of the Reagan–Bush years has been abandoned, with drugs control now presented as merely one piece of a larger foreign policy agenda for the Americas which also very much includes the promotion of democracy and free-market economic reforms. Yet Clinton's first drug budget was virtually a copy of the Bush plan he inherited; the funding for interdiction efforts has been cut, but not by much; and the administration apparently plans to tighten up the certification process by which the provision of other forms of US aid is made conditional upon the undertaking of satisfactory anti-drugs activities by the recipient country. Above all, attempts to eliminate the production of drugs in key source countries like Colombia, Bolivia and Peru are still focused on military support for local anti-drug operations.

Interestingly, in a shift of discourse, the US now claims that its support for liberalisation and democratisation in the Americas contributes to the fight against drugs. According to the most recent National Drug Control Strategy Report, 'the United States finds that democratic, market-oriented governments are much easier to work with and more willing to co-operate with the international community in a common effort against the illicit drug industry'.[33] That may be so, but at the same time there are obvious problems. In particular, market deregulation as a general process makes the specific task of drugs regulation harder. For example, NAFTA could well ease access to the US drugs market because any increase in the overall flow of goods crossing the US–Mexican border will unavoidably make it harder, indeed almost impossible, for customs officials to weed out the illegal items. One can also go further with the argument: Mark Peceny of the University of New Mexico has suggested that the drugs issue is the dark side of the new liberal inter-American order. From his point of view, 'drug cartels are transnational actors responding to liberal market forces'.[34] At best, therefore, there may be emerging an equivocal relationship between the new political economy of the Americas and the drugs problem. Either way, the longstanding supply-side logic of US policy looks increasingly inappropriate.

Immigration

The US has had to have a set of policies on the question of regional immigration from the Americas from the moment when large-scale flows began to build up after the Second World War. The scale and growth of the US economy during the years of hegemony acted as an extraordinarily powerful magnet, attracting professional talent but in the main sucking in the huge reservoirs of unskilled low-wage labour needed by its expanding agricultural, industrial and service sectors. This general trend was also neatly integrated into the anti-Communist agenda because differential access to immigration could then be used either to help or hinder LAC governments in the task of warding off the social pressures of underdevelopment.[35] This regime has now been undermined and contemporary US immigration policy is full of contradictions. The problem is that the economy of the US and, perhaps even more, US society as a whole, no longer has the same capacity to absorb large inflows of migrant labour; and yet both still unquestionably act as a powerful draw, ideologically and practically, to many, many of the inhabitants of the rest of the Americas. As a consequence, the new security problem, as perceived by the US, has become how to limit *illegal* immigration into the US by Mexicans, Dominicans, Salvadorians, Haitians, Cubans and the like.

In this cause over the last few years the US has been prepared to spend substantial resources, financially and morally. For example, it has continued to police the Mexican border, routinely returning to Mexico each morning dozens of illegal immigrants who have crossed the Rio Grande during the night, even as it has been engaged in the developing process of economic and political integration with Mexico which NAFTA represents. In fact, representatives of the Bush administration used frequently to say that one of the merits – indeed one of the aims – of NAFTA was that it would inhibit illegal Mexican immigration by contributing to greater Mexican prosperity. Bush was also prepared to return to Haiti the so-called 'boat people' who fled the poverty of that island for the hope of a better life in the US. They were deemed by US law to be economic migrants and therefore ineligible for admission, a stance which seemed to many to contrast harshly with the welcome given in the US to political refugees who succeeded in escaping from revolutionary Cuba. Once again candidate Clinton promised to overturn Bush's policy on Haitian immigration, only to back away from the commitment when in office for fear of setting off a major exodus of impoverished and persecuted Haitians and an angry reaction amongst white Floridans.[36] In the end, Clinton could not escape the vortex which the combined Haitian economic and political crisis constituted and sent in US troops in an attempt to restore sufficient order, if not democracy, in the island to keep most Haitians there. In similar fashion, and for largely similar reasons, he was also driven to amend traditional US immigration policy towards Cuba. Alarmed by the growing numbers of ordinary Cubans who were setting sail for the US on flimsy rafts during 1994, Clinton eventually ordered that all those captured *en route* or on landing be detained at the US naval base at Guantanamo in Cuba prior to their return to Cuba proper. In deference, however, to continuing Cold-War sensibilities towards Cuba (the one part of LAC where this agenda has not been extinguished) he did also agree to increase considerably the number of legal Cuban immigrants which the US would take each year.[37]

In other words, it is apparent that much of recent US immigration policy has been made in extempore fashion in response to crises occurring in different parts of LAC. As *Newsweek* rather gruesomely put it, 'instability in the Caribbean doesn't stay there – it washes up, dead or alive, on the Florida shore'.[38] Instability may or may not grow in the coming years: whether it does or not very much depends on how well neo-liberal development works, especially in the smaller and poorer parts of the Caribbean Basin located within reach of the US. To a substantial extent, therefore, the immigration strand of US security policy towards the Americas has now become the prisoner of its broader economic strategy.

The environment

Lastly the US has been required of late to incorporate into its security policies towards the Americas a new concern for environmental protection. This is a genuinely novel feature of the security agenda which cannot be related to any aspect of Cold-War policy. It has been forced upon the US government primarily by the actions and lobbying of domestic environmental groups who have seen in the lower environmental standards pertaining within LAC a threat to US achievements in this sphere of policy. They have drawn attention in particular to the high levels of pollution and generally appalling environmental conditions which exist on the Mexican side of the US border as a consequence of many years of uncontrolled *maquiladora* development and have argued effectively that this gives an indication of the sorts of environmental damage which can emanate from too unthinking a connection with LAC. The threat was not only seen to be immediate and direct through the contamination of water and air in border areas; it was also perceived as a long-term warning of the insidious effects on the prospects of achieving tougher US environmental legislation of US companies arguing that the price of such legislation would be a greater drain of investment to Mexico and other parts of LAC with more lenient environmental frameworks.[39] This pressure secured the adoption of an environmental side-agreement to NAFTA, connected to but not strictly part of the treaty. More generally, it has meant that all official US arguments about the benefits of freer trade and more market-oriented development in the hemisphere have to be scrutinised against the threat they might pose to the US environment. As and when this is done, it becomes apparent that environmental considerations not only come into frequent conflict with the philosophy of the market but also inexorably bring forward deeper democratic questions than are raised within most establishment US usages of that concept. Once again, then, the security and economic agendas proposed for LAC by the US emerge as somewhat less than consistent.

The new political sociology of the US

As has been seen, contemporary US policy towards the Americas is required to address a very wide range of issues and not every aspect of policy necessarily coheres. There does not exist a single US national interest in the making of foreign policy towards LAC. In fact, the reverse is true: this whole arena of policy has fully exposed the many cross-cutting cleavages which presently run through US politics and society. This links what we have called the US enterprise for the Americas to the debate about 'the disuniting' of contemporary US society which has been launched by Arthur Schlesinger's recent polemical essay of that title.[40] Although the ramifications of this latter debate cannot be fully considered here, the point is that the recent and continuing arguments about NAFTA, about the invasion of Haiti and about drugs and immigration have highlighted – and exacerbated – many of these fissures. All of these items of policy connect in different ways to the various constituencies which constitute the new and highly complex political sociology of the US in the 1990s. Although, as indicated, this section can do no more than sketch in the outlines of these social and political divisions, a sense of the domestic base out of which US policy towards the Americas emerges is indispensable to understanding its meaning and indeed its limitations.

Bush vs Clinton vs Perot

The most visible level at which divisions surfaced was the personal political rivalry between Bush, Clinton and their independent rival in the 1992 presidential election, Ross Perot. Whatever was said in that campaign, Clinton has ended up adopting very large parts of Bush's agenda for LAC. He responded to pressures from the labour unions and environmental groups, both of which played prominent roles in his electoral coalition, and insisted on the negotiation of side agreements to NAFTA in these two areas. Once that was done, he worked hard, using all the prestige and patronage of the presidency, to secure a majority for NAFTA in the crucial November 1993 votes in the Congress. The opposition to the Bush/Clinton approach came from Perot, a Texan billionaire whose populist programme took 19 per cent of the vote in the presidential election. After his defeat, he seized on the NAFTA issue, charging that it would be accompanied by a 'giant sucking sound' as US jobs were pulled down the plug-hole towards Mexico by the lure of cheaper wages.[41] He also tried to tie NAFTA to the drugs problem by alleging that it would help Mexican dealers offer 'door-to-door delivery' anywhere in the US and, in general, did not refrain from subliminally racist observations about Mexicans. Perot used his wealth to buy enormous amounts of US television time and appeared for a while as if he could stop Congressional ratification of NAFTA. In the end, he fell foul of his own favoured political medium, being widely perceived to lose an ill-tempered debate about NAFTA with Clinton's Vice-President, Albert Gore, on *Cable Network News* (CNN). Immediately after the debate polls showed public support for NAFTA rising from 34 per cent to 57 per cent.

Capital vs labour

NAFTA, predictably enough, brought out sharp differences between the forces of capital and labour in the US. Most of the major US business groups vigorously endorsed the idea, believing that freer trade generates growth and arguing specifically that the agreement would improve the US economy's ability to compete in world markets and was thus vital to the country's future. They paid for extensive press advertisements promoting this message, as well as other forms of lobbying designed to facilitate the treaty's passage. Organised business associations supporting NAFTA included the National Association of Manufacturers, the US Chamber of Commerce, the Business Roundtable and the Council of the Americas. By contrast, organised labour, principally the American Federation of Labor–Congress of Industrial Organizations (AFL–CIO), fought fiercely against the agreement, arguing, like Perot, that it would lead to many US companies relocating to Mexico and thus shedding jobs in the US. In that sense, the unions were doing no more than seeking to protect their members. But they also sought to raise the debate to the ideological level, suggesting that a wider capitalist agenda underpinned NAFTA. Lane Kirkland, the AFL–CIO leader, put the point typically when he said that NAFTA would 'give corporate America a virtual veto over every piece of social and economic legislation designed to establish minimum conditions of life and labour in this country'.[42] Although the charge was not unfair, it missed one subtext of the NAFTA debate within the US, which was a difference of view between internationally-oriented capital, concerned to see new export markets opened up, and nationally-oriented capital, concerned to protect its domestic markets against competitive foreign imports. In particular, growers of fruits and vegetables in Florida and California opposed NAFTA and were sufficiently effective for a number of safeguards of their interests to have to be inserted into the final text of the treaty.

Anglos vs Hispanics vs Blacks

The arguments about NAFTA and other aspects of US policy towards LAC have been read differently again by the various

major ethnic groupings in US society. This has certainly cut
across the class divisions highlighted in the capital–labour split.
Broadly speaking, the growing Hispanic community in the US
has welcomed the high profile attached to policy towards the
Americas since the EAI was announced by Bush in 1990 and
naturally favours the closer integration of Mexico into US life.
Aware that many of its members are Hispanics, the AFL–CIO
tried to tackle this by arguing that NAFTA would harm Mexican workers by, in effect, turning the whole of Mexico into a
kind of huge *maquiladora*. The Black Caucus in Congress was
also uneasy about NAFTA, with some members worried by the
threat to the jobs of Afro-Americans posed by what was often
portrayed in black circles as huge, new incoming flows of
Hispanics. Indeed, immigration has proved domestically to be
a highly divisive feature of US policy towards LAC. Quite apart
from the displaced racism which might be said to be connected
to many of the other objections which were mounted against
NAFTA, radical-right politicians like Pat Buchanan (who challenged Bush for the 1992 Republican presidential nomination)
openly raised the spectre of mass immigration within the Anglo
community. This anxiety has subsequently been given new legitimacy by the support given to Proposition 187 in California at
the time of the mid-term elections in November 1994. Although
it is being challenged in the courts, this denies access to welfare services to illegal immigrants in California, who are mostly
of course Mexicans.[43] It heralds the advent of an era of more
open racism in US politics, something which was apparent too
in the condemnation heaped upon Clinton's decision to send
troops to the (black-populated) island of Haiti by several white
Republican politicians. The heavy implication of much of this
criticism was that Haiti was not a place which could ever be
made democratic. Equally, and to some extent paradoxically,
Clinton's concern with Haiti cannot be separated from an
awareness of the considerable influence which the Black Caucus continues to hold within the Democratic Party.

South and West vs North and East

These various fissures can be alternatively expressed in terms
of competing subregional interests within the US. This has

generally been described as a conflict between the south and west of the country (the 'sunbelt') against the north and east (the 'rustbelt') and draws attention to the contrast between subregions likely to experience economic growth as a result of developing closer connections with LAC economies and subregions in decline and geographically less well positioned to take advantage of the new markets opened up by NAFTA. There is clearly something in this: in the final vote on NAFTA in the House of Representatives, 24 of the 30 Texas representatives voted for the agreement, whereas 10 out of 15 Michigan representatives voted against. Yet Florida and California's delegations, although supportive, were noticeably more evenly divided, splitting 13 to 10 in favour in Florida's case and 31 to 21 in favour in California's. It must be remembered that these parts of the country also bear the brunt of the flows of drugs and people from LAC into the US and of the hostility that is consequently generated and that they are additionally the home states of some of the agricultural interests most threatened by Mexican production. There are further subtleties too to the pattern of subregional reactions. Whereas Los Angeles and San Antonio have become Mexican cities, Miami has turned into a Caribbean and Central American city. In fact, Florida has been concerned that the Caribbean Basin countries with which it has close and beneficial connections will be relatively disadvantaged by the way that NAFTA opens up Mexico.[44] Its representatives in Washington in both the Senate and the House have even joined with some Caribbean Basin governments in pressing upon the Clinton administration the case for parity legislation which gives the former beneficiaries of the CBI much the same access to the US market as Mexico has been granted.[45]

Producers vs Consumers vs Environmentalists

If business and labour in their different ways represent the organised economic and political interests of producers, then both have been confronted in the NAFTA debate by consumers and environmentalists. The latter have been especially active and successful in opposing NAFTA. They initially ensured that the Bush administration built a measure of safety and environmental regulation into the text of the treaty and latterly forced

Clinton to negotiate a separate side agreement on the environment.[46] Indeed, some environmental groups nearly undermined the whole pact when they persuaded a federal judge to order the preparation of a full environmental impact statement on NAFTA before it could be approved. This judgement was subsequently overturned and in the end some environmental groups, such as the National Wildlife Federation, did not oppose NAFTA's legislative passage, claiming that their concerns had been met in the side agreement. Some radical groups who were opposed to NAFTA for other reasons or who were opposed to US capitalism in general tried to use the environment issue to create a broader (red–green) front linked to workers worried about their jobs. Even the AFL–CIO engaged in a somewhat strained attempt to make joint cause with environmentalists. It did not work in either case and, with NAFTA, as so often, the cleavage between producers and environmentalists remained one that could only be compromised, not bridged.

Democrats vs Republicans

NAFTA had eventually either to stand or fall in votes in the Senate and House of Representatives. President Bush did not find it at all easy to get fast-track authority to negotiate NAFTA in 1991, although he eventually succeeded. (This meant that any treaty subsequently brought forward could not be amended but had to be passed or rejected by Congress as a whole.) Yet such was the opposition that was generated during 1992 that for a long while many observers felt that NAFTA would never be approved. As already indicated, President Clinton lobbied hard for the bill when his administration finally decided to push it through and the final votes in November 1993 saw a comfortable majority in the Senate, which was by then expected, but also an ample majority of 34 votes – much larger than anticipated – in the House. The key point about the latter was that Clinton only achieved his majority with Republican votes. 132 Republicans and 102 Democrats voted in favour; 156 Democrats, 43 Republicans and one Independent voted against. The roots of this pattern of voting will already be apparent from the preceding discussion of the various cleavages in contemporary US society which NAFTA brought to the fore. Most

Congressional Democrats were, at least in the abstract, in favour of free trade and they understood the risks posed by an unstable Mexico; at the same time they had close links with the unions and faced strong protectionist demands from older industries located in Democratic political strongholds in the 'rustbelt' of New England and the Midwest. They also had to make a calculation as to how many Hispanic voters they had in their electoral districts. For their part, Congressional Republicans saw NAFTA and the hemispheric free-trade strategy which attached to it as a Bush initiative and were more widely committed in any case to a business view of the world. At the same time Republican members from states with strong grower interests like Florida had to take note of these reservations. As regards leadership, both the Democratic Majority Leader and Majority Whip in the House started out opposed and remained opposed, notwithstanding blandishments, which meant that Clinton was forced to work more closely with, and ultimately rely on, the Republican Minority Leader, Newt Gingrich. In the final analysis, then, NAFTA only passed through the Congress on the back of a complex cross-party coalition – in David Calleo's telling phrase, 'the serendipitous result of innumerable private bargains'.[47]

Conclusion

At this stage in the unfolding of events all that a conclusion can hope to do is offer a balance of judgements about the prospect of a 'regional bloc' being created in the Americas by the US. There certainly cannot be any doubt that the US has been particularly active in relating to LAC in a variety of areas of policy since the beginning of the 1990s and that relations between the US and the rest of the Americas are closer now than for many years. As the Summit of the Americas in Miami showed, the dominant political discourse in the region is currently characterised by notions of 'partnership', 'synergy' and 'co-operation'. Old Cold-War concepts like 'threat', 'war' and 'subversion' have been banished. It also seems likely that the Bush administration, so often derided for its lack of vision, did develop a distinctive view of the way it wanted LAC to develop over the final years of this century. In that sense the EAI bids to be seen as a genuinely historic speech which picked up existing trends and assembled them into a new agenda for the Americas. In more theoretical terms, it can be said to represent the initiation of a US project to offset the loss of global hegemony by the establishment of a regional hegemony in the Americas across the economic, security and ideological agendas. The Clinton administration was initially slow to see the implications and benefits of such a project but it eventually caught up and has now etched out a policy framework for the Americas which links free trade, democracy and security in a more direct fashion than Bush ever managed to do.

As Andrew Hurrell has noted, 'neither partnership nor co-operation is incompatible with continued U.S. hegemony'.[48] In fact, in neo-Gramscian terms the dominance of the notion of partnership is evidence of the existence of hegemony. As we have seen, there is plenty of other evidence too to suggest that, over the last few years, the US has succeeded to a remarkable extent in laying down the parameters within which economic and security policies are conceived by LAC political élites. The objective has not been to create a closed regional bloc, but rather to organise the Americas in a way consistent with and supportive of US global strategy. Again to quote Hurrell, 'structured free-trade agreements offer the United States both economic benefits (market access, the ability to ensure compliance with a favorable investment regime and adequate patent protection, and a means to promote microeconomic adjustment and increased international competitiveness) and a political framework for the effective management of other issues (drugs, migration, and environment)'.[49] In short, Bush and Clinton, between them, have been able to advance quite significantly the regional project set out in the EAI. But they cannot be said yet to have fully succeeded in engineering a US regional hegemony in the Americas. In fact, there are some reasons for believing that the extent of US influence over LAC may have already reached something of a high tide and that the trend over the remaining years of the decade may accordingly be one of retreat and growing difficulty.

Three such reasons stand out, all of which have been flagged in the preceding analysis. Firstly, there are real contradictions between the economic and security agendas of the US. As argued earlier, liberalisation and democratisation are far from being comfortable bedfellows; drugs control is not made easier by the freeing of markets; and environmentalism, if taken seriously, challenges many of the favoured prescriptions of the neoliberal economic consensus. Thus far these incongruities have been covered over, but that cannot necessarily be maintained for much longer. Secondly, the US is not equally concerned with all parts of the Americas. It does not any longer have to take a view of LAC as a whole, something which it felt it necessary to do by way of example in the era of global hegemony; instead one has a growing sense that the signal of concern weakens the further it moves away from US territory. Mexico is thus crucial, overwhelmingly so. The small states of the Caribbean Basin cannot be forgotten, much as some in the US government would wish it. But Latin America south, say, of Colombia and Venezuela is not such an important economic partner for the US, certainly when compared with other parts of the world outside the Americas, and it is not that much of a security threat either. Pressures to differentiate US policy *vis-à-vis* the various subregions of the Americas can therefore be expected to grow. Thirdly, and perhaps most importantly, the Americas project is not grounded domestically on a firm social and political base. As again we have seen, the regionalist option has been deployed by a variety of groups for different, often mutually exclusive, reasons. The coalitions that passed NAFTA or supported the invasion of Haiti were at best fragile. At worst, the policy issues of the Americas have the capacity to penetrate and divide US society and politics in a very harmful fashion. Either way, the increasingly fragmented nature of the US state/society complex does not augur well for the further and full development of the US enterprise for the Americas.

Notes

*   The author would like to thank the United States Institute for Peace for the award of a research grant relating to this research.
1. The region under discussion in this chapter is the Americas, that is North, Central and South America, plus the Caribbean. Central and South America and the Caribbean are collectively de-

scribed as Latin America and the Caribbean (LAC) or sometimes simply by the shorthand Latin America. Pan-American relations refer to the body of relations within the Americas as a whole.
2. L. D. Langley, *The United States and the Caribbean in the Twentieth Century* (Athens: The University of Georgia Press, 1982) pp. 13–4.
3. For an account of US policy in this period, see G. Connell-Smith, *The Inter-American System* (New York: Oxford University Press, 1962).
4. For a good statement of this argument, see P. K. Sutton, 'The Caribbean as a Focus for Strategic and Resource Rivalry', in P. Calvert (ed.), *The Central American Security System: North-South or East-West?* (Cambridge: Cambridge University Press, 1988) pp. 18–44.
5. See G. P. Atkins, *Latin America in the International Political System* (New York: The Free Press, 1977).
6. A brillant 'insider' account of US relations with Nicaragua in the Carter period is provided by R. A. Pastor, *Condemned to Repetition: The United States and Nicaragua* (Princeton: Princeton University Press, 1987).
7. One notable exception was E. Pantojas Garcia, 'Restoring Hegemony: The Complementarity among the Security, Economic and Political Components of US Policy in the Caribbean Basin during the 1980s', in J. Rodriguez Beruff, J. P. Figueroa and J. E. Greene (eds.), *Conflict, Peace and Development in the Caribbean* (London: Macmillan, 1991) pp. 22–61.
8. For a discussion of the US role in the debt crisis, see M. Shepherd, 'U.S. Domestic Interests and the Latin American Debt Crisis', in R. Stubbs and G. R. D. Underhill (eds.), *Political Economy and the Changing Global Order* (London: Macmillan, 1994) pp. 302–12.
9. R. Roett, 'The Debt Crisis and Economic Development in Latin America', in J. Hartlyn, L. Schoultz and A. Varas (eds.), *The United States and Latin America in the 1990s* (Chapel Hill: The University of North Carolina Press, 1992) p. 136.
10. Again, see, amongst many possible sources, Shepherd, 'U.S. Domestic Interests and the Latin American Debt Crisis' for the details.
11. See J. Petras, 'The Metamorphosis of Latin America's Intellectuals', *Latin American Perspectives*, 17, 2 (1990) 102–12.
12. See J. Sachs, 'Making the Brady Plan Work', *Foreign Affairs*, 68 (1989) 87–8.
13. J. H. Jackson, 'Multilateral and Bilateral Negotiating Approaches for the Conduct of U.S. Trade Policies', in R. M. Stern (ed.), *U.S. Trade Policies in a Changing World Economy* (Cambridge, Mass: MIT Press, 1987) and J. J. Schott, 'More Free Trade Areas?', in J. J. Schott (ed.), *Free Trade Areas and U.S. Trade Policy* (Washington DC: Institute for International Economics, 1989).
14. W. E. Brock, 'U.S. Trade Policy toward Developing Countries', in E. H. Preeg (ed.), *Hard Bargaining Ahead: U.S. Trade Policy and Developing Countries* (Washington DC: Overseas Development Council, 1985) p. 38.

128   *The United States and its Enterprise for the Americas*

15. For a useful discussion of US–Canadian trade, see W. Diebold, Jr. (ed.), *Bilateralism, Multilateralism and Canada in U.S. Trade Policy* (Cambridge, Mass: Ballinger, 1988).
16. Confidential interviews, Mexico City, July 1991.
17. See R. A. Pastor and J. G. Castenada, *Limits to Friendship: The United States and Mexico* (New York: Alfred A. Knopf, 1988).
18. For a fuller account of events leading up to the EAI speech, see M. D. Baer, 'North American Free Trade', *Foreign Affairs*, 70 (1991) 132–49; R. B. Porter, 'The Enterprise for the Americas Initiative: A New Approach to Economic Growth', *Journal of Interamerican Studies and World Affairs*, 32 (1990) 1–12; and S. Weintraub, 'The New US Economic Initiative toward Latin America', *Journal of Interamerican Studies and World Affairs*, 33 (1991) 1–18.
19. White House press release on The Enterprise for the Americas Initiative, Washington DC, June 1990.
20. For a discussion of the competing interests of the three states, see D. Leyton-Brown, 'The Political Economy of North American Free Trade', in Stubbs and Underhill (eds.), *Political Economy and the Changing Global Order*, pp. 352–65.
21. Statement of P. Hakim, Inter-American Dialogue, to the Subcommittee on Foreign Relations, US House of Representatives Hearings on 'External Debt and Free Trade in the Americas', Washington DC, March 1991.
22. S. Weintraub, 'The North American Free Trade Debate', *Washington Quarterly*, 13 (1990) 119–30; and A. P. Maingot, 'The Offshore Caribbean', in A. J. Payne and P. K. Sutton (eds.), *Modern Caribbean Politics* (Baltimore: The Johns Hopkins University Press, 1993) pp. 259–76.
23. F. L. Lavin, 'Clinton and Trade', *The National Interest*, 32 (1993) 29.
24. White House press release – 'Clinton Envisions Partnership for Prosperity at Summit' – Washington DC, 9 December 1994.
25. *Miami Herald*, 12 January 1995.
26. A. F. Lowenthal (ed.), *Exporting Democracy* (Baltimore: The Johns Hopkins University Press, 1991); T. Carothers, *In the Name of Democracy* (Berkeley: University of California Press, 1991); and R. A. Pastor, *Whirlpool: U.S. Foreign Policy toward Latin America and the Caribbean* (Princeton: Princeton University Press, 1992).
27. White House press release – 'Clinton Envisions Partnership for Prosperity at Summit' – Washington DC, 9 December 1994.
28. For an insightful discussion of recent trends and possible options in US policy towards Cuba, see Cuban Research Institute, *Transition in Cuba: New Challenges for US Policy* (Miami: Florida International University, 1994).
29. A helpful, but optimistic, assessment of the potential of the OAS in this regard is given in H. Munoz, 'A New OAS for the New Times', in A. F. Lowenthal and G. F. Treverton (eds.), *Latin America in a New World* (Boulder: Westview Press, 1994) pp. 191–202.

30. B. M. Bagley and J. G. Tokatlian, 'Dope and Dogma: Explaining the Failure of U.S.–Latin American Drug Policies', in Hartlyn, Schoultz and Varas (eds.), *The United States and Latin America in the 1990s*, p. 224.
31. See R. L. Millett, 'The Aftermath of Intervention: Panama 1990', *Journal of Interamerican Studies and World Affairs*, 32 (1990) 1–15.
32. P. Andreas and K. Doyle, 'The Drug War is Dead . . .', *Hemisphere*, 6, 2 (1994) 34.
33. Cited in ibid., 37.
34. M. Peceny, 'The Inter-American System as a Liberal "Pacific Union"?', *Latin American Research Review*, 29 (1994) 197.
35. For a review of policy in this area, see R. L. Bach, 'Hemispheric Migration in the 1990s', in Hartlyn, Schoultz and Varas (eds.), *The United States and Latin America in the 1990s*, pp. 262–81.
36. See *Caribbean Insight*, February 1993.
37. *Miami Herald*, 10 September 1994.
38. *Newsweek*, 14 September 1994.
39. See R. A. Pastor, 'NAFTA as the Center of an Integration Process: The Nontrade Issues', in N. Lustig, B. P. Bosworth and R. Z. Lawrence (eds.), *North American Free Trade: Assessing the Impact* (Washington DC: Brookings Institute, 1992) pp. 176–209.
40. A. M. Schlesinger, Jr., *The Disuniting of America: Reflections on a Multicultural Society* (New York: W. W. Norton & Co, 1991).
41. *Miami Herald*, 25 March 1993.
42. Cited in *The Economist*, 20 November 1993.
43. *International Herald Tribune*, 10 November 1994.
44. See M. B. Rosenberg and J. T. Hiskey, 'Interdependence between Florida and the Caribbean', *Caribbean Affairs*, 6 (1993) 12–30.
45. See *Caribbean Insight*, December 1993.
46. For an account of these pressures, see J. Gilbreath and J. B. Tonra, 'The Environment: Unwelcome Guest at the Free Trade Party', in M. D. Baer and S. Weintraub (eds.), *The NAFTA Debate: Grappling with Unconventional Trade Issues* (Boulder: Lynne Rienner, 1994) pp. 53–93.
47. D. P. Calleo, 'America's Federal Nation State: A Crisis of Postimperial Viability?', *Political Studies*, 42, Special Issue (1994) 28.
48. A. Hurrell, 'Regionalism in the Americas', in Lowenthal and Treverton (eds.), *Latin America in a New World*, p. 173.
49. Ibid., p. 185.

5 Latin America and the Remaking of the Americas

JEAN GRUGEL

This chapter seeks to analyse Latin American and Caribbean responses towards the new region-building initiatives in the Americas. It tries to link the responses to the new regionalism in Latin America and the Caribbean (LAC) with the economic liberalisation which has characterised the policy reforms undertaken within LAC since the mid-1980s. It is our contention that LAC is seeking to move towards 'open regionalism' as a response to the complex transformation of the political economy of the Americas which is underway.[1] Once in place, 'open regionalism' should mean, first, the application of trade policies at the regional level between LAC states or between some LAC states and the US and/or Canada which do not discriminate in trade or investment terms against non-members of the bloc, and second, trade policy agreements which are prepared to accept new members into the bloc if they demonstrate preparedness to abide by the same rules of engagement as the existing members. According to its proponents, it is compatible with multilateralism, in line with newer theories of trade which challenge the orthodox insistence on the incompatibility of regionalism and global free trade.[2]

This trend is, however, neither completely straightforward nor completely assured of success because of the political, economic and ideological complexities which attach to it. Subregional integration is a particularly complicated issue in LAC; additionally, the broader sphere of inter-American relations has traditionally been antagonistic rather than co-operative. And a climate of uncertainty persists in LAC over whether the US will actively promote regional free trade although President Clinton insisted on the US commitment to hemispheric free trade at the Americas Summit in Miami in December 1994.

Regional and subregional initiatives have received an enormous boost in the 1990s as a result of, among other factors, the transformation of the US strategy towards LAC effected by the announcement by President Bush in June 1990 of an 'Enterprise for the Americas Initiative' (EAI), and the subsequent negotiations for a free trade agreement (FTA) with Mexico, followed by Mexico's accession to a trilateral free-trade agreement with the US and Canada. The North American Free Trade Agreement (NAFTA) is potentially both an encouragment to 'open regionalism' and a challenge to it: will NAFTA lead to free trade between the participant countries but raise barriers to non-members or will it signal a move towards hemispheric free trade and perhaps even a push in the direction of global liberalisation?

NAFTA does not represent the first attempt at subregional integration in the Americas. But it is the first subregional bloc which includes the US and Canada as partners with a country south of the Rio Grande. As such, it signifies a paradigm shift within LAC in official thinking about models of economic development. It also suggests the possibility of the emergence of a new agenda of relations within the Americas on a broad range of issues from production, investment and trade to the role of the state and immigration policy. According to Lowenthal, there could now be the option of a 'partnership' between LAC and the US in place of the conflict and mistrust of the past.[3] This new era of inter-American consensus perceived by Lowenthal could extend from trade policy to agreement on regional political and security systems. It is being built on two twin processes: a transformation of US strategy towards the region, and a radical change in LAC's political economy and external relations.

New political and security agendas are also emerging in the Americas. These address, primarily, regional democracy, the environment, immigration and illegal drug trafficking. These political and security questions are not directly tied into the framework of regional economic policy, though efforts are being made by policy makers across the region to argue that there is a substantive and causal link between political democratisation, regional co-operation and economic liberalisation. But the extent to which it is possible to talk at present of the existence of an integrated and coherent policy agenda in the Americas is doubtful.

Finally, we will suggest in the chapter that, though inter-American relations have been more harmonious since 1989–90, this does not mean that they are more equal. The US retains hegemony in the area and the new regional initiatives are ways of reproducing and updating power relations to fit a new global order.

The inter-American system and LAC responses to US dominance

The inter-American relationship, which was put in place after 1945, confirmed the patterns of interaction between the US and LAC established from the end of the nineteenth century. Power relations were unequal, and the US followed a series of strategies to confirm dominance over LAC, ranging from the buying of élites to outright intervention. Individual LAC states either resisted or capitulated to demands from Washington, which covered a range of issues from the kind of political systems operative in LAC to security, external relations and economic policy. The response to Washington's dominance from LAC depended partly on the ideological orientation of the LAC government in office at the time. For oligarchical or military governments, the anti-Communism which formed the overarching framework of the relationship offered the opportunity for the repression or even the elimination of reformist groups internally. For democratic or reformist governments, the objective economic and military dependence of LAC on the US meant that Latin American governments would, however reluctantly, eventually toe the Washington line.

Because LAC fell so clearly into the US sphere of influence, the Cold War also cut LAC off from the possibility of relations with other regions. This was particularly detrimental on the one hand for the states of the Southern Cone which had previously had close relations with Europe, and, on the other, for those states which attempted consciously to reduce their dependence on the US through a diversification of external relations (Cuba after the revolution; Chile 1970–73; Nicaragua after 1979). Inter-American relations, in sum, rested on a security agenda, established from Washington, with trade issues and the question of economic development, which mattered far more to LAC, playing a very secondary role.[4]

Among the basic institutions of the relationship established after 1945, the Organisation of American States (OAS), created in Bogata in 1948, occupied a particularly important symbolic role.[5] It served mainly as a transmission belt for decisions previously taken in Washington, rubber-stamping US policy in the region. After the US-backed coup overthrowing President Arbenz in Guatemala in 1954, the OAS justifed the action, ratifying the struggle against Communism in the Americas; in 1962 Cuba was excluded from the organisation because of US hostility; and the 1989 invasion of Panama met with swift OAS approval. At the same time, there were important areas of tension in the regional system, especially in the 1970s. Apart from the political challenges posed by the emergence of nationalist regimes – in Peru, Chile and Venezuela, for example – the bigger of the LAC states also sought to loosen the bonds of US dominance through a search for alternative economic and political associates. Brazil in particular sought to diversify its markets into Europe with deepening industrialisation in the 1970s.[6] And in the broadest sense the emergence of a situation of 'complex interdependence'[7] – or 'complex dependence'[8] as it has also been called – between the US and LAC, mediated largely by non-state actors such as transnational corporations, modified the absolute power of the US state in determining the agenda of regional relations.

The question of economic development in LAC was a central issue in the conflicts which arose in the relationship. It was important to Washington only to the degree to which decisions about economic policy making, trade and other such matters taken in LAC might impinge on the security agenda. But for LAC, as a developing area, the question was vital for political and economic reasons and in order to position LAC globally. LAC intellectual élites used the question of development to challenge Washington's dominance in the region. The UN Economic Commission for Latin America (ECLA), created in 1948 to provide development recipes for LAC, created a space for indirect opposition to the US which was legitimated through its being a part of the UN. Nef describes ECLA as 'a distinct Latin American "counter-culture" to the dominant Manifest Destiny-cum-anti-communism and *laissez-faire* themes of the inter-American system'.[9]

ECLA was to have a major impact over LAC's turn towards regional integration. LAC states were encouraged to see subregional integration as a way of modifying the power structures in inter-American relations. Particularly for medium-sized, middle-income developing economies, it was seen as a way to promote industrialisation which would, ultimately, enable LAC to resist US coercion. Integration projects, therefore, were implicitly predicated upon the idea of integration as a means of opposing US dominance and a belief in the value of collective negotiations with the regional superpower. Moves towards subregional integration form part of a pattern of external relations inside LAC which were intellectually conceived principally as a search to defend itself from US dominance in this period.

The drive for integration led to the establishment of the Latin American Free Trade Association (LAFTA) in 1961, the Central American Common Market (CACM) in the same year, the Andean Pact in 1969 and the Caribbean Community (CARICOM) in 1973. The rationale for these projects was in all cases the extension of the protective benefits of import-substitution industrialisation (ISI) to larger markets than simply national ones. At the same time, the members of the pacts perceived advantages in collective trade bargaining with the developed world.

In all cases, the objectives of the pacts were only partially achieved. LAFTA, which originally proposed the establishment of a free-trade area and industrial planning between the largest of the Latin American economies, moved slowly in the direction of simply promoting bilateral trade agreements until around 40 per cent of intra-Latin American trade was eligible for preferential tariffs by the mid-1980s. The CACM, in some ways the most successful of these subregional pacts, led to an increase in intra-isthmian trade from 6.5 per cent of CACM members'

overall trade in 1960 to 26.7 per cent in 1971. But industrialisation was inefficient and dependent on external financing and
protection. External vulnerability was actually increased by
integration in some cases. The high level of external vulnerability
coupled with the excessive dependence on the US for capital
investment created a situation in which 'the regional institutions
[operated] like foreign enclaves'.[11] Other regional groupings
had much poorer results even than the CACM. Trade between
the CARICOM countries increased only marginally as a result
of integration: from 4.2 per cent of members' external trade
in 1970 to 7.9 per cent in 1989, since all countries inside the
Community continued to produce a similar range of goods for
export.

Regionalism effectively collapsed in the 1970s as a result of:
(1) a lack of agreement on the economic direction within the
groupings; (2) protectionism; (3) the loss of competitiveness
of industry; and (4) growing indebtedness.[12] Because of these
factors, trade within the subregions could not operate as a viable
alternative to trade with industrialised countries, particularly
the US. Regional integration could not therefore offset the dis-
advantages of ISI. LAC's share of the global economy continued
to shrink as a result of the tariff and non-tariff protectionism
implicit in integration. Despite industrialisation, and with the
partial exceptions of Mexico and Brazil, LAC continued to participate in global trade as a supplier of primary goods. By the
early 1980s, after the terms of trade for traditional exports had
fallen by about 40 per cent and world interest rates had risen
precipitously, integration became a mechanism for transmitting
recession and came to a halt.

Other explanations of its collapse are less deterministic, however, in that they put equal emphasis on political problems in
LAC, including instability and inconsistent implementation of
policies.[13] The new regionalism, built on a fresh political commitment and a more effective environment for policy implementation, may have more chance of success. At the very least,
if it fails, it will not be for the same reasons.

The 1980s: recession, restructuring and the reshaping of the inter-American relationship

LAC has had to respond to the EAI and the US reversal of its stance on multilateralism – what has been termed Washington's 'conversion' to the new regionalism[14] – in the context of a radically different regional political and economic environment. More than simply recession, the 1980s signifed a total crisis of confidence within LAC in all spheres – politics, economics and international relations. This was a result of the debt crisis. The LAC economies crashed into profound recession, one after another, following Mexico's open declaration of its inability to keep up the interest payments on its international debt in 1982.

The crisis shook the foundations of LAC society, casting doubt on all aspects of the economic models of the previous 30 years and especially the strategies for industrialisation. The crisis also threatened the power of the political élites inside LAC. This affected primarily the governments in office (overwhelmingly military regimes). Moreover, the economic collapse emphasised the urgent need to rethink development models in the region. However, the recession was such that there was little possibility of rethinking development from within LAC. Rather, external prescriptions were sought, principally in the shape of assistance from multilateral donors and the US, the effect of which was to impose orthodox solutions on the region.

The debt crisis in LAC was attributed not only to extremely high levels of external borrowing, but also more fundamentally to the common economic model of regional development through ISI, which led to uneven growth through massive public-sector borrowing and protection of embryonic industries with a variety of tariff and non-tariff measures. ISI, as it was implemented in LAC, was dependent on high levels of foreign capital. Nowhere was ISI pursued primarily through local saving and domestic capitalisation – mainly for reasons of a political veto by élites on the parameters of fiscal policy. It was complemented by political systems which were either corrupt or authoritarian or both.

Restructuring in the wake of the crisis which erupted in 1982 brought stabilisation in which the IMF and other multilateral donors played a critical role. The stabilisation programmes intensified the social problems caused by unemployment, the bankruptcy of domestic industry and the collapse of domestic and regional markets. Nevertheless, in the absence of any workable alternatives, the adjustment of the mid-1980s settled into a new economic orthodoxy around export promotion and deregulation of the economy, first in Chile, where the initial phase of privatisation was implemented between 1976–82, followed by a more pragmatic application after 1985. Bolivia followed in 1985, then Mexico after 1986, as the model slowly spread throughout LAC, most latterly to Argentina after 1990 and Brazil in 1993. This new economic orientation has created a regional consensus on the need for foreign investment, the destatisation of the economy and the centrality of the market in policy making.

The result of the new economic focus has been for most (though not all) of LAC a sharp increase in dependence on the US as a trading and investment partner. Chile stands out as an exception in that it has been able to use export promotion to diversify trading partners. 'Throughout the 1980s, in contrast to previous years, the importance of the United States both as a supplier and as an outlet for regional exports has increased, with the share of two-way trade rising from below a third of total Latin American external trade in 1980–2 to 37 per cent in 1987–9 . . . US exports to Latin America increased even more sharply, with the US share rising from 31.9 per cent in 1980–2 to 36.7 per cent by the end of the decade'.[15] All of this has made LAC more vulnerable to changes in US trade policy than ever before. One consequence has been a desire, especially strong in Mexico where the importance of the US as market and supplier is greatest, to lock the US into trade with LAC in a stable, definitive and, if possible, contractual way.

Transformation of a second kind occurred in LAC in the 1980s: democratisation. Starting with the collapse of the Argentine dictatorship in military defeat in 1982, a variety of factors including economic collapse, domestic opposition and international pressure ushered in fragile new democracies throughout LAC. By the beginning of the 1990s, elected civilian governments were evident even in Central America, limited and crisis-prone but apparently prepared to undertake some kind of political opening.[16] This has created new possibilities for co-operation within the Americas and inside LAC, and made it possible for LAC to engage in dialogue, on political and security matters especially, within the international system as a coherent bloc. The Rio Group, representing the South American states, plus one representative from Central America and one from the Caribbean, was created for the purpose of deepening contacts within LAC and in order to act as a representative for LAC outside the inter-American system.

LAC governments have moved more closely together on political issues; they have also tilted towards Washington. In quite spectacular and public acts of contrition, they now suggest that Washington was correct all along in its support of market economics as a strategy for development, instead of the protectionist policies favoured by LAC in the past. At the same time, the collapse of the USSR, which has freed LAC from the pressure to align itself alongside the US in the East-West conflict, has enabled Washington to take a more unambiguous stand on regional democracy.[17] In this way, the image of the US in official LAC circles has undergone a momentous transformation.

But while democratisation lends opportunities for co-operation within LAC and within the inter-American system, the region is also being reshaped by the new political economy which suggests a break-up of the idea of a homogeneous LAC bloc. Varas goes as far as seeing the end of LAC as a coherent unit and talks of a 'post-Latin America . . . characterised by several sub-regional systems with different economic, political and strategic weights. In addition to the region of North American hegemony, which includes Canada, Mexico, the Caribbean and Central America, it is possible to identify a depressed Andean subregion, an embryonic Brazilian–Argentine axis, and individual countries such as Chile looking for the best way to integrate into world, economic, political and strategic affairs'.[18]

We will come back to this new map of the Americas later and see how the different areas of LAC fit in. But it should be made clear here that what we are witnessing is a reordering of hegemony in the wake of the break-up of the previous model of inter-American politics and the collapse of the search for autonomous LAC strategies for development. Whereas, once, it was necessary for the US to shore up security throughout LAC, whatever the cost, now Washington has only fragmented demands to make on LAC: the opportunity to deepen trade and investment with some LAC states; the need to resolve immigration problems with others; and the maintenance of historical links and commitments left over from the past with a third group. The new system of dominance rests on the deconstruction of 'LAC' itself, as a bloc antagonistic to the US. The new map of the Americas creates a small group of privileged LAC states, ideologically and economically located in close proximity to the US, with access to Washington, and a hinterland of others, which may adapt to the new agenda but have little to gain from it.

NAFTA: the emergence of a new subregion in the Americas

A new impetus in integration is apparent throughout the Americas; but the most dynamic version is the North American axis. Although linked in the economic sphere by foreign investment and *maquiladora* plants which have long been able to export tariff-free into the US, Mexican–US interdependence is also a result of complex social, environmental and security factors which go beyond the economic. The border has been a defining feature of bilateral relations, as Mexican immigrants have crossed in their thousands in search of jobs. There are now more than two and a half million legal Mexican immigrants in the US without including the huge numbers who either reside illegally or move between the two countries. More recently, the border area has become a prime site of environmental degradation as US firms have taken advantage of Mexico's more lax implementation of laws on industrial waste.

Negotiations for NAFTA began in 1991 after the June 1990 decision between Presidents Bush and Salinas to push for a comprehensive free-trade agreement between the two countries. Although, in economic terms, the main beneficiaries of interdependence have been and still are the transnational corporations, NAFTA was a state-led strategy and, for all signatories, was about governmental perceptions of national interest. It could be interpreted, even, as an attempt by states to reassert control over an integration process dominated so far mainly by transnationals.

Trade and investment issues

NAFTA was not the cause but rather the consequence of a *de facto* deepening of long-standing trans-border ties which gathered greater pace after the start of Mexican liberalisation in 1986. Analyses of the NAFTA factor in trans-border trade during the negotiations were on the whole exaggerated. Even before NAFTA came into effect, overall tariffs between the two countries were low. 80 per cent of Mexican exports entered the US with a 0.5 per cent tariff and half of Mexican imports from the US came duty-free, with low average tariffs for the rest at 9 per cent.[19] 1994, the first year of implementation, registered only a modest increase in two-way trade. In some cases, in fact, the agreement is slowing down cross-border trade as a result of the new regulations which mean more checks and more paperwork. NAFTA's main impact, then, will not be to increase massively cross-border trade. Rather, it will lock in the new economic policy in Mexico and it will commit Washington irrevocably to the relationship.

The provisions of NAFTA refer mainly to how the transition to free trade should be managed. Implicitly, NAFTA also deals with creating a regional investment climate by removing barriers to foreign investment. There are only a few areas where the origin of capital investment remains subject to national control: oil and gas, and the media, for example. In sensitive sectors, including the automotive industry, an adjustment period was negotiated before the NAFTA provisions become operable. For some agricultural products, the US insisted on 15 years to adjust to the effects of free trade. Additionally, there are complex rules of origin, especially in textiles, which aim to prevent Mexico serving as a launching pad for Asian assembly plants, especially in textiles, selling into the US market. Again as a result of US pressure, NAFTA has clauses relating to the environment and to labour standards.

Integration, at its most profound level, in the past has been through US investment, especially in the *maquiladora* border plants, which are tariff-free export processing zones established in some cases as long ago as the mid-1960s. *Maquiladora* plants have traditionally been viewed as offering Mexico little in development terms, except jobs in the border area where they are primarily located. The plants, of which there were around 2000 before NAFTA, employing around half a million people, were not integrated into the domestic economy in that they mainly assembled for export. Although this remains true for the most part, some diversification in investment took place during the 1980s in that sophisticated production processes and capital investment increased, making *maquiladoras* less labour intensive. This opened up a debate within Mexico about whether new *maquila* investment could contribute to national development by offering technology transfer, training and stimulation of local production. The Mexican government decided that it could. It has been argued that up to 30 per cent of the parts used in technological *maquila* production is Mexican.[20] In traditional *maquiladoras* this is as low as 3 per cent, with all other parts used in production imported. Economic liberalisation and the signing of NAFTA, therefore, are not designed simply to attract foreign investment, since that has been a feature of the Mexican economy since the 1960s. Rather, by effectively ending the *maquila* provisions (since everything is now tariff-free), the Mexican strategy is to encourage the shift of foreign capital out of cheap-labour, export-processing zones into high-tech investment, spatially distributed throughout the country.

Mexican–US interdependence has always been *asymmetric* or 'subordinate' integration and NAFTA implies no direct action by the parties to alter that.[21] In effect, Mexico chose to push for an integration agreement which is based on maintaining unequal bilateral power. This strategy rests on the idea that integration, even asymmetric integration, is not a zero-sum game and that there are economic benefits which could fall to Mexico, including an increase in Mexico's share of production and exports within North America. Before liberalisation, Mexico accounted for only 3 per cent of North American output; this will certainly increase.[22] Mexico will also look to NAFTA to stop the US protecting itself from Mexican manufacturing exports such as televisions, cars, computers and fridges, products in which the country is highly competitive. It is in this sense a defensive strategy, designed to prevent the US from protecting itself from competition from Mexico. For Mexico, with over 70 per cent of its trade already with the US before NAFTA, this guarantee was vital to encourage industrial investment.

But, in the long run, Mexican domestic capital will face greater competition from foreign investors than before and US investment will probably move beyond production, to services and distribution, government procurement, insurance and finance, sectors which Mexico agreed to open up to foreign investment during the NAFTA negotiations. But, the Mexican proponents of NAFTA would be quick to point out, this would have happened anyway, since there appears to be no possibility that the ruling party, the *Partido Revolucionario Institucional* (PRI), will reverse its stand on economic liberalisation.

Liberalisation, plus the promise of NAFTA, turned Mexico into a prime site for private investment between 1990 and 1993, fuelling expectations inside Mexico itself, and in Washington, that Mexico was poised for rapid, relatively stable, externally-funded, export led growth. The currency crisis of January 1995 exposed how exaggerated these hopes were. In April 1994, Mexico's NAFTA partners, the US and Canada, had, in fact, put together a US$8.8 billion facility to defend the Mexican peso against anticipated falls caused by speculation as a result of a rise in US interest rates. The decision to devalue the peso taken by Ernesto Zedillo in December 1994, just six weeks into the presidency, proved too much for the confidence of international investors. Mexico experienced a sudden and massive withdrawal of private investment, indicating the extreme fragility of a model of growth which is dependent upon volatile capital investment flows which leave deregulated markets as easily as they enter. The crisis not only forced the Mexican government to request an IMF loan and put together a hasty package of tight austerity measures in order to reduce consumption internally. It also set in train a series of talks between Mexico and the US in which it was clear that the Mexican response to the crisis was the result of a bilaterally negotiated strategy. The Clinton administration put together a package of emergency lending of US$20 billion to Mexico in order to stem the flow of capital out of the Mexican economy, an arrangement which has been underwritten with future revenues from Mexico's oil.

The crisis has tested NAFTA on a number of levels. First, by raising the question of how far neo-liberal economic models can guarantee sustained growth, it questions the basic Mexican assumptions about NAFTA. Second, the crisis begs the question as to how often, and to what degree, Washington will underwrite Mexican financial instability, if it becomes apparent that integration brings only limited economic gain to the US. And, thirdly, it raises the issue of the costs inside Mexico of 'open integration': in view of the PRI's precarious hold on power already, will it be able to resist popular opposition to the deepening of austerity measures in order to shore up an economic model which appears to bring few rewards to the mass of citizens?

Non-trade issues

From the US perspective, the two major non-trade issues which arise from integration with Mexico relate to the environment and to labour. Environmental concerns were surfacing anyway before NAFTA was signed, as a consequence of industrialisation on the border. Offering action by the federal government on the environment was therefore necessary as a way of ensuring NAFTA's safe passage through Congress. Dealing at least minimally with labour issues was seen as a contribution to slowing down trans-border immigration and was again vital to win sufficient support for NAFTA. For Mexico, by contrast, the important non-trade issue referred to the question of sovereignty.

Environmental concerns are part of the new agenda generally in the Americas. The Rio summit of June 1992 on the environment and development, sponsored by the UN, demonstrated how important this issue has become. Nevertheless, it remains true to say that, although there is a green constituency in most LAC countries, it is still generally an issue put on the agenda by developed countries to which LAC responds.[23] It is clear that Mexico was prepared to take action on environmental degradation in the border area and such matters as the setting of standards for toxic emissions, providing they came in a package addressing trade issues. The latter mattered a great deal more to the PRI which had little need to respond to demands from Mexico's own environmental movement because of its overall control over the Mexican political system.

The Salinas government took much more seriously environmental concerns on the border, where it directly affects the US, than contamination in Mexico City, which is in fact far worse. Still, the problems on the border are substantial enough to warrant extensive action, with contamination levels in some areas 1650 times higher than those recommended by US law. Plans for cleaning up the border area date from 1992, when NAFTA was still under discussion, with a budget of over US $900 million to be spent over three years. And if the Mexican strategy of using NAFTA to shift foreign investment out of the border area favoured by the *maquiladoras* and across the country actually works, then this could have a positive effect on contamination along the frontier.

The push for more effective labour legislation in Mexico has come from US unions who fear jobs crossing the border in search of cheaper labour. Taking action in labour-related areas, however, runs contrary to the ethos of NAFTA which is about freeing the market for trade and investment. Mexican unions, tied and controlled for the most part by the PRI, hope US fears are correct and that NAFTA does lead to job creation, and are therefore not prepared to push for higher wage levels in case that spoils the possibilities. So, to the degree to which the impact of NAFTA on trade and investment is only incremental – along the lines of 1994 – we should hear only rhetorical protests in the US about Mexican labour standards.

In Mexico, by contrast, controversy over NAFTA focused on the sovereignty debate. NAFTA – and other subregional pacts – are forcing the Mexicans, and by extension LAC, to address the issue of what exactly constitutes sovereignty, really for the first time since independence in the nineteenth century. Sovereignty has always been interpreted in LAC to mean non-intervention in internal affairs. Grand proclamations of national sovereignty have obviously been a defensive strategy to protect against US interference. Indeed, the PRI has been able to silence critics in the past simply by accusing them of being unpatriotic, of trying to 'sell out' sovereignty. So it was perhaps inevitable that the debate over NAFTA in Mexico would focus on the degree to which the deal constituted a betrayal of historic principles. Opposition from the left-wing *Partido Revolucionario Democrático* was phrased in exactly these terms and the January 1995 deal, which ties future oil revenues to paying back US aid, means that this issue will be kept to the forefront of the minds of the Mexican public.

Undoubtedly, NAFTA has legitimated US concern with at least some aspects of Mexican policy and mandates the Mexican government to deal with these issues in co-operation with the US and Canada. Trade policies and the environment are the clearest examples. NAFTA – in fact just the decision to negotiate – also opened Mexico up to international pressure to reform the political system. But it should be borne in mind that economic integration had reduced the autonomy of the Mexican state anyway and the entire development thrust of the reforms after 1986 was bound to erode autonomy still further. It could even be argued that, by signing a formal agreement with the US, the Mexican state has been trying to assert control over the integration process and therefore demonstrate its sovereignty albeit in the changed framework of transnational capitalism. To argue this, however, requires a less traditional view of sovereignty than has hitherto emerged in Mexico, or indeed LAC.

The Mexican gamble

The Mexican strategy has been shaped from the first by the neo-liberal policies it adopted after 1986. The government believes that more pro-active social and regional policies by the state to compensate for the costs of integration would detract from the possibilities of growth by interfering too much with market allocation. Neo-liberalism is also the origin of its confidence that, as the poorest member of an asymmetric pact, Mexico will grow fastest if the conditions for investment are equalised and the barriers to free trade removed.

The essence of NAFTA is that it is an attempt, using a neo-liberal perspective on the global economy, at maximising national benefits by assuring partnership (albeit unequal) with the largest economy in the world. Its novelty lies in the fact that, as a long-term strategy, it is an attempt consciously to use asymmetric integration as a means to economic growth. However, there is little consensus among economists about the effects of this kind of 'asymmetric reciprocity' between a developed and a developing society; will it lead to an increase in already existing inequalities, to relative gains, or even to absolute gains for the developing country?

There is not yet enough empirical evidence of asymmetric integration on this scale to constitute firm evidence and the Mexicans are taking an enormous gamble. A strong possibility exists that the Mexican government may have overcalculated the benefits of open integration. For example, the PRI presumes that competition will make Mexican capital competitive. But, equally, it might turn out that most Mexican capital, apart from a few flagship groups, will withdraw from high-competition, high-profit and high-risk areas of the economy and that there will be an increase in joint ventures with US capital and invasive US investment.

The Mexican government hopes that liberalisation, plus access to the US and Canadian market, will make the country a globally competitive site for foreign investment. Mexico expects to diversify the sources of foreign direct investment – Germany and Japan are currently the second and third largest investors in the country – by offering the US market as bait. In the run-up period to NAFTA, 1990–4, Mexico did indeed become, after China, the developing country which attracted most flows of private investment. The immediate draw for productive investment is the income gap between Mexico and the US and Canada. Mexican labour costs are around an eighth of labour costs in the US. Crucially, wage differentials apply to skilled as well as unskilled labour. NAFTA will not mean that Mexican wages converge with those in the US and Canada. NAFTA will have to create a huge number of jobs for it to have any possibility of shifting wage levels upwards in Mexico. And, in any case, if the wage gap is operating as a draw for investment, the Mexican state has an interest in stopping wages from rising too fast.

To sum up, then, Mexico is engaged in an enormous gamble: first, that growth will occur through liberalisation and integration; second, that it will resolve Mexico's pressing social problems; and, third, that growth will thereby limit the political demands on the system and allow the PRI to retain political control over the country. Underscoring the whole gamble is the conviction that NAFTA now means that the US is firmly and permanently engaged in Mexican development. Essentially, for Mexico, it is a leap of faith.

Responses to the new regionalism

Globalisation has meant the subordination of most external initiatives in LAC to the need to promote domestic growth and integration into the international system. In sharp contrast to the period of ISI, foreign policy throughout LAC has become a channel for the negotiation of institutional mechanisms which consolidate economic reforms. On the one hand, most of LAC joined GATT from the mid-1980s onwards in a search for multilateral agreements to compensate for unilateral liberalisation of tariffs.[24] On the other, as the GATT negotiations stalled between 1988 and 1992 especially, the concept of open agreements within the Americas was taken on board.

A revision of subregional integration within LAC was already underway before the EAI speech. In fact, the option of open integration emerged first as a way of revitalising existing blocs.[25] However, the main stimulus to integration came from the EAI. The concept of hemispheric free trade was received with enthusiasm throughout LAC. Its attraction lay not only in the idea of trade access to the US and Canada, but also in that it constituted some reciprocity from a developed country for LAC's unilateral economic opening in the 1980s. More particularly, it offered the option of a new deal generally in inter-American relations after the tensions of the 1980s.[26] Enthusiasm was fuelled as World Bank analyses estimated that some countries – Brazil, Mexico, Paraguay, Uruguay and Argentina especially – would find their exports boosted significantly by the dismantling of US tariffs. Bouzas and Ros similarly concluded that the overall benefits from hemispheric liberalisation – in both trade and investment terms – would be felt by the larger semi-industrialised countries.[27]

But the details of any deals that might be offered through the EAI were always vague and poorly thought out in Washington, and the push for hemispheric free-trade negotiations soon dissolved into a series of bilateral discussions between individual LAC countries and Washington in which it was clear that only the least protectionist members of the region would be rewarded with a substantive deal. Free trade through bilateral deals with the US in this way would create a 'hub and spoke' pattern of integration in which the US remained the regional hub. But, despite enthusiastic verbal endorsements of the idea from President Clinton at the 1994 Miami summit, there are no indications that negotiations which include all the Americas in a regional free-trade agreement will take place.

LAC states are limbering up to demonstrate their readiness for at least a bilateral deal, either individually or through reinvigorated subregional pacts, and ultimately perhaps for incorporation into NAFTA. So far, only Chile has been promised a firm negotiating date for accession into NAFTA. But Chile is a small economy by regional standards; the real test will come if one of the larger, semi-industrialised LAC states such as Brazil or Argentina is admitted. There is no indication that Mexico or the US is prepared to extend membership of NAFTA to potential competitors, in contradiction to the principle of 'open regionalism'. NAFTA privileges Mexico within LAC and any advantages would be dissipated if NAFTA was extended. Otherwise, so far, there are only FTAs between LAC countries, and a series of framework FTAs signed between LAC countries/subregions and the US which promise talks on trade liberalisation providing domestic economic reform is carried out.[28] There are problems with this approach. First, a proliferation of separate FTAs, each with its rules, could actually complicate hemispheric trade; second, for most (though not all) of LAC, trade is with the US, not other LAC states; and, third, LAC is looking to attract investment, not simply lift tariffs, so an FTA with the US is vital.

The trend throughout LAC is towards economic liberalisation but *successful* liberalisation, as Carlos Moneta put it succinctly, 'can be reproduced but not generalized. Only a certain number of countries, not all, can hope to enter the club.'[29] In other words, there will be winners and losers within LAC as a result of the new political economy. We look now briefly at the differential impact in LAC of the new political economy of the Americas and try to identify who those winners and losers are.

Chile

Structural reform is at its most advanced in Chile where it has a 16-year history. Partly because liberalisation began long before the rest of the region and under a diplomatically isolated dictatorship, reform has gone hand in hand with a 'go it alone' approach and Chile has remained outside formal subregional arrangements. Chile is also unique in LAC in that the state has 'managed' liberalisation in order to promote the diversification of export markets as well as encouraging non-traditional export products.[30] As a result, approximately 45 per cent of Chilean exports are now directed at EU markets and around 30 per cent of exports go to Japan. It has become a 'global trader' and, as such, the model for the rest of LAC. Chile exports mainly primary goods, however. It would be difficult for a more industrialised LAC state to reproduce this success.

Democratisation after 1989 has not changed the export focus of the economy.[31] Instead, it has made the country more interested in cooperation within the Americas. This has essentially taken two different forms: an interest in diplomatic co-operation with LAC through the Rio Group, which is discussed later, and the pursuit of bilateral FTAs throughout the region. Chile has signed FTAs with Colombia, Mexico and Venezuela and has been promised that an FTA will be concluded with the US by the end of 1995. This will mean, in effect, membership of NAFTA. The Miami summit of 1994 ended with the US promising to seek approval from Congress for 'fast track' negotiation of an FTA for Chile.

The benefits to Chile of successfully concluding an FTA with the US, as with Mexico, do not relate just to trade. World Bank estimates point only to a potential 3 per cent increase in exports to the US,[32] though Butlemann argues that there could be some impact on the composition of exports and an increase in manufactured goods destined for the US market.[33] The more important impact of an FTA would be to guarantee stable Chilean access to the US and, psychologically, to reward Chile's long-standing liberalisation, signal US government approval and strengthen Chile's hand in trade and investment negotiations globally. In terms of looking for a larger market for its manufactured products, however, Chile would do better to negotiate access to MERCOSUR since Brazil and Argentina are Chile's largest trading partners within LAC. But until MERCOSUR lowers its tariffs overall, Chile will resist full incorporation because of the implications a common external tariff would have on its global trade.

MERCOSUR

The origins of MERCOSUR lie in the Integration Act signed between Argentina and Brazil in 1986. This was conceived in order to create a regional arena for support for new and fragile democracies, rather than to make a major contribution to trade. It took the neo-liberal governments of Carlos Menem in Argentina and Fernando Collor in Brazil after 1989 to use the agreement as support for liberalisation policies internally. In 1990, Argentina and Brazil agreed to a programme of tariff reduction and abolition of non-tariff barriers. Spurred on by the EAI, Uruguay and Paraguay joined in March 1991. In 1992, a timetable for the establishment of a customs union – with a common external tariff, therefore – was agreed, which formally entered into operation in January 1995.

MERCOSUR's common external tariff marks it out from NAFTA. And it may make it difficult for individual members of the pact, such as Argentina, to conclude a successful FTA with the US. Also, the external tariff would have to be abandoned within any future hemispheric free-trade project. In reality, what Argentina and Brazil are doing is holding off definitive plans until both the global framework of future trade becomes clear with the implementation of the Uruguay Round and the establishment of the World Trading Organisation (WTO), and until the US defines less ambiguously its attitude to free trade within the Americas. According to Felix Peña, Argentina's negotiator within MERCOSUR, Argentina's strategy has so far been to search for simultaneous reciprocal agreements, even if they appear contradictory, in what he terms a 'poligamy'.[34] In this strategy, subregional agreements are a first step to hemispheric free trade and, ideally, to multilateralism.

MERCOSUR has an additional function in the subregion: it holds the members to strict economic orthodoxy. If the only way an FTA with the US can be negotiated is through negotiations between the US and all members, then pressure will be immediately created, from Argentina in particular as the least protective of all,[35] for the rest to toe the line. At present, however, there is no timetable for such negotiations and, although Menem has unilaterally sought to improve relations with the US on all fronts, the question of access to the US for

Argentina's competitive temperate agricultural production will make the securing of a deal difficult.

The apparent lack of US interest in MERCOSUR may reflect, at least in part, the restructuring of the security agenda in the Americas. The end of the Cold War brought to an end the US need to ensure loyalty throughout the region, and the Southern Cone, geographicallly far removed from the dynamic North American axis, may now simply be less important for Washington. The fear of this has led to a revival of contacts with European countries, the source of foreign capital and the most important markets for Argentina, Brazil and Uruguay until the 1930s. As a result, a framework agreement for a common market between the EU and MERCOSUR was signed in October 1994, to be effective from 2001.

MERCOSUR's place in the new regionalism is further complicated by the presence of Brazil, the largest economy in LAC and the only LAC country with the potential to challenge the regional dominance of the US. Brazil has been slow in expressing enthusiasm for the new liberalism, preferring instead to maintain vestiges of ISI as a way of preserving at least part of the country's industrial base. Consequently, governmental and industrial élites were less than enthusiastic about the implications of EAI. One reason is that 'for Brazil, because of its higher tariff and the importance of non-US trade, joining an FTA would have costs similar to a non-discriminatory unilateral liberalisation'.[36] The policy dilemma now facing Brazil is, in fact, rooted in a long-term debate within the country about how to achieve development and about the country's role in the inter-American system. Brazil remains the LAC state most committed to industrialisation as a path to development.[37] And the country has a tradition of independent foreign policy making, resisting US dominance within LAC on a number of occasions, even during the Cold War, on issues ranging from questions of external trade to security. It is unlikely, therefore, that Brazil will now support an integration strategy which reproduces rather than challenges US hegemony. So, while there would be some benefits from increasing exports to the US if an FTA were to be signed, it may be that Brazil would prefer to act as the pole of a new subregional bloc, grouping together the states south of NAFTA. The possibility of a South American Free Trade Area (SAFTA) is currently under discussion within the new Brazilian government headed by Fernando Enrique Cardoso.

The Andean Pact

The Andean Pact, created in 1969 to consolidate ISI, soon split into two blocs: Colombia, Venezuela and Ecuador, trading 70 per cent of their goods within the Pact; and Peru and Bolivia, trading with Argentina, Brazil and Chile. There were some efforts to revive the Andean Pact along more liberal lines after 1989 but the disparities between members and their different trading patterns made it difficult. Colombia has been the most enthusiastic member of the Pact in terms of pursuing open regionalism, signing FTAs with Chile and Central America as well as with Venezuela and Mexico.

The Peruvian and Bolivian economies plummeted into deep recession through the 1980s as a result of the collapse of prices for traditional exports – the terms of trade declined around 60 per cent for these two countries between 1985 and 1993 – and the emergence of an informal economy based on coca. The gap widened within the Pact and Colombia and Venezuela turned northwards to formalise the alliance with Mexico established during the 1980s within the framework of the *Contadora* peace initiative for Central America.

As the international agenda of the Americas changed with the peace settlement in El Salvador in 1992, the new political economy focus of interregional relations, and the discussions following the EAI speech, the Group of Three expanded its area of concern towards economic issues. Colombia and Venezuela are obviously directly affected by Mexico's membership of NAFTA. On the debit side, NAFTA makes clear that Mexico has prioritised the North American axis. But more positively, through membership of the Group of Three, Colombia and Venezuela edge closer by proxy to the US market – for both countries, a crucial one – and, critically, towards a US seal of approval. However, the provisions of NAFTA will be two-way, so any tariff reduction between Colombia, Venezuela and Mexico will not only mean more of their products entering the NAFTA market but will also, inevitably, mean stiffer competition inside

Colombia and Venezuela from cheaper and more efficient production located in Mexico.

Few concrete integration measures have come out of the Group of Three and those that have been most effective have been bilateral agreements between Venezuela and Colombia or Colombia and Mexico over Colombian coal exports, for example. For the next few years, a divergence of the Group's trading patterns towards other partners, or at least a failure to deepen them beyond what is already in place, is perhaps the most likely scenario. This will be a consequence not only of NAFTA, but also of Venezuela's turn towards protectionism in 1994, a temporary measure according to the government, and Colombia's search for hemispheric allies on a bilateral basis. But the Group of Three remains important as a diplomatic forum and brings together three heavyweight countries within LAC whose voice carries weight in regional affairs. Mexico has declared its interest in maintaining close relations, especially on a political and diplomatic level, with Colombia and Venezuela as a way to counterbalance the US's expanding role in Mexican external relations. For Colombia and Venezuela, foreign policy is still about much more than trade and investment. So in some ways, then, the Group will act to promote LAC solidarity around more than economic issues.

For Peru and Bolivia, the outlook is much bleaker. Both countries are now committed to liberalisation of the economy and privatisation ('capitalisation', as it is called in Bolivia). In Bolivia, for example, where stabilisation has been a feature of policy since 1985 when inflation reached 23 000 per cent, maximum tariffs are now only 10 per cent. But growth has been slow and export performance poor.[38] Bolivia has found it difficult to attract foreign capital, particularly outside the privatised sector, and will find it impossible to compete for foreign investment with larger economies with better infrastructure, a more skilled and integrated workforce and more responsive élites inside a putative western hemispheric free-trade bloc. The gains from an FTA with the US would also be low. Non-traditional exports, especially in agriculture, are already exported unilaterally duty-free to the US as a result of the Andean Trade Preferences Act, an initiative aimed at promoting diversification out of coca. But only around 24 per cent of all Bolivian trade is with the US and Bolivia would stand to gain more from pursuing options within LAC which accounts for 40 per cent of all its exports overall. Still, at best, liberalisation will find more markets; it will do nothing to change the basis of Bolivian exports which are natural resource-based (metals; natural gas) or non-traditional agricultural products, providing few jobs and with few linkages to the rest of the domestic economy. The liberalisation programme carried out since 1985 has simply increased the precariousness of daily life for a majority of Bolivians without generating any hope for the future.

CACM

For the CACM countries (Nicaragua, El Salvador, Costa Rica, Honduras and Guatemala), for whom access to the US is primordial with over 40 per cent of exports US-directed, NAFTA represents a frightening prospect. It means the erosion of privileged access to US capital and investment which the Caribbean Basin Initiative (CBI) guaranteed. Pacification in Central America has led to a revival of the CACM, this time in a more open mould, with the hope that the subregion as a whole could become more competitive in international markets. But increased competition from Mexico will certainly mean a diversification of trade and investment away from CACM and towards Mexico. NAFTA puts around 60 per cent of CBI exports at a disadvantage *vis-à-vis* Mexican exports.[38] Although the CACM has signed an FTA with Mexico, CACM exports to Mexico are small in number and cannot be re-routed to the US via Mexico.

As a result, the CACM is pushing for its own FTA with the US. But FTAs are reciprocal, unlike the CBI arrangements, so the adjustment costs for the CACM as US imports come in duty-free would be high. In trade terms, the benefits are unclear since US tariffs are already low and many products are tariff-free. The only dynamic effect could come from increased investment, which will depend at least as much on other factors such as long-term stability and development in the isthmus. Along with the CARICOM countries, the CACM is the most directly disadvantaged within LAC by NAFTA provisions. Its strategy, which is in effect to win back priority status in Washington, only indicates the poverty of development options within the isthmus. And although NAFTA can hardly be held responsible for the precipitous decline in living standards in the subregion, which is the result of the conflicts of the 1980s, the deterioration of the terms of trade for traditional products, and the application of structural reform without compensating social spending, it will not make life any easier for economically disenfranchised Central Americans. In the new political economy of North America, Central America remains peripheral.

CARICOM

The CARICOM countries are directly and negatively affected by NAFTA because it puts Mexico on a level footing with CARICOM in terms of tariff-free access to the US. Since Mexico has distinct advantages as a producer in other areas, this will lead to trade and investment diversion to Mexico. 50 per cent of CARICOM trade is with the US – and over 70 per cent of GDP is trade. The effect, therefore, could be disastrous.[40] CARICOM is, in fact, potentially worse positioned in the international economy even than Central America, because of the possible phasing out of Lomé provisions from the EU after the year 2000. CARICOM has taken steps to improve relations with bigger LAC states, including Mexico, Colombia, Venezuela and the Central American countries,[41] but nonetheless is unlikely to survive in its present form in a trading environment which denies the usefulness of non-reciprocal preferences. The emerging Americas bloc, or rather subregional blocs, aimed at reordering US hegemony in the area, are freezing the small Caribbean states out and condemning them to an existence as services and tourist-based outposts from which out-migration will continue unabated.

The new political agenda

The essence of the new political agenda in the Americas relates to democratisation. There are at least three levels of consensus around the issue: first, in almost all LAC states there is domestic commitment to maintaining electoral forms of government; second, there are now intra-LAC organisations which underwrite diplomatically the democratisation process, most notably the Rio Group; and third, the US and the OAS have committed themselves to policies which reward regional democratisation and punish authoritarianism. At the same time, as LAC has embarked consciously on policies of internationalisation, it has needed to apply more strictly the criteria of the new international order in which the construction of at least formal democracy is crucial.

Democratisation, then, is clearly a *sine qua non* of the new regionalism. But to talk of liberalisation and democracy as sections of the same agenda can also be misleading if it is taken to suggest a conscious and integrated framework of interlocking political, economic and international policies. This is evidently not the case. Democratisation emerged as a trend within LAC as early as 1982, long before any new regional consensus developed around security and economic issues. The movement towards democracy was prior to, and independent of, a commitment to a market-based economic policy. Ten years ago, it was still unthinkable in LAC that policy makers would try to insist on a causal relationship between the market and deregulation on the one hand and democracy on the other. The general thrust of research into the political sociology of LAC was, in fact, to suggest that capitalism, especially of the free-market variety, led consistently to authoritarianism.

However, there have been more recent attempts to establish functional links between the democratisation process and the advance of market-based reforms in the region. Domestic LAC governments, needing to put to use the political capital gained domestically as democratisers in order to legitimate economic reforms which might otherwise be unpopular, have suggested that open economies make for stable democracies. For support, they are drawing on revisionist thinking in development studies. And the democracy-market connection has also been consistently pushed by the US. Nevertheless, the evidence for establishing a causal relationship between economic liberalisation and democratic transition is, in LAC anyway, weak and counter-factual. Only in the unique case of Mexico is it possible to argue that market opening is occurring alongside timid and increasingly perilous moves towards political change, and even in this instance there is no indication of causality.

The idea of regional – and indeed, international – mechanisms which act as supports for democratisation, with the ultimate option of ousting authoritarian governments through intervention, represents a substantial modification of the concept of sovereignty because it legitimates concern on the part of outside bodies with internal affairs. Nevertheless, LAC has not, on the whole, resorted to nationalist positions that see democratisation as a form of US intromission, but has co-operated in the new regional pro-democracy organisations. The OAS, in particular, has taken on a new role as a support organisation for democracy. The *Unidad para la Promoción de la Democracia* (UPD) was created in 1990, and has organised OAS observation in elections in Costa Rica (1990), the Dominican Republic (1990), Guatemala (1990), Honduras (1990), Panama (1990 and 1992) and Venezuela (1993). The UPD also collaborated in long-term projects related to electoral preparation in Nicaragua (1989–90), Haiti (1990–91), El Salvador (1991), Surinam (1991), Paraguay (1991 and 1993) and Peru (1992 and 1993).[42] Canada, interestingly enough a new member of the OAS, has been particularly active in supporting the UPD. The Santiago Declaration and the OAS Resolution 1080 of 1991 have established automatic mechanisms which suspend members who interrupt the democratic process. So far Guatemala, Peru and Haiti have all been suspended from the OAS as a result of the application of this resolution. The Rio Group has adopted similar mechanisms in support of regional democracy.

While there is a consensus throughout the region around the importance of democracy, debates are still going on about what kind of democracy best fits LAC. This is nothing new. What is new, however, is that the debates are played out internally within LAC states between governmental and intellectual élites on the one hand and a marginalised and defensive left on the other, with popular levels of participation very low. In the past, discussions of democracy took place inside a framework of antagonistic inter-American relations which posited one version of democracy, supported by the US, against another 'Latin American' democracy. In the Cold-War era, before the push for democratisation in the 1980s, the US had frequently tried to impose liberal democracies on the region, which meant in fact recognition of any pro-US president who came to power through elections, however corrupt the elections had been or however militarised and abusive the state. LAC political élites preferred either outright dictatorship or, if they were leftist, to argue for democracies which addressed the social and economic needs of Latin Americans and reflected LAC political culture (popular participation; local democracy; community-based organisations) rather than worrying too much about the creation of party systems, independent judiciaries and a free press. It would be true to say that debates about democracy in the inter-American system until the 1980s constituted a dialogue of the deaf.

Currently, however, there is a baseline consensus which covers most LAC political and intellectual élites and the US government about regional democracy: elections play the key role, though, ideally, governments should also work towards establishing a free press, an independent judiciary and should guarantee basic human rights. Alternative visions of democracy, where the state promotes welfare and alleviates poverty, and where the formal structures are underwritten by some kind of wealth redistribution, have been stranded on the periphery of national and regional politics. The kind of democratisation which has taken place in LAC, in which the traditional left has come to be seen as just another kind of dictatorship, and the context of democratisation, namely the devastating economic collapse of the 1980s, have combined to push the nationalist or statist left to the edges of the political system, or even outside it, from Mexico through to Argentina. In order to survive electorally, the new LAC left has embraced liberalism and abandoned ideas of welfare and the specificity of Latin American capitalism. There is a danger that, with political and intellectual élites all offering more or less the same kind of policies in the context of fragile party structures, the articulation of alternatives will come from outside the formal political system and may even threaten the consolidation of democracy in the future. The rebellion in Chiapas, Mexico, which started on 1 January 1994, the day NAFTA entered into effect, is an example of the kind of popular protest, removed from the traditional left, which could erupt throughout LAC.

Security in the new regionalism

A new security system in the Americas is in the process of construction. The need for this is obvious in the light of global transformation. 'Security' now more than ever needs to be understood in more than military terms and embrace issues like the use of natural resources, the sustainability of development projects, immigration and narcotics, areas where the decisions taken in one country have implications for the populations and the state in others. In fact, the old security agenda in the Americas had begun to fragment before the demise of the Soviet bloc and new themes began to emerge in the inter-American relationship in the late 1980s.[43] This was the result of the diversification of LAC's external contacts which was in turn the result of growing multipolarity and a relative decline in superpower politics.[44] The new framework does, however, depend on LAC co-operation. For Varas, this implies a return on the part of the US to 'hegemonic control', exercised through regional leadership and regional institutions, instead of the 'coercive control' favoured by Washington during most of the 1980s.[45] Other analysts, however, are less convinced that the US strategy of hegemony will be sufficient and admit the possibility that Washington may return to imposing policies on LAC unilaterallly.[46]

The changes are a result of the new phase of interdependence in the Americas, whereby some LAC countries have become strategically more important to the US than before, especially in the economic sphere in view of the US perception of its vulnerability to challenges from other emerging economic superpowers. 'Complex interdependence', an explanatory model frequently used to examine the new relationship of co-operation within the Americas, does not of course mean *equal* dependence. So a move towards a more co-operative framework of relations does not necessarily imply a power shift, since the exercise of hegemony is consistent with co-operation. What seems clear is that any renegotiation of power within the regional relationship will only take place between the US and the larger and more dynamic LAC states or subregions.

The new security agenda fragments LAC still further. The outcome appears to be 'a series of sub-systems with fragmented interests and competing policies', in which some countries or subregions emerge as primordial in security terms for Washington – but not necessarily in any other way.[47] The outlines of a new regional security map are just emerging, representing those areas of the Americas in which Washington is particularly interested. To be the object of 'privileged' attention from Washington in a security sense is of course very different from being a partner (however unequal) in the new political economy. Moreover, the emerging security map of the Americas is very different from the political economy map. The issues which the US defines currently as central to its security – immigration, the environment, narcotics dealing – require the design of policies to be applied on the periphery of the new political economy: the Caribbean, Central America and the depressed Andean countries of Bolivia and Peru. The degree to which relations with these countries therefore move out of the coercive mode and into a more co-operative framework, as anticipated by Varas, should be questioned. Only in relation to Mexico does the US recognise the need to respond with an integrated set of policies from trade and investment to immigration and narcotics.

Underpinning the new security focus is an insistence on the centrality of *development* in inter-American relations. This takes us back to democratisation and market economics, which is how *development* is currently conceived. These thus become, yet again, the overarching perspective through which all the issues in the Americas relate. Put at its most simplistic, free trade will create development, which will keep potential migrants at home, establish democratic accountability, and create functioning party systems and interest groups to press governments on issues like environmental degradation. New aid policies, combined with pressure on states to democratise and establish legitimate forms of effective governance, will also make it possible for LAC to clean up its narcotics problem. It should strike observers that this is hardly a new set of policies: they are rather part of the conventional wisdom of modernisation theory within which capitalism and democracy are thought to exist in symbiotic dependence. In fact, US policy today resembles some aspects of the 1960s focus in the Alliance for Progress. Then, however, free-market capitalism and liberal democracy were only supposed to solve political instability and the threat from the left, not environmental waste and drug trafficking as well.

It should be clear that we are expressing a certain scepticism about whether the new agenda can really deal with the development problems of the region. In fact, the new focus ignores much that is known about LAC development over time. It bypasses research into the cyclical nature of LAC economic expansion from the 1880s to the present day which should have taught us to be wary of proclamations that 'take-off' is just around the corner. It ignores too the thorny question of political culture in LAC, social relations within LAC states and the consequences of LAC's reliance on the expansion of primary commodities for the international economy. Yet the 'new' focus also echoes the present convictions of LAC élites. This convergence is being built on the crisis of confidence in LAC following the economic collapse of the 1980s and the apparent bankruptcy of the LAC intellectual élite. It is also constructed over deep divisions in LAC societies between the beneficiaries of the new model of 'open regionalism' and those excluded from it, between those individuals who are able to consume and those who manage merely to subsist uneasily inside the new free-market economies. The new development focus, therefore, may also bring with it in the future the need for policies of internal security in order to contain popular opposition to the costs of restructuring.

Tentative conclusions: the costs and benefits of the new regionalism in LAC

The new regionalism is a fascinating debate because it goes to the heart of the central issues of LAC political economy. It pulls together the debates of 35 years in development studies in the region: the private vs. the public, the state vs. the market, and democracy vs. authoritarianism. What is emerging is an outcome which would have been completely unexpected even ten years ago: a regional consensus around the importance of the market and the centrality of export development and foreign capital, which governments believe is guaranteed by the democratic transitions. This new consensus has eliminated many of the old tensions in inter-American relations and paved the way for a new articulation of regionalism within the Americas.

By bringing LAC political economy into line with the US, doubts about LAC loyalty to Washington have largely disappeared. So have tensions over political models in LAC as democratisation, understood in exclusively liberal terms, has swept the region. LAC appears now to seek full incorporation into a global system through insisting on its Western credentials – liberal economics and democratic politics. It thereby ends a longstanding tension implicit in LAC models of development, between those who argued that LAC was an outpost of Western culture – 'Europe in exile', in the phrase of Borges, the celebrated Argentine writer – and those who postulated the need for specifically Latin American models of development, which took on board the peripheral nature of capitalism as well as the specificity of LAC cultural practices. The conflict appears to have been resolved in favour of the Westernisers. Nowhere is this more apparent than in Mexico, Argentina and Brazil, the giants of LAC. The Mexican government is dismantling the pillars of the revolution – anti-Americanism, communal agriculture and the one-party system; the Peronists in Argentina under Menem, once thought of as representing a return to the traditional insistence on national capitalism and statism, have presided over the most rapid of all liberalisations in LAC; and the Brazilian president, Fernando Enrique Cardoso, the apostle of dependency theory, is shaping the Brazilian economy to attract foreign investment. In sum, the options appear to governing élites to have shrunk to either successful liberalisation or unsuccessful liberalisation; any search for alternatives has disappeared from domestic agendas.

But there are enormous social costs involved in integration through open regionalism. And the costs are borne most heavily by those groups which fit least well with the idea of LAC as unequivocally and exclusively 'Western'. The new regionalism consecrates economic orthodoxy, the costs of which are paid for by already marginalised social groups: women, ethnic minorities, the urban unemployed and rural labour. The reordering of the Americas is, in this sense, a particularly brutal project of social restructuring. There is nothing new, of course, in the fact that the poorest and most vulnerable groups in LAC underwrite economic expansion. In Brazil and in Central America, for example, the economic growth of the 1960s was built on a redistribution of income upwards and a corresponding intensification of rural poverty. Stabilisation in the 1980s, throughout LAC, was also paid for by the poorest social groups. What is new, however, about this particular set of policies is that it couples impoverishment with democratisation, and it leaves the poor with representatives who are themselves committed to the idea of the market as a tool for deepening democratisation. It makes opposition to liberal policies and 'open regionalism' difficult to articulate from within the new political systems and therefore makes them limited and, ultimately, potentially unstable.

Yet there are clear reasons why LAC governments are attracted to the new regionalism. If the full ramifications of the EAI are ever carried through into practice, they will cement the US into a new pattern of trade and investment through which the larger and more successful economies of LAC assure themselves of stable access to a vital market, and through which they hope to prevent the US closing off its market to competitive goods produced in Latin America. It thus appears potentially as a strategy for deepening some industrial production inside the larger LAC states. The gains are less than clear for the smaller countries, though staying outside the new framework appears even less appealing than taking the risks of incorporation. For the smallest states, in the Caribbean for example, or for the poorest states, such as Bolivia, it is unlikely that integration will do anything at all to reverse economic decline and it may even prevent states from adopting pro-active policies to diversify production.

Finally, we should note that the new regionalism is not founded on a transformation of power relations within the Americas. It is clear that, especially with Mexico, the US is opting for integration as a way of dealing with interdependence. The US remains the regional hub of the new Americas. The break-up of the idea of LAC into subregions, each with a different economic or security agenda and each with different relations with Washington, may well only increase both the bargaining *and* coercive power the US wields in the Americas. In this sense, although regionalism is by no means zero-sum, the biggest winner will be the US.

Notes

1. G. Rosenthal, 'ECLAC Advocates Open Regionalism', statement by Mr Gert Rosenthal, Executive Secretary of ECLAC on the Occasion of the Presidential Summit of the Rio Group, Santiago, Chile, 16 October 1993, *CEPAL Notas Sobre la Economía y el Desarrollo*, no. 551 (November 1993).
2. A. Dunkel, 'Address to the 26th General Meeting of the Pacific Economic Council in Seoul', GATT Press Communiqué 1582, 1993, Geneva.
3. A. Lowenthal, 'Latin America: Ready for Partnership?', *Foreign Affairs*, 72, 1 (1992–3).
4. L. Schoultz, *National Security and US Policy Towards Latin America* (Princeton: Princeton University Press, 1987).
5. G. P. Atkins, *Latin America in the International Political System* (New York: The Free Press, 1977).
6. P. Evans, *Dependent Development: The Alliance of Multinational, State and Local Capital in Brazil* (Princeton: Princeton University Press, 1979).
7. R. O. Keohane and J. S. Nye, *Power and Interdependence: World Politics in Transition* (Boston: Little, Brown, 1977).
8. J. Nef and F. Rojas, 'Dependencia Compleja y Transnacioalizacion del Estado en America Latina', *Relaciones Internacionales*, 8/9 (1984).
9. J. Nef, 'The Political Economy of Inter-American Relations: A Structural and Historical Overview', in R. Stubbs and G. R. D. Underhill (eds.), *Political Economy and the Changing Global Order* (London: Macmillan, 1994).
10. United Nations Economic Commission for Latin America (ECLA), *Recent Developments and Trends in Latin American Trade with the European Community*, Doc E/CN 12/631, New York, 1962.
11. V. Bulmer-Thomas, *The Political Economy of Central America Since 1920* (Cambridge: Cambridge University Press, 1987) p. 177.
12. J. M. Insulza, 'Mexico and Latin America: Prospects for a New Relationship', in R. Roett (ed.), *Mexico's External Relations in the 1990s* (Boulder: Lynne Rienner Publishers, 1991).
13. E. Grilli, 'Regionalism and Multilateralism: Conflict or Coexistence?', paper delivered to VIIth General Conference of the European Association of Development Research and Training Institutes (EADI), Berlin, 15–18 September 1993.
14. J. Bhagwati, *Regionalism and Multilateralism: An Overview* (New York: Colombia University Discussion Paper Series No. 603, 1992); and C. Bradford, 'Tendencias y problemas de la regionalizacion y el

nuevo orden internacional', *Capitulos de SELA*, 36 (July–September 1993).

15. R. Bouzas 'US–Latin American Trade Relations: Issues in the 1980s and Prospects for the 1990s', in J. Hartlyn, L. Schoultz & A. Varas (eds.) *The United States and Latin America in the 1990s: Beyond the Cold War* (Chapel Hill: University of North Carolina Press, 1992) pp. 156–157.

16. See L. Whitehead, 'The Alternatives to "Liberal Democracy": A Latin American Perspective', *Political Studies* Special Issue *Prospects for Democracy*, XL (1992) for a good overview of the nature of Latin American democratisation.

17. T. Carothers, *In the Name of Democracy: U.S. Policy Toward Latin America in the Reagan Years* (California: University of California Press, 1991).

18. A. Varas, 'From Coercion to Partnership: A New Paradigm for Security in the Western Hemisphere?', in Hartlyn, Schoultz and Varas (eds.), *The United States and Latin America in the 1990s*.

19. G. Szekely, 'Forging a North American Economy: Issues for Mexico in the 1990s', in Roett (ed.), *Mexico's External Relations in the 1990s*.

20. H. Shaiken, *Mexico in the Global Economy: High Technology and Work Organization in Export Industries* (San Diego: Centre for US–Mexican Studies, University of California, Monograph Series no. 33, 1990).

21. A. Frambes-Buxeda, 'Moving Towards a Sociology and Theory of Subordinate Integration: Implications for Latin America and North America', paper delivered to XVIIIth Latin American Studies (LASA) Congress, Atlanta, 10–12 March 1994.

22. R. Roett, 'Mexico's Strategic Alternatives in the Changing World System: Four Options, Four Ironies', in Roett (ed.), *Mexico's External Relations in the 1990s*.

23. H. Munoz, 'El Debate Comercio Internacional vs. Ecologia', *Estudios Publicos*, 54 (Autumn 1994).

24. A. Jara, 'Bargaining Strategies of Developing Countries in the Uruguay Round', in D. Tussie and D. Glover (eds.), *The Developing Countries in World Trade* (Boulder: Lynne Rienner Publishers, 1993).

25. G. Rosenthal, 'Treinta Años de Integración en America Latina: Un Examen Crítico', *Estudios Internacionales*, XXVI (1993) 101.

26. P. Hakim 'Western Hemisphere Free Trade: Why Should Latin America be Interested?', *Annals of the American Academy of Political Science*, 526 (1993).

27. R. Bouzas & J. Ros, 'The North–South Variety of Economic Integration: Issues and Prospects for Latin America', Workshop on *Economic Integration in the Western Hemisphere*, Kellogg Institute, 17–18 April 1993.

28. R. Bouzas & N. Lustig (eds.) *Liberalización Comercial e Integración Regional: De NAFTA a Mercosur* (Buenos Aires: FLACSO-Grupo Editor Latinoamericano, 1992).

29. C. Moneta, 'Los Probables Escenarios de la Globalización', *Capítulos de SELA*, 39 (July–September 1993).

30. E. Aninat, 'El Futuro de la Insercion Internacional de Chile: Elementos para un Debate', *Sintesis*, 19 (January–June 1993).
31. P. Yangara, 'Market Economy, Social Welfare, and Democratic Consolidation in Chile', in W. Smith, C. Acuna and E. Gamarra (eds.), *Democracy, Markets and Structural Reform in Latin America* (New Brunswick: Transaction Publishers, 1994).
32. S. Saborio, *The Premise and the Promise: Free Trade in the Americas* (New Brunswick: Transaction Publishers, 1992).
33. A. Butlemann, 'Some Elements of Chilean Trade Policy', Workshop on *Economic Integration in the Western Hemisphere.*
34. F. Pena, 'MERCOSUR y NAFTA: Dos Realidades Hemisfericas', *Contribuciones*, 2 (1993).
35. R. Bouzas, 'Mas Alla de la Establzacion y la Reforma: Un Ensayo Sobre la Economia Argentina a Comienzos de los '90', *Desarrollo Economico*, April–June 1993.
36. M. de Paiva Abreu, 'Trade Policies and Bargaining in a Heavily Indebted Economy: Brazil', in Tussie and Glover (eds.) *The Developing Countries in World Trade.*
37. W. Fritsch and G. Franco, 'The Progress of Trade and Industrial Policy Reform in Brazil', *Pensamiento Iberoamericano*, 21 (1992).
38. V. Palermo, 'Programas de Ajuste y Estrategias Politicas: Las Experiencias Receintes de la Argentina y Bolivia', *Desarrollo Economico*, 30 (1990).
39. E. Rodriguez, 'Central America: Common Market, Trade Liberalization, and Trade Agreements', Workshop on *Economic Integration in the Western Hemisphere.*
40. R. Bernal, 'CARICOM', Workshop on *Economic Integration in the Western Hemisphere.*
41. Caribbean Basin Technical Advisory Group (CBTAG), *Status Report*, Dept of State, Commonwealth of Puerto Rico, September 1992.
42. J. L. Ramirez, 'La OEA, los Paises Latinoamericos y la Democracia cn cl Hemisferio', *Sintesis*, 21 (May–December 1994).
43. R. Russell, 'La Agenda Global den los Años 90: Antiguos y Nuevos Temas', in R. Russell (ed.), *La Agenda Internacional en los Años 90* (Buenos Aires: Grupo Editor Latinoamcricano, 1990).
44. See C. Portales (ed.), *El Munod en Transicion y America Latina* (Buenos Aires: Grupo Editor Latinoamericano, 1989).
45. A. Varas, 'From Coercion to Partnership: A New Paradigm for Security in the Western Hemisphere?'.
46. A. Hurrell, 'Regionalism in the Americas', in A. Lowenthal & G. Treverton (eds.), *Latin America in a New World* (Boulder: Westview Press, 1994).
47. H. Molineu, 'The Inter-American System: Searching for a New Framework', *Latin America Research Review*, 29, 1 (1994).

6 Japan and the Construction of Asia-Pacific

GLENN HOOK

The spatial focus of this chapter is more contested than others in this volume, taking as its referents the national space 'Japan' along with the non-Western cultural space 'Asia' and the oceanic space 'Pacific'. The articulation of Japanese identity as part of the regions 'Asia-Pacific', 'East Asia' or the Eurocentric 'Far East' symbolises the construction of contending regional orders, which are shaped by military, political, economic and socio-cultural relations and motivations rooted both inside and outside these amorphous areas. Whether we take as our reason for focusing on this part of the globe the spectacular economic performance, first of Japan, then of the Newly Industrialising Countries (NICs), now of key members of the Association of Southeast Asian Nations (ASEAN), China, and Indochina; or the complex legacy of the Cold-War era in the shape of the surviving socialist and divided nations of China and North Korea, and socialist Vietnam, which appear set to hold on to power in the transition to a market economy; or, again, Huntington's apocalyptic warning of future global politics being dominated by 'a clash of civilizations' as evident, among others, in the incompatibility between American civilisation and Japanese civilisation,[1] not least one might add in the different models of capitalist development represented by American theories of 'trickle-down' modernisation and Japanese theories of a 'flying-geese' pattern of growth,[2] this region is likely to exert a profound influence on the shape of the world as we move towards the twenty-first century. For these reasons, we will here examine Japan as the 'core' of a region embracing the NICs (Hong Kong, Singapore, South Korea, Taiwan), ASEAN (Brunei, Indonesia, Malaysia, Philippines, Thailand, with the 'dual member' Singapore being considered in the former group), as well as to a limited extent China. We will refer to this grouping of states and territories as 'East Asia', a term now commonly used in Japanese academic, economic and political circles to reflect the dynamic economic relations shaping the region in the 1980s and early 1990s. The term 'Asia-Pacific' will be used in connection with the role of the United States, as the US is central to the recent attempts to puncture the East Asian identity and reconfigure it around 'Asia-Pacific' or 'Pacific-Asia'.

Whatever terminology we adopt, the reconfiguration of geographic space into a regional form challenges the spatial identities of all of these sovereign states and territories by investing value in military, political, economic and socio-cultural links of an international or transnational nature. These identities are most forcefully articulated by the states and territories which make up these regions as well as by the actors who are building the links at their heart. A dialectical process can be said to be at work between the reconstruction of a regional identity and the strengthening of these links; that is, their deepening and widening within regional parameters gives substance to an identity on the regional level. This is nowhere clearer than in the recent competitive attempts by political and business leaders to construct the regional identities 'Asia-Pacific' and 'East Asia' out of the growth of economic and other links in this part of the globe. At the core of their discourse is Japan, just as at the core of the war-time attempt to form another regional identity, the Greater East Asia Co-prosperity Sphere, was the 'Empire of Japan'.

Historical background: from Meiji to the early Cold-War order

Where is 'Japan', deprived by defeat of its name as well as its territories, located? Although in geographic and cultural space Japan is in Asia, the Western advance into this part of the world in the nineteenth century starkly revealed the vulnerability of a late-comer in the 'Far East'. The Japanese leadership's response to imperialism was to prioritise the state's congruence of interests with the West by importing Western learning at the same time as it sought to maintain an indigenous cultural identity – *wakon yōsai* (Japanese spirit, Western learning) in the expression of the early years of the Meiji period (1868–1911). This dichotomy between a spatial and cultural location in Asia and a military, political and economic identification with the advanced West led the Meiji political thinker, Fukuzawa Yukichi, to call on his countrymen to 'leave Asia and join the west' (*datsua nyūō*). With victory in the Russo–Japanese war (1904–5), following on from the earlier success in the Sino–Japanese war (1894–5), Japan did indeed 'join the west' in a military sense, the war of 1904–5 making the Japanese the first Asian nation to defeat a Western power. Having thereby learned from the West the value of military conquest in a late-comer's struggle to catch up with and overtake (*oitsuki, oikose*) the early starters, Japan's attempt to reach this goal by military means was continued into the 1930s and early 1940s through the 'Greater East Asia War'. The ideological underpinning of this war was Japan's shared identity with its 'Asian brothers', who were to be freed from the shackles of Western imperialism.

The Greater East Asia Co-prosperity Sphere was a regional answer to the question of Japanese identity, for essentially the 'sphere' reconfigured the Chinese World Order around Japan as the new 'core'.[3] Although such a spatial reconfiguration linked Japan to other parts of Asia through the ideological embrace of *co*-prosperity, the relationship was nevertheless asymmetric, with the 'sphere' subordinated to the 'core' as in the Chinese World Order. Geographic propinquity and a sense of Japanese superiority help to explain why those in the 'sphere' were to be vertically integrated into the military, political, economic and socio-cultural space of the Japanese Empire, even down to the eradication of Korean ethnic identity under a policy of the forced adoption of Japanese names. Japan's territorial ambitions, mounted on the backs of belligerent expansionists, were expressed in the attempt to conquer physically the geographic space identified as 'Greater East Asia' in order to impose a congruence between physical and ideological space.

The empire's defeat at the hands of the Allies doomed this attempt to integrate the region through military aggrandisement, although it did not bring about the immediate death of the ideology which underpinned the co-prosperity sphere, as seen in the periodic but continuing attempts of leading conservative politicians to legitimise the war.[4] The ideology could nevertheless not be trotted out to legitimise the new regime. In this ideological climate, the Japanese psychologically withdrew from Asia. In its place appeared the United States in the concrete form of the Allied occupation of Japan (1945–52). Thus, in the years immediately following the defeat, instead of facing the legacy of colonisation and war in Asia, Japan faced a US attempt to 'remake' it by demilitarising and democratising both state and society.[5] The result was the imposition of a framework of restraint on its dealings with the former victims of imperial aggression, simultaneously depriving state and society of the ability to define their relations with the outside world. Unlike European imperial powers, which faced colonial struggles far from home and divisive debates right at home, Japan was initially severed from an Asia of which it was an integral part. In this process, state and society failed to address the role the empire had played in ending European colonisation by starting the war and ending the Japanese imperium by losing the war. In a fundamental sense, these questions were overshadowed by the regional emergence of the Cold War.

The Cold War split Asia ideologically and some parts of it physically in a way which reconstituted Japan's relations with the nations it had conquered along lines largely charted by the anti-Communist strategy of the United States. The 'reverse course', which placed higher priority on the country's role as a capitalist bastion in the 'Far East' than on the demilitarisation and democratisation of state and society, locked Japan into an anti-Communist alliance.[6] In the discussions leading up to the adoption of NSC 48/1 in December 1949 – 'a document so important it might be called the NSC 68 for Asia' – the triangular structure between the United States (core), Japan (semi-periphery), and Southeast Asia (periphery) began to take shape.[7] Japan was firmly anchored to the United States, politically with the conclusion of the 1951 San Francisco Peace Treaty on US terms, as evident in the absence of a Soviet signature on the treaty and the later signing of the treaty by Taiwan rather than mainland China; and militarily with the simultaneous signing of the US–Japan security treaty, thereby ceding Okinawa and bases on the main islands for the exclusive use of the United States in prosecuting both conventional and nuclear war.[8] This led to Japan's ideological as well as economic, political and military integration into the capitalist confrontation with Communism. Thus, in the Cold-War ideological climate of the early 1950s, regionalism in Asia was suffocated under the weight of bilateralism, with the division of the region in terms of 'capitalism' and 'Communism' reconstructing 'Asia' as 'East Asia'; East Asia as 'divided' East Asia; and divided East Asia as 'capitalist' East Asia. This obfuscated the need for state and society to face the question of wartime responsibilities for Asia as a whole.

For all that, the nature of the post-war settlement, the aims of NSC 48/1, and the rebuilding of the Japanese economy, still laid the foundation upon which Japan was to gradually renew its relationship with the nations of East Asia. First of all, the US perceived a need to prevent the communisation of Japan and maintain domestic stability under a political party supportive of capitalism. This led to the external Cold War being reproduced domestically, with the United States and the Soviet Union allegedly pouring funds into the coffers of their chosen collaborators, which by the mid-1950s had coalesced into the conservative Liberal Democratic Party (LDP), on the one hand, and the Japan Socialist Party (JSP) and Japan Communist Party (JCP), on the other.[9] One of the reasons for the US support of the LDP was to ensure Japan remained 'a bastion against communism in Asia'.[10] Second, in order to play this designated role, the US perceived a similar need to rebuild the economy and turn Japan into a capitalist nation of the second rank.[11] This would reduce its own financial burden as well as establish a framework for integrating the East Asian economies. The Communist victory in China in 1949 meant Japan's economic revival would depend on developing bilateral links with the capitalist nations of East Asia, which the US viewed as possible targets for communisation. The 1949 pegging of the yen at a low exchange rate of 360 yen to the dollar thus aimed to facilitate Japanese exports to these nations. This rate of exchange remained stable until the break-down of the Bretton Woods system in the early 1970s.

The absorption of relatively cheap made-in-Japans, economic development and the maintenance of political stability were seen as ways to contain Communism in the region. In line with this goal, the US took on the role of political and military leader for the region's anti-Communist regimes, becoming a major supplier of weapons, aid, capital and technology. Not that such a role was necessarily unwelcome. The conservative, nationalist leaders of capitalist East Asia shared a fear of militarism and Communism. This meant a continual need to balance their concern over a revival of the past (Japanese militarism) with the imposition of the present (Communist victory). Still, Japan loomed large in the field of economics, both as an exporter of finished products and as an absorber of the region's resources.

Resistance in the region nevertheless precluded economic integration centring on Japan: for the victims of Japanese aggression, the 'new Japan's' economic penetration not only engendered fears of a recrudescence of the 'old Japan's' co-prosperity sphere, but also ran up against the forces of nationalism, born of the goal of casting off the last shackles of imperialism and building an independent nation. In this situation, the nationalist goals of the former colonies, and the demands of nation-building in Thailand (which though not colonised ceded territory), precluded a declared political or military place for Japan in the region, with economic links developing only gradually. In this way, the regional order to emerge in the early 1950s was not only determined by the nature of the Cold-War confrontation, but also by the decolonisation struggle and the demands of economic development among the newly emerging nations.

Economic links with East Asia

Aid

As symbolised by the reparation payments the government made to the former victims of the Japanese empire, bilateral links were rebuilt with East Asia from the mid-1950s onwards, starting with Burma (1955), the Philippines (1956), Indonesia (1958), South Vietnam (1959) and through cash grants (though not formal reparation payments) Laos and Cambodia (1959). Others followed.[12] The normalisation of relations in 1965 was the starting point for aid to South Korea. This is the same year an economic co-operation agreement was concluded with Taiwan. These forms of 'economic co-operation' (aid), which were an obligation under Article 14 of the Peace Treaty, gave shape to the developing economic links with capitalist East Asia. The reparation payments led to a major increase in exports to the region, which from around 1957 came to include the export of metal products, machinery, and chemicals as well as consumer goods – the start of a increasingly profitable relationship for Japan. At the same time, economic links were gradually rebuilt with Communist China from the late 1950s onwards under a policy of separating politics and economics (*seikei bunri*).[13]

The role assigned to the region by the Japanese government in its struggle to catch up with and overtake the West is evident from the first post-war economic plan drawn up by the Economic Planning Agency in 1955. In essence, Asia was regarded as a target of economic diplomacy and trade promotion.[14] By the 1960s, with the rise to power in the ruling LDP of Ikeda Hayato, an aid policy towards Asia had started to take shape. It was nevertheless the 1970s before the role of aid as a tool of foreign policy became salient.[15] The focus of Japanese aid on economic infrastructure projects within the region facilitated Japanese manufacturers' entry into the blossoming markets of East Asia. The trend continued: as Ensign shows in a study of Japanese aid in the 1980s, 'Japanese aid and trade are linked. Specifically, aid to infrastructure projects in Indonesia, Malaysia, the Philippines, Thailand, China, and Korea is positively correlated with trade in infrastructure. Tied aid benefits the Japanese economy and industries. Capital projects support the exports of Japanese goods.'[16]

The focus on capitalist East Asia as the destination for Japanese aid fulfilled a strategic role in supporting US allies in the region, especially pro-Western authoritarian regimes, with South Korea, the Philippines, and Indonesia as major recipients in the 1960s. In 1970 as much as 98.3 per cent of Japanese aid went to Asian countries, especially Indonesia (33.8 per cent) and South Korea (23.3 per cent).[17] In the aftermath of the 1973 oil crisis Prime Minister Tanaka Kakuei perceived a need to diversify energy sources. As a result, Japan's aid started to break out of this regional mould and become more global. Even so, the regional focus fundamentally remained unaltered. Although by 1980 South Korea's share of total aid had fallen to 3.9 per cent and Indonesia's to 17.9 per cent, over 60 per cent of Japanese aid went to Asia even in the late 1980s. Following the signing of the Peace and Friendship Treaty and Trade Agreement of 1978, aid to China started to take on an increasingly important role within aid to Asia. The newly emerging giant was soon one of the major recipients: in 1982, for instance, China's share was already 15.6 per cent. The focus on Asia has continued into the 1990s, with over 60 per cent of Japanese aid still going to Asia in 1992, suggesting the continued importance of the region to Japan. With the ending of the Cold War Vietnam has joined China as a target for Japanese aid in line with the government's policy of promoting the economic development of the 'socialist' as well as capitalist market economies of the region.

The theory of the 'flying geese' model of development, with Japan as the lead goose, is an ideological thread tying the aid Japan is extending to East Asia to the Greater East Asia Coprosperity Sphere. In this sense, even though it is correct to point to the decentralised, overlapping and competitive nature of decision making on aid, involving the Ministry of Foreign Affairs, the Ministry of International Trade and Industry (MITI), the Ministry of Finance, and the Economic Planning Agency, the importance of the shared belief in the 'flying geese' model of development should not be overlooked.[18] 'At the very least,' states Korhonen, 'the idea of an inevitable process of development in Asia seems to have spread among academic, bureaucratic, and political elites in Japan during the 1950s and 1960s.'[19] Certainly, Japan's entry into the OECD in 1964 symbolised to other Asian states how economic development was possible for the 'lead goose', so why not aid to assist the followers?

Foreign direct investment

Along with the role of government aid, foreign direct investment (FDI) by Japanese companies has been crucial in shaping economic links in East Asia. These investments started on a small scale in the 1950s and were initially focused on resource exploitation, as in the development of the Sumatran oil fields in the early 1950s and similar investments following the start of reparation payments in 1955. It was the early 1970s before Japan became a major investor in the region, however, when the first wave of Japanese FDI occurred in response to the negative impact of a rise in the price of the yen caused by the 'Nixon shocks', which ended fixed parity at 360 yen to the dollar. In comparison with 1971, for instance, investments in Southeast Asia were up fourfold in 1973, from 0.15 billion dollars to 0.63 billion dollars.[20] Japanese companies were moving offshore in order to reap the benefits associated with the cheap price of capital resulting from the yen's rise to set up low-cost export bases in the developing parts of East Asia. The winding down of the Cold-War confrontation with China increased the region's attractiveness for Japanese FDI, which with the withdrawal of the United States after defeat in the Vietnam War gradually opened the way for further penetration into the region. US military disentanglement from East Asia created new opportunities for strengthening Japanese economic control, with Japanese companies able to exploit and benefit from the infrastructure built with Japanese aid as well as the links developed through the reparation payments.

Moreover, by investing in the developing economies of the region these companies were able to take advantage of cheap wages in labour-intensive manufacturing industries such as textiles and electronics, as well as set up new launch platforms to penetrate the American market. The US–Japan economic relationship had been transformed in the process of Japan's own rapid economic development. This was concretely manifested in trade conflict after trade conflict starting in the 1960s. The 'textile wrangle' symbolises the challenge the late-comer was now mounting on the early starter.[21] The movement of textile makers to developing East Asia, which had taken a step forward with the Japanese recession of 1965, took a further major stride

after the Nixon shocks. Although the United States had maintained a deficit in textiles throughout the post-1945 period, in
1972, after the textile wrangle, the Japanese government was
forced to accept the imposition of 'voluntary export restraint'
(VER) on textile exports to the United States. Within the newly
emerging relationship, exports from Japanese manufacturing
bases located in developing East Asia offered another way into
this market.

The second wave of FDI started in 1978 after a decline in
FDI in the mid-1970s following the downturn in the Japanese
economy due to the impact of the oil crisis. The successful
return to economic health by Japanese companies after imple-
menting slimline management and ruthless labour policies saw
FDI in East Asia climb again. The investment in electronics
continued, along with investments in new areas such as chemicals, machinery, automobiles as well as in the service sector
(for example, finance, insurance). In contrast to the first wave,
the second wave of investments from 1978 until the next wave
of currency-driven investments after 1985 resulted from the
restructuring of the Japanese economy followng the rise in
the price of oil as well as the increasing trade conflict with the
United States. FDI in Southeast Asia grew from 0.64 billion
dollars in 1977 to 2.84 billion in 1981, before dropping rapidly as the trade conflict with the United States led Japanese
companies to boost FDI there and in the European Community.
This second wave of investment was set to transform Japanese
companies into multinational corporations, with production
facilities being established in the three core regions of the global
economy.

The third and biggest wave of Japanese investment followed
the Plaza Accord of 1985, which led to a further increase in
the value of the yen from around 250 yen to the dollar in
April 1985 to around 150 yen to the dollar in July 1987, an
increase of about 70 per cent. This again forced Japanese corporations to seek to maintain international competitiveness by
moving production offshore. The pattern of investment post-
1985 was much broader than in the 1970s, with small and
medium-sized companies and component makers also playing
a bigger role. FDI in Southeast Asia shot up from 0.94 billion
dollars in 1985 to 2.71 billion in 1988. Much of the new in-

vestment came to be directed at ASEAN, with a drop in investment to the NICs. For instance, of the total Japanese manufacturing investment in the NICs, ASEAN and China, investment in the NICs fell from 15.1 per cent in 1986 to 5.6 per cent in 1988, whereas that in ASEAN more than tripled from 5.1 per cent in 1988 to 18 per cent in 1992.[22] With the intensification of management–labour strife following the move to more democratic forms of government in Taiwan and South Korea, wage hikes, the rise in the value of their own currencies after the Louvre Accord of 1987, and the increasing economic conflicts with the US, the NICs had by this time lost much of their attraction for Japanese investors. Indeed, in 1989 the United States removed the NICs from the Generalised System of Preferences (GSP), with the resulting loss of trading advantages associated with the GSP.

A fourth wave of investment appears to be following the currency realignment of 1992–4, with the yen rising from 130 yen to the dollar in April 1992 to 108 yen to the dollar in October 1993, an increase of around 20 per cent, with the months in between seeing the yen break the barrier of 100 yen to the dollar for the first time. The yen stood at around 100 yen to the dollar at the beginning of 1995. What is striking about the recent investment pattern is the growing weight of China, along with the continuing importance of ASEAN economies such as Thailand. In the 1980s investments in China were around 1 per cent of the total manufacturing investment in the NICs, ASEAN and China, but these increased to 2.5 per cent in 1991, 6.5 per cent in 1992 and 12.4 per cent in 1993, reflecting the shift of Japan's East Asian investments to this country. The change from 1985, when only 19.6 per cent of Japan's total global investment in manufacturing was in East Asia, to 1993, when 32.9 per cent was in the region, is graphic testimony to the enormous change in the global pattern of Japanese investment. In short, East Asia has come to play an ever more important role in the investment and production strategies of Japanese industries.

The case of consumer electronics illustrates the outcome of the above type of investments. By the 1970s Japan had eaten into the US market in televisions. This erosion of a key consumer industry provoked calls by US industrialists and their

political allies to restrict exports from Japan. As a result, an
agreement to accept voluntary export restraint on televisions
was reached in 1977.[23] The production of colour televisions in
the US, Europe and East Asia went forward thereafter, with
Japanese transplants in East Asia exporting their products to
third countries as well as reimporting them into Japan. Overall, the share of Japanese electrical machinery produced offshore increased from 7.4 per cent in 1985 to 10.8 per cent in
1992. Already by the late 1980s the offshore production of televisions had not only led to a reduction in domestic production, but Japan had become a net importer of colour televisions.[24]
In other words, these changes in the economic structures of
the region's economies have led to the 'hollowing out' of the
Japanese television industry.

The example of the electronics giant Matsushita shows how
Japanese corporations developed a strategy to deal with these
changes in the electronics industry during the 1980s and early
1990s. Matsushita has invested in the offshore production of
colour televisions, refrigerators, vacuum cleaners, air-conditioners
and other consumer electronics. Before the yen appreciation
following the Plaza agreement the plants it set up in Southeast
Asia assembled home electronic products without being a part
of any overall regional strategy. After the rise in the yen, however, the company moved the production base of electrical
appliances such as air-conditioners to Malaysia. This enabled
the company to export 'made-in-Malaysia' air-conditioners to
the United States. Such type of home appliances are also being increasingly reimported into Japan. Reflecting the globalisation of its business operations, in 1981 the company established
Asia Matsushita in Singapore, and in 1991 went on to set up a
research and development centre for air-conditioners in Malaysia.

The president of a semi-conductor company conveys the dynamic links these sorts of strategies set in motion for other
Japanese companies. In this case, after building his first semi-
conductor factory in Malaysia in the 1980s, at the end of 1992
he completed another in Bangkok in order to be able to supply the electronic consumer makers now located in the region.
As he states, 'with just our Malaysian factory we could not fill
Asian demand [for semi-conductors]. We advanced into Asia
not because of the cheapness of labour but because our cus-

tomers are there.'[25] In the case of another electronics giant, Sharp, we find 'calculators produced for export on an OEM basis by a Taiwanese company located in Thailand using Japanese components and Thai labour'.[26] In this way, electronics-industry components are being shipped inside the region before final assembly and then exported to a third country outside the region or increasingly to other markets within the region.

With the rise in the value of the yen in 1994, together with intense competition in the domestic market due to the recession and penetration by overseas multinationals, ever-higher levels of Japanese technology are being moved to other parts of East Asia. In October 1994, for instance, Fujitsu announced that production of its hard-disk drives would be moved to Thailand. It plans to produce about 80 per cent of group requirements there by 1995. In addition to the rise in the value of the yen, the increasingly severe price competition with US computer makers motivated Fujitsu to move production off-shore.[27]

Significance of economic links

The point is that Japanese corporations have moved production to other parts of East Asia variously to take advantage of the low cost of capital and cheap labour, to move into new markets, to remain competitive, to ameliorate trade conflict with the United States, and so on. Clearly, trade conflict and protectionist pressures arising from within the United States have been crucial, suggesting how Japanese investments in East Asia and elsewhere are intricately linked to global dynamics. In a sense, it has been the development of the Japanese economy beyond second rank which has led to the numerous US–Japan trade conflicts, with internationally competitive made-in-Japans penetrating the American market in increasing quantities in the decades since US policy makers envisaged Japan as nothing more than a second-rank power.

The establishment of research centres, the relocation of high-technology industries such as hard-disk drives, and the general increase in technologically sophisticated industries being located in other parts of East Asia suggest these economies are not so much following Japan as the 'lead goose' in the 'flying geese' model of economic development so much as 'leap frog-ging' into advanced industries, at least in the electronics field. The 'flying geese' model of locating high-technology produc-tion processes in Japan, standardised technology production processes in the NICs, and labour-intensive production pro-cesses in ASEAN, certainly does not characterise the recent trends in the Japanese electronics industry.

What we do find is that current Japanese FDI in East Asia points to the movement of labour-intensive production from the NICs, then to ASEAN, now to China, and next perhaps to Vietnam and other parts of Indochina. Despite the drop in Japanese investments after becoming the number one in world FDI in 1989, following the bursting of the economic 'bubble', a 5 per cent increase occurred in 1993, with the investment focused on China. In this case, Japanese imports of manufac-tured goods centring on textiles has shot up in the past few years. The rise of the yen in 1993 and 1994 has further pushed Japanese companies overseas, with small and medium-sized companies, as well as the giants, heading into the China mar-ket. This highlights how a complex division of labour is devel-oping in the region.

One of the noteworthy outcomes of Japanese investments after the mid-1980s and especially the beginning of the 1990s has been an increase in investment-related intraregional trade. As a result, Japan is rapidly taking on a role as an absorber of exports from the NICs, ASEAN and China. In 1985, for in-stance, the share of manufactured goods as a share of Japan's total imports was 31 per cent, but by 1991 this had reached 50.8 per cent, with a particularly sharp rise in manufactured imports from the NICs – from 57.8 per cent in 1985 to 73.9 per cent in 1991 – ASEAN – from 8.4 per cent in 1985 to 28.4 per cent in 1991 – and China – from 27 per cent in 1985 to 58.1 per cent in 1991.[28] By the first half of 1994 manufactured products had reached 54.6 per cent of total imports, the highest level ever recorded, with large increases in imports from the region's economies.[29] This reflects the rapid growth in the share of industrial products in many of the ASEAN economies, with a jump from 40 per cent in 1982 to 68 per cent in 1989 in Thailand, from 27 per cent to 51 per cent in Malaysia, and from 11 per cent to 50 per cent in Indonesia. In ASEAN as a whole the exports of machinery components nearly tripled, from 8.5 per cent in 1985 to 22.5 per cent in 1989. In short, the ASEAN nations and China are following the NICs as exporters of manufactured goods, with Japan becoming an increasingly important absorber for the economies of the region.

The triangular structural links created by the aid policy of the Japanese government, the investment focus of Japanese multinationals, and the export strategies of manufacturers located in the NICs and ASEAN have given rise to interpenetration between Japan and the other East Asian economies. As with the LDP during the period of single-handed rule (1955–93), Japanese infrastructure projects and aid in general have provided the ruling élites in the NICs and ASEAN with the patronage to help stabilise their regimes.[30] In this sense, aid, investment and trade have played a role in laying a corrupt pipeline between the Japanese government, Japanese corporations and the regimes of East Asia. In this context, the numerous scandals surrounding the use of Japanese aid suggests the scale of the problem.[31]

Finally, the structural links between Japan and the other economies of East Asia are not simply a one-way process of an 'activist' Japan and a 'passive' East Asia: the governments in the region have often acted swiftly in response to changes in the global economy. In the first place, although the developing East Asian economies pursued different types of economic strategies during the Cold-War era, by the early 1970s they had generally abandoned the import-substitution policy and moved to export-oriented development. Since this meant a need to attract foreign capital they had to create the political and economic environment for that capital. The building of export zones was one way forward. The first zone built in Asia was in Taiwan in 1965; by the mid-1970s, export manufacturing zones were under operation in South Korea, the Philippines and Malaysia, as well as to an increasing extent in Taiwan. The Chinese decision in 1978 to adopt an open-door policy was crucial in making China an attractive investment area for Japan, the NICs and the overseas Chinese in ASEAN. Second, Japan has served as a model for the newly developing economies of the region, at least in the minimalist sense of a demonstration effect, if not in the concrete form of a 'Look East Policy' as in the case of Malaysia. The policies pursued by the regional economies promoted their level of industrialisation, making them export-ers of manufactured goods. In this sense, the 'Japanese model' can be said to have extended an ideological influence in the region, even if the path of development did not follow the pattern of the 'flying geese'.

Security links in Asia Pacific

The Cold War

The above-mentioned economic links between Japan and other parts of East Asia are in sharp contrast to the almost total lack of any military links during the Cold-War era. In essence, Ja-pan's main role in the security sphere was to make an indirect rather than direct contribution to maintaining the regional order by providing the United States with the military infrastructure needed to meet challenges to its hegemony in Asia-Pacific. The legacy of the war, in terms both of the opposition from former victims in East Asia as well as the principles of the anti-milita-ristic 1947 Constitution, precluded Japan's inclusion in any collective security arrangement. The 1951 bilateral security treaty with the United States was pivotal but only part of a wider 'hub and spokes' security system established by the US involv-ing security treaties with the Philippines (1951) and South Korea (1953) as well as a trilateral treaty with Australia and New Zea-land (ANZUS, 1951). Thus, unlike the Cold-War confrontation in Europe, which linked geographically proximate states to the rival pillars of the United States and the Soviet Union, the American security framework established in Asia-Pacific during the early 1950s centred on tying Japan and the other anti-Com-munist regimes of the region into bilateral not collective secu-rity arrangements, with China as the major threat and the fear of Communist revolutions at home a strong incentive for the region's leaders to develop close links with the United States.

In this way, Japan was tied into a bilateral security arrange-ment, which concomitantly precluded its development of an independent security role and prevented a strong sense of re-gional identity between the 'spokes'. The US–Japan security treaty was pivotal to US prosecution of the wars in Korea and Vietnam. The provision of bases and other facilities by the Japanese government thus contributed to the preservation of the regional order as defined by the United States. With the Nixon Doctrine of 1969, Japan was pressured to make an even greater contribution to security in the region, in line with the idea of Asians shouldering the burden for Asian security. The weakening of US power in the wake of defeat in the Vietnam War, and the economic rise of Japan, led the US government to make increasingly vociferous calls for the Japanese to do more. Why, the argument ran, should Japan take a 'free ride' on the security treaty at the same as it chalked up enormous trade surpluses and destroyed sector after sector of the US economy? Indeed, in both war and peace Japan stands out as a major beneficiary of the Cold-War confrontation in Asia-Pacific.

The Sino-American accord of the early 1970s meant that, so far as the main regional antagonist was concerned, the Cold War was over. But US interests in the region were global as well as regional, with Japan set to play an increasingly important role in protecting those as well as its own interests. The latent fear of US retaliation in the area of trade made the Japanese government vulnerable to pressure to play a direct as well as indirect regional role. Over the years, this has meant boosting the Japanese military budget, increasing defensive strength, and assuming important naval and other military duties. After the implementation of the US–Japan Guidelines for Defence Cooperation in 1979 this came to include the Self Defence Forces (SDF) patrolling the sea lines of communication up to 1000 nautical miles from Japan, which put the sea in the region under Japanese military patrol for the first time in the Cold-War era.

The Japanese government's vulnerability to US pressure is not to suggest a lack of domestic political ambition to turn the nation into a political and military as well as economic force in the region. Within the ruling LDP, certain leading politicians supported the idea of Japan playing a direct political and military role in East Asia. This is the key to understanding the success of US pressure in reshaping Japan's regional role in the 1980s.[32] The defence build up under Prime Minister Nakasone Yasuhiro (1982–7) is here crucial, as his idea of

Japan playing a more prominent political and military role in the world was grounded in an attempt to revive the 'community' idea at the base of Greater East Asia Co-prosperity Sphere. In other words, Nakasone strove to build up Japan's military and political, as well as economic, influence in East Asia and more generally the world.

Post-Cold War

The question of whether Japan should play a direct security role in the region remains one of the sources of division in the rapidly shifting landscape of Japanese domestic politics in the 1990s. The ending of the Cold War and the outbreak of the Gulf War has destroyed the domestic political consensus on the role of the SDF. In 1991 the taboo on the SDF being despatched overseas, which was established in 1954 to prevent the further use of the military to try to create a Greater East Asia Co-prosperity Sphere, was broken. The despatch of Japanese minesweepers to the Gulf after the end of the Gulf War marked the first time that Japanese military forces had been despatched in force since Japanese minesweepers secretly took part in operations to clear Korean ports at the time of the Korean War. In 1992 the then ruling LDP was able to pass Diet legislation enabling the government to despatch troops to East Asia, when the SDF were sent to Cambodia on UN peace-keeping duties. In neither case did these decisions meet with the type of vociferous opposition which might have been expected from domestic opinion or the governments and people in the region. Indeed, the Japanese minesweepers sent to the Gulf were permitted to make port calls in Southeast Asia and the role of the SDF in UN peace-keeping in Cambodia has been regarded favourably both at home and abroad. With the ending of the global Cold War, the twin brakes on the Japanese military – anti-military public opinion at home and the fear of a revival of Japanese militarism in East Asia – have not been applied with as much force as before. In this sense, a regional security role for Japan is becoming more acceptable, although opposition to an independent role remains strong.

This new Japanese role marks an important change in the regional security environment, for Japan is starting to become more active militarily, at the same time as it continues to support US regional strategy. This is occurring against a background of change in US military commitments in the region. The withdrawal of American forces and the closure of bases in the Philippines is part of a wider programme of US force reductions. Paradoxically, however, their closure means that US bases in Sasebo and Yokosuka are likely to take on greater importance, as these are now the only ones in the region capable of repairing, servicing and resupplying naval forces of the size and class of the US seventh fleet. Even in the post Cold-War era, therefore, the US–Japan security system continues to tie Japan into US strategy.

Indeed, it is actually Japan which provides the United States with a virtual free-ride in its pursuit of regional and global interests. In this latter regard Japanese bases functioned as important strategic points for deployments against Iraq at the time of the Gulf War and the Japanese government made a major contribution to the cost of that war. Moreover, the host nation support given by the Japanese government means that stationing troops in Japan is more economical than stationing them in the United States. Since one of the reasons for a reduction in US deployments overseas is the financial burden, this makes deployment of troops in Japan especially attractive. As it stands, Japan is contributing the equivalent of over 66 000 dollars per soldier stationed in Japan.[33] The presence of the US military after the end of the Cold War highlights the continuing role of the alliance as a means to maintain order both inside and outside Asia-Pacific. In this sense, the security framework emerging in the post-Cold-War era is a condominium centring on the US, with Japan playing a supporting role. As we have seen, Japan pays for the stationing of American troops and, as at the time of the Gulf War, sometimes their deployment, bearing joint responsibility for military actions launched from US bases in Japan. The US Department of Defense's 1992 announcement that it will take account of 'the ability of our allies and friends to share responsibility in shaping the new era' suggests Japan is expected to continue to play such a role.[34]

Thus, despite the end of the Cold War, and the disappearance of the reason why the alliance was established, the US–Japan security system continues to limit Japan's freedom of action in developing a regional security role. This is revealed in a comment made by the US Marine Corps Commander in Okinawa, Lieutenant General Henry Stackpole, who stated in 1990 that the deployment of US troops in Japan acts as a 'cap in the bottle',[35] precluding the government's development of an independent defence role. For the treaty ties Japan into a subordinate, albeit gradually more powerful, position in US strategy in Asia-Pacific. This subordination is manifested in a variety of ways, ranging from the integration of the Japanese military into US force structures, to restrictions on the independent development of weaponry. Japan remains one of the US's best weapons customers, and interoperability helps to ensure a continuing flow of weapons across the Pacific. What is more, as the previously mentioned Department of Defense report makes clear, the United States continues to oppose Japan's acquisition of the ability to project power overseas and aims to prevent 'one state's dominance of the region'.[36] In short, Japan continues to be controlled within the framework of the US–Japan security system, restricting if not totally precluding any attempt to pursue an independent security policy.

In a wider context, this helps to explain why the US–Japan security treaty is supported by other states in the region. At a minimum they harbour a residual fear concerning what kind of military role Japan would play if the US withdrew and Japan acquired aircraft carriers and other means to 'project power' in Asia-Pacific. To make this less likely, both Singapore and Malaysia have offered the US navy the use of port facilities, albeit on a commercial basis. The growing military might of China is another source of concern leading to support for a US presence, especially by ASEAN. Outstanding territorial questions like the problem of sovereignty over the Spratly Islands and the apparent Chinese willingness to use force in its resolution, strengthen this support for a US presence. The remaining legacies of the Cold War, as with the divided Korean peninsula and China, bring a similar result, as with the possibility of the North Korean development of nuclear weapons. Finally, unlike in the case of the Conference on Security and Co-operation in Europe, no clear political framework exists in Asia-Pacific for concrete discussions on disarmament involving the CIS (or Russia) and the United States. This lack of a clear framework leads to fears that any change in force structures brought about by 'unbalanced' reductions in armaments in the region might encourage Japan or China to move to fill the 'vacuum', again prompting support for a US presence.

It is thus the United States and not Japan which continues to shape the security regime in Asia-Pacific. The Japanese dependency within this structure seems set to continue, not least as a result of the end of political opposition to the security treaty: all of the main political parties in Japan now support its continuation. Likewise, the legacy of the war in East Asia still rules out the independent use of Japanese military forces to maintain the regional order, and thus protect the regional interests of Japanese corporations. At the same time, however, there remains the possibility of Japanese forces being used in the maintenance of the regional order under the umbrella of the United Nations. In 1994 the Japanese government expressed a formal interest in gaining a permanent seat on the UN security council. A role Japan might plausibly play in the region in the future is thus as part of a UN-backed co-operative endeavour to maintain the regional order. The Yomiuri newspaper company's recently announced proposal to revise the Constitution seeks to remove the constitutional impediment on Japan taking part in such actions.[37] This highlights the attempts conservative domestic forces are making to drum up support for Japan to play an active military and political as well as economic role in Asia-Pacific. We will return to this issue in the conclusion.

Regional organisations

The attempts made during the Cold War to build regional organisations tended to focus on economics, exclude Japan, or give centrality to Asia-Pacific, rather than East Asia, as the regional identity. In the same way that states invent traditions and impose histories in their struggle to create national identities, so regional organisations promote values and images to create regional identities. As we will see below, 'Asia-Pacific' and 'East Asia' are the cores around which attempts are now being made to reconstruct regional identities, with discourses of regionalism centring on inclusion, in the case of the Asia Pacific Economic Co-operation (APEC), and exclusion, in the case of the East Asian Economic Caucus (EAEC), offering alternative visions of the regional projects.

The regional organisations which developed over the course of the Cold War formed identities around the divisions imposed by the East–West as well as the North–South divides. Some of these, such as the United Nations Economic and Social Commission for Asia and the Pacific (1974, ESCAP), and its predecessor, the Economic Commission for Asia and the Far East (1947, ECAFE), are intergovernmental and reflect both these divisions in the region. So too with the Asia Development Bank (ADB), which was set up to promote economic development and co-operation in the region covered by ESCAP. In an early attempt to define itself as both 'West' and 'North', Japan played 'a leading role in planning, designing, and founding the bank in 1966', and has become increasingly active in shaping the bank's agenda from the mid-1980s onwards.[38]

Other organisations involving business leaders, academics and government officials acting in their private capacity have been at the heart of the practical task of creating networks linking together the 'West', 'North' and 'South'. These organisations have helped to spread the values of market-oriented economies to the 'East' as the core of an inclusionary identity embracing different political regimes, cultures and geographical locations. One example is the Pacific-Basin Economic Council (PBEC), a group set up in 1968, in which Japanese business leaders have been part of a regional attempt to build up a network identifying with 'Asia-Pacific' as the region. At the May 1994 meeting in Malaysia this groups clearly expressed its support for APEC, and announced a wish to be given observer status in the future.[39] Similarly, the Pacific Economic Co-operation Conference (PECC), a group set up in 1980 after a proposal by then Prime Minister Ohira Masayoshi, following a joint initiative by Japan and Australia, identified capitalist 'Asia-Pacific' as the region, with this network drawing together business leaders, academics and policy makers participating in their private capacity. In an attempt to influence policy in the region, the reports drawn up by PECC working groups are submitted to intergovernmental organisations such as ESCAP and the World Bank. Finally, following the 1965 initiative of Japanese economist Kojima Kiyoshi, who proposed a Pacific Free Trade Area (PAFTA) along with Okita Saburo (later to become a foreign minister of Japan), the Pacific Trade and Development meetings were set up in 1968 following developments outside the region, particularly the establishment of the European Community.[40] The aim was to promote economic integration in line with Japan's identity as one of the industrially developed, capitalist Asia-Pacific economies. The twenty-first meeting of PAFTAD, held in June 1994 in Taiwan, drew over 70 economists and researchers together from Asia and the Pacific to discuss, 'Corporate Links and Direct Investment in Asia and the Pacific'.

ASEAN and Japan

While the above organisations can be seen to reflect both Cold-War and developmental concerns, dividing identities in terms of 'capitalism' and 'Communism', 'developed' and 'developing', they at the same time reflect the reconfiguration of Japanese identity within an Asia-Pacific, as opposed to an East Asian, framework. Until the end of the Cold War, however, the main regional organisation was rooted in an East Asian identity, the Association of Southeast Asian Nations (ASEAN). During the Cold-War era the Japanese government treated ASEAN as not much more than a target for Japanese aid, giving support to the capitalist regimes in the region within the Cold-War framework established by the United States. The end of the Cold War has galvanised Japanese interest in the association as a partner with which to work in addressing international issues of common concern. The interest in ASEAN also reflects the successful economic growth of most members, which means they are increasingly facing the same type of difficulties in maintaining export-oriented economic growth as Japan. The success of ASEAN's export-led strategy in penetrating the US market has engendered the same sorts of economic and political fears seen earlier in the case of Japan and the NICs. Thus Japan and ASEAN have a shared interest in resisting US pressure. As seen at the first meeting of the Japan–ASEAN Economic Ministerial Conference in October 1992, Japan and ASEAN both oppose 'the formation of new regional blocs', highlighting their commonality of interest as global exporters.[41]

The ASEAN post-ministerial meetings have institutionalised ASEAN's dealings with key actors outside of the organisation, with Japan participating along with the US, Canada, Australia, New Zealand, South Korea and the EU as dialogue partners. Bearing in mind ASEAN sensitivities, the Japanese role in these meetings during the Cold War was largely restricted to making an announcement of aid to the members. In 1991, however, the Japanese Foreign Minister Nakayama Tarō proposed a region-wide political and security dialogue be set in motion.[42] This was the first time Japan had taken the initiative in the more sensitive area of regional security, widening the focus of the meetings beyond economics. In the following July, a consensus was reached to hold a meeting in 1993 to discuss regional security issues. Finally, in 1994 the Nakayama proposal took on life as the ASEAN Regional Forum (ARF), despite initial wariness on the part of some ASEAN members that Japan might take over leadership of the new organisation. In this way, the Japanese government played a crucial role in setting up the first multilateral meeting to discuss security in the Asia-Pacific.

As the Forum's name suggests, ASEAN has been able to limit the possibility of its domination by Japan or the other big powers. This fear of big-power domination nevertheless restricts the Japanese government in any attempt to take a major initiative in the Forum. In the first meeting in July 1994 in Bangkok, for instance, Japanese Foreign Minister Kono Yohei did little more than call for transparency in military relations, concretely suggesting that the members produce annual defence white papers. To what extent the Forum will pursue this issue, or indeed to what extent it will come to play a major role in tackling regional security issues, remains to be seen. What is clear, however, is that a reliance on bilateral security frameworks, which characterised the Cold-War era, has come to an end in Asia-Pacific.[43] With the success of ASEAN in bringing China within this multilateral dialogue framework, the Forum has been able to take up security issues such as sovereignty over the Spratly Islands, which has risen to prominence in the post-Cold-War era.[44] In this new framework, Japan and the other big powers will be able to work to restrain Chinese behaviour at the same time as all participants build up trust, discuss confidence-building measures, and deal with problems like the Spratlys. At the same time, Japan can co-operate with the association in trying to construct a new security system in the region which includes both China and Vietnam.

APEC and Japan

APEC was established in 1989 on the initiative of then Australian Prime Minister Bob Hawke, who proposed that 12 nations of the Asia-Pacific region – Japan, South Korea, the ASEAN six, the US, Canada, Australia and New Zealand – form an organisation to promote economic co-operation in line with 'open regionalism'. In essence, APEC started out as a market-led understanding of the identity of the region, with an inclusionary rather than an exclusionary framework for multilateral dialogue and policy co-ordination. In the same way as PAFTAD, the initiative was a response to developments outside of the region, especially the possibility of the formation of regional economic blocs in Europe (EU) and North America (NAFTA) and the ASEAN proposal for an ASEAN Free Trade Area. Despite the initial Australian initiative, increasingly the United States has taken over the leadership role in APEC and has used the organisation as a forum to maintain US power, embrace the exclusionary East Asian identity within an inclusionary 'Asia-Pacific' identity, and thereby prevent the creation of a regional identity centring on East Asian capitalist values – i.e. EAEC.

The initial Japanese reaction to the APEC proposal was 'wait-and-see'. Following US backing of APEC as the core regional organisation, however, the government has come to give preference to APEC, thereby further identifying itself with Asia-Pacific as opposed to East Asia. The Japanese government has started to play an active role in the organisation. In April 1992, for instance, Japan put forward the idea of setting up a secretariat in order to strengthen the functioning of APEC. Likewise, at the 1994 meeting of APEC in Indonesia, the Japanese proposed a plan for co-operation on energy. This followed an initiative by MITI to establish a research database on transportation technology in APEC in order to promote exchange of

technology amongst the members of APEC.[45] The APEC meetings are becoming increasingly important for Japan as the key
forums for multilateral dialogue on regional issues, particularly
economics, with Japan set to host the 1995 meeting of APEC
in Osaka. In this way, the government's commitment to APEC
has grown.

EAEC and Japan

The East Asia Economic Caucus, proposed by the Malaysian
foreign minister at the 1991 post-ministerial meeting of ASEAN,
originates from the proposal for an East Asian Economic Bloc
put forward in December 1990 by Malaysian Prime Minister
Mohamed Mahathir to Chinese Premier Li Peng. Despite the
change in the name, scope and function of EAEC due to pressure from both inside and outside the region, with the idea of
'bloc' being replaced with 'dialogue on economic co-operation',
Malaysia has consistently excluded the United States from the
proposed membership. The United States immediately expressed
opposition to the idea as dividing the Pacific and driving a
wedge in US–Japanese relations.

As with APEC, the Malaysian initiative was a response to fears
of protectionism and the formation of economic blocs centring on the EU and NAFTA, as well as an attempt to slow the
flow of local Chinese capital back to the mainland by integrating China into a network of economic co-operation. At the
same time, the initiative was a counterproposal to APEC, as
surfaced in 1994. Despite the compromise position of subsum-
ing EAEC under the APEC umbrella, the ASEAN secretariat
presented a document to the US government on the setting
up of EAEC, suggesting as members only the ASEAN six, Japan, South Korea and China. What this exclusionary group seems
to suggest is a perception of the regional economies as being
driven by Japan and South Korea as regional investors and China
as a disinvestor, pulling capital from the local Chinese in ASEAN
back to China, along with an understanding of Chinese sensibilities over Taiwan and Hong Kong (originally proposed as
members). While the declared aim of 'promoting economic
co-operation and the liberalisation of trade in East Asia' is
unproblematic, the document proposed that EAEC maintain a

high degree of independence within the APEC framework. For instance, it stated that EAEC is not a 'subordinate organisation of APEC, and has no obligation to report on agenda items'.[46] This has hardened US opposition to EAEC, even though the Clinton administration softened its stance for a time in 1993.

As the only industrially developed country in the EAEC proposal, Prime Minister Mahathir gave a central place to the role of Japan as leader of the group, both in an economic and a political sense, including the possibility of Japan acting as the 'voice of Asia' in the G7 meetings.[47] This 'voice of Asia' would naturally be a different voice to APEC. From the start the Japanese government has been ambivalent about EAEC: neither expressing support for the Malaysian proposal, nor open opposition. In other words, the need for Japan to remain sensitive to an East Asian regional identity precluded the sort of hostile response evidenced in the United States. However, the implications of the idea for the United States were such that, fearing a split between the US and Japan, and Japan's increasing commitment to the East Asian region, the US put pressure on the Japanese government to stay outside of the EAEC framework, as became clear in November 1991.[48] The American opposition was crucial in shaping Japanese attitudes, and thereafter the government grew more negative, not even discussing the topic when Mahathir visited Tokyo in December 1991. What is more, the position formally taken by the Japanese government, as expressed over the last few years by Prime Ministers Miyazawa, Hosokawa, Hata, and Murayama, has been to continue to place the highest priority on multilateral forums which include the United States. In other words, despite the end of single-handed LDP rule and the creation of coalition governments, maintaining close relations with the United States has continued as the core of Japanese policy.

Two examples should suffice. As part of the 'Miyazawa doctrine' the last LDP Prime Minister, Miyazawa Ki'ichi, called in 1993 for the maintenance of the US presence and the promotion of a system of open economic co-operation in Asia-Pacific, and expressed support for APEC over EAEC. This was despite a change in the nature of the EAEC proposal, which was in line with the 'open regionalism' supported by Japan.[49] In other words, of crucial concern to the government was not so much the nature of EAEC but its membership. Second, as part of his policy speech to the Diet in September 1994 the first socialist Prime Minister since 1947, Murayama Tomi'ichi, declared a commitment to 'active participation' in the ASEAN Regional Forum and APEC and the promotion of 'open regionalism'. Although both the ASEAN Regional Forum and the ASEAN post-ministerial meetings remain under ASEAN auspices, both include the United States. In other words, although the EAEC supporters and Japan share a common agreement on the need to maintain a US militeray presence in East Asia, when it comes to an economic forum the Japanese government wants to include and the Malaysian government wants to exclude the United States. As it stands, the Japanese government is still to give a formal answer to the EAEC proposal.

As we can see from Table 6.1, all of the policy co-ordination forums in Asia-Pacific of which Japan is a part also involve the United States. The creation of a forum excluding the United States in the name of an independent EAEC would weaken the US's power to influence developments in East Asia. In response to the EAEC proposal President Clinton has put forward the idea of a new Asia-Pacific Community. The idea is similar to Kojima's idea of PAFTA, but the 'community' at its base would serve as a way for the US to limit Japan's autonomous actions, enabling it to exert influence over Japan in multilateral as well as bilateral forums. What is more, as EAEC proposed including both Japan and China, the successful formation of the organisation would limit US ability to play the 'China card' against Japan and the 'Japan card' against China. Accordingly, we can expect the United States to continue to oppose the formation of an independent EAEC.

The significance of the Cold War's end

The above introduction of some of the most important regional organisations sheds light on the important initiatives Japan has taken as well as the limitations on its role. With the ending of the Cold War the government has come to play a wider role in the region, moving beyond the mainly economic concerns of earlier decades. In a sense, the recent creation of regional organisations such as APEC represents an attempt to bind the

TABLE 6.1   Important Regional Organisations in Asia-Pacific (1994)

Organisation	ASEAN (1967)	PAFTAD (1968)	PBEC (1968)	PECC (1980)	APEC (1989)	AFTA (1992)	EAEC (1993)	ARF (1994)
Japanese initiatives		i	i	i				i
Members								
Japan	+	x	x	x	x		*	x
South Korea	+	x	x	x	x		*	x
North Korea							?	
Taiwan		x	x	x	x		?	
China	#			x	x		*	□
Hong Kong			x	x	x		?	
United States	+	x	x	x	x			x
Canada	+	x	x	x	x			x
Mexico			x	x	x			
Peru			x	x				
Chile			x	x	x			
Thailand	x	x		x	x	x	*	x
Indonesia	x	x		x	x	x	*	x
Philippines	x	x	x	x	x	x	*	x
Malaysia	x	x	x	x	x	x	*	x
Brunei	x	x		x	x	x	*	x
Singapore	x	x		x	x	x	*	x
Vietnam	# x(1995?)			x(1995?)			?	□
Laos	#						?	□
Cambodia							?	
Mynmar							?	
Australia	+	x	x	x	x			x
New Zealand	+	x	x	x	x			x
Pacific Islands (Papua New Guinea)	#			x	x			□
Russia	#			o				□
European Union	+			o				x

x – member; + – dialogue partner; ASEAN Post-Ministerial Meeting; o – observer; * – ASEAN's proposed members; □ – guest; # – guest at 1993 ASEAN Foreign Ministers Meeting

centripetal forces of economics, to a large extent set in motion by the Japanese economy, in order to keep the centrifugal forces of politics under control. This is critically important to the United States in the wake of the ending of the Cold War and the disappearance of the reason for the establishment of the bilateral security framework in Asia-Pacific. In this respect, the political behaviour of the Japanese government continues to be constrained by the legacy of the Cold War in its relationship with the United States.

This is evident in the US opposition to the creation of EAEC. The proposed members of EAEC are all dependent on the US market to one degree or another. All except China are similarly dependent on the United States in the field of security. This implies a dual vulnerability to US pressure. Despite the collapse of single-handed LDP rule in Japan, all of the new coalition governments have declared their support for the preservation of the US–Japan security treaty. Neither the LDP's Ozawa Committee nor the prime minister's advisory group on defence, which submitted its report to Prime Minister Murayama in 1994, have come forward with any vision of Japan playing an independent security role in the region.[50] With the continuing role of the United States in the security of the region, as well as the important role of the US market as an absorber of East Asian products, Japan and most other states in the region are unwilling to risk joining a regional organisation opposed by the United States. The pragmatic concern over not being seen to support an exclusionary organisation, even if the rhetoric is one of open regionalism, can be expected to ensure an increasingly important role for APEC in the future.

Given the historical legacy of the war, why is Japan now becoming a more acceptable partner for its former victims? In the first place, the ending of the global Cold War has ended the attendant Cold-War divisions in Japanese domestic politics, thereby creating space for debate on Japan's future regional role. The political leaders who have taken power in the aftermath of single-handed LDP rule, such as Prime Minister Hosokawa Morihiro, have made more forthright apologies for Japan's wartime aggression than heretofore. For without addressing the outstanding issue of wartime responsibility, no Japanese government will be able to play a full political and military role in the region in the post-Cold-War era. In this sense, the recent attempts to deal with the legacy of the war are not so much a result of reflecting on the horrors of Japanese aggression and the subjective need to come to grips finally with the 'war's legacy, but derive more from a pragmatic need to do the minimum required to mollify Japan's victims so that a new role can be taken up.

Despite the progress made in coming to grips with the past, however, unresolved issues remain. The issue of the mostly Korean sex-slaves used by Japanese soldiers during the war, and reparations for North Korea, to mention two of the most intractable legacies of the war, continue to influence Japan's relations with its former victims. North Korea's forthright opposition to a permanent seat for Japan on the United Nations security council, together with the more circumspect opposition of South Korea, is in stark contrast to the support given by members of ASEAN. The division of opinion developing within East Asia over Japan's role in the region is symbolised by Mahathir's 1994 call on Prime Minister Murayama to stop apologising for the war, a sentiment hardly likely to meet with sympathy in South Korea or China, two of the core states in the EAEC proposal.

Conclusion

What, then, can be said about the possibility of an East Asian or Asia-Pacific regional bloc forming as part of a new world order? The following troika of expressions suggest the answer: competing identities, functional links, reactive strategies. First, competing identities: the spatial identity of the region is contested, as we have seen. Japan is at the core of competitive projects to reshape relations around the regional identities of 'East Asia' and 'Asia-Pacific'. The Cold-War strategies pursued by the United States, on the one hand, and the legacy of the war, on the other, have constrained Japanese relations in East Asia, with an economic rather than a military or political role being pursued in the Cold-War era. The ending of the global Cold War, however, has given rise to the possibility of Japan playing a new regional role: first, because of the change in attitudes within the region, making Japan more acceptable to East Asian governments; second, because of a change within Japanese popular opinion, making such a role more acceptable at home. What continues as a restraint on Japan playing an independent role is the US determination to exploit the legacy of the Cold War in dealing with Japan and the region. Embedding Japan in Asia-Pacific institutional frameworks, on the one hand, and maintaining its military subordination within the bilateral security framework, on the other, restrains Japan's independent action. Thus, in pressuring the Japanese government to identify with Asia-Pacific not East Asia, the United States has been acting to prevent the creation of a common East Asian identity incompatible with US interests, where Japan might strive to develop an independent role. In the immediate future, Japan can be expected to act within these frameworks: not one of the new coalition governments has crossed the taboo line of proposing a reconfiguration of relations with the United States in order to reflect the changes of the new post-Cold-War era.

Second, functional links: we have seen how Japan, the NICs, ASEAN and recently China are becoming increasingly integrated economically. The waves of investments from Japan (later followed by the NICs and Chinese capital in ASEAN) have been crucial in reshaping regional industries and trade patterns. What we are here witnessing is how the functional dynamics of regional interactions have fundamentally transformed the relationship between Japan, the advanced economies of the west, the NICs and the developing economies of East Asia. The catch-up process has generated pressures on the regional economies to restructure, but rather than this moving forward in line with the 'flying geese' model of economic development, the functional links within and between industries are generating the 'leapfrogging' of high technology sectors of the Japanese economy to other parts of East Asia. What is developing, therefore, is not a Japanese 'core' and a developing East Asian 'periphery', but a complex division of labour involving symmetric as well as asymmetric relationships between and within economies, industries and firms, with Japanese industries being 'hollowed out' in certain instances. Functional links in the economic sphere continue to play a crucial role in strengthening the integrative characteristics of the regional order. Given the functional basis of these links, however, an end to regional growth may well slow down or end this integrative process. In this sense, the predictions of continued high economic growth in East Asia suggest a further strengthening of economic integration.

Third, reactive strategies: we have seen how the surges in the value of the yen after 1972, 1985 and 1993 were pivotal in

determining the investment orientation of Japanese corporations. They reacted to these exogenous pressures by relocating
production facilities in Europe, the United States and overwhelmingly in East Asia, especially after 1985. In this sense,
the regional linkages built up in investment and trade have
been driven by global forces. Similarly, the attempts to create
regional organisations, whether it be in the 1960s with PAFTAD,
1989 with APEC or 1991 with EAEC, were a response to forces
outside of the region. The dynamic interaction between regional projects in one part of the globe with regional projects
in other parts of the globe highlights the interactive nature of
global processes. In this sense, regional organisations in Asia-
Pacific can be expected to continue to be shaped by developments in other regions of the globe, with the Japanese state,
corporations and society reacting to global as well as regional
pressures.

These three points in no way gainsay the fact that, in the
late 1980s and especially in the post-Cold-War era, the Japanese government has taken a number of regional initiatives.
What we would stress, however, is the overall compatibility of
the actions taken so far with the interests of the United States.
In other words, this greater show of independence presently is
not aimed at replacing the United States and establishing an
independent regional role for Japan. The nation's role in regard to security in the region, as seen in the case of Cambodian peace-keeping operations and the initiative to promote a
multilateral security dialogue in the region, for instance, are
not a challenge to the interests of the United States; rather
they are supportive of those interests.

As it stands, no domestic consensus yet exists on the future
military and political role Japan should play in the region and
the world. In the post-Cold-War era we can nevertheless point
to a number of competing scenarios around which political
forces appear to be coalescing in the fluid political landscape
of the early 1990s: first, a 'Gaullist option', with Japan moving
forward with an emphasis on becoming an independent military and political as well as economic big power. On the regional level this scenario implies the possibility of military and
political rivalry developing between Japan and China over leadership in East Asia. Second, there is an internationalist politico-

military option, with emphasis on Japan playing a larger military and political role as a permanent member of the United Nations Security Council. As touched on above, on the regional level this implies the possibility of Japanese military forces being deployed in East Asia with the backing of the security council. Third, there remains a 'middle power' option, with an emphasis on non-military contributions to international society outside the security council. On the regional level this implies the possibility of Japan strengthening its supply of aid, capital and technology – not weapons, in distinct contrast to the United States – and carving out a lead for itself in promoting environmental protection and non-proliferation in East Asia.[51]

Although no consensus yet exists on Japan playing a larger global or regional role, the anti-militarist tendencies of the Japanese public, and even leading politicians, remain and bear note. In this respect, Foreign Minister Kono's speech at the United Nations in September 1994 suggests the present government's attraction to a fourth scenario – a big power playing a limited military role as a permanent member of the UN Security Council. For Kono declared the Japanese constitution prevented Japan from playing a military role, even as a permanent member of the UN Security Council. On the regional level this implies the possibility of Japan emphasising a non-conventional, 'military' role in the region as at the time of the Cambodian settlement, when the Japanese Self Defence Forces were restricted in their role, in this case mainly carrying out such activities as high construction. The Kono statement demonstrates how the post-war settlement continues to act as a source of legitimacy as well as restraint on the government's actions. Although the debate over Japan's entry into the Security Council as a permanent member is still continuing, and the longevity of the present coalition government remains unclear, the United Nations may turn out to be an important forum where Japan attempts to reshape its political and military relations with East Asia and the world.

In the end, the nation is still faced with resolving the question political leaders from Meiji onwards have faced: how to balance relations between Asia and the West? We have seen how the Japanese state and society responded the first two times this question was addressed: in Meiji, the response to the Western

imperial advance was to learn from the West and try to reshape the region through military aggrandisement; in the Cold-
War era, the response to the defeat was to rebuild relations
based on bilateralism and economism, giving priority to relations with the United States and economic activity above all
else. In the post-Cold-War era, Japan is now called upon again
to reshape its relations with Asia and the West. We have suggested a number of possible scenarios for the future. Although
the present restructuring of the Japanese political system will
determine the outcome, the response of the East Asian victims
of Japanese imperialism will continue to play a crucial role. In
this sense, Malaysia's call for the Japanese government to act
as a regional leader cannot be answered fully until the problem of Japan's wartime responsibilities have been addressed.
The fiftieth anniversary of the war's ending provides an opportunity for both the Japanese state and society finally to come
to grips with this question.

Notes

* The author wishes to thank the Japan Foundation and the Japan
  Foundation Endowment Committee for financial support to carry
  out the research on which this chapter is based.

1. S. P. Huntington, 'The Clash of Civilizations?', *Foreign Affairs*, 72,
   3 (1993) 22–49.
2. On the 'flying geese' model, see P. Korhonen, 'The Theory of
   the Flying Geese Pattern of Development and its Interpretation',
   Journal of Peace Research, 31, 1 (1994) 93–108; and P. Korhonen,
   Japan and the Pacific Free Trade Area (London: Routledge, 1994).
3. On the Chinese World Order, see J. F. Fairbank (ed.) *The Chinese World Order* (Cambridge, Mass: Harvard University Press, 1968).
4. The recent case of Nagano Shigeto, the Minister of Justice in the
   Hata Cabinet, who in May 1994 was forced to resign after refer-
   ring to the Nanjing massacre as a 'hoax' is illustrative.
5. T. Cohen, *Remaking Japan: The American Occupation as New Deal*
   (ed. H. Passin) (New York: Free Press, 1987).
6. On the reverse course, see J. Dower, *Empire and Aftermath: Yoshida
   Shigeru and the Japanese Experience, 1878–1954* (Cambridge: Harvard
   Council on East Asian Studies, 1979) pp. 305–68; and J. Dower,
   'Occupied Japan and the Cold War in Asia', in M. J. Lacey (ed.)

The Truman Presidency (Cambridge: Woodrow Wilson International Center for Scholars and Cambridge University Press, 1989) pp. 366–409.

7. B. Cumings, 'The Origins and Development of the Northeast Asian Political Economy: Industrial Sectors, Products Cycles, and Political Consequences', in F. C. Deyo (ed.), *The Political Economy of the New Asian Industrialism* (New York: Cornell University, 1987) p. 62. For a discussion of NSC 48, see H. Kinouchi, 'Reisen to Tonan Ajia', in T. Yano (ed.), *Tonan Ajia no Kokusai Kankei* (Tokyo: Kobundo, 1991) pp. 199ff.

8. For details, see J. Welfield, *An Empire in Eclipse: Japan in the Postwar American Alliance System* (London: Athlone Press, 1988).

9. For a discussion of the Soviet case, see K. Nagoshi, *Kuremulin Himitsu Bunsho wa Kataru* (Tokyo: Chūō Kōron, 1994). For the recently revealed US case, in which the details are more sketchy, see *Asahi Shimbun*, 10 October 1994, and *New York Times*, 8 October 1994.

10. *Asahi Shimbun*, 10 October 1994.

11. Cumings, 'The Origins and Development of the Northeast Asian Political Economy', p. 60.

12. For details on reparation payments, see S. Hasegawa, *Japanese Foreign Aid: Policy and Practice* (London: Praeger, 1975), chapter 4.

13. On the policy of separating politics and economics, see L. Newby, *Sino-Japanese Relations: China's Perspective* (London: Routledge, 1988).

14. A. Rix, *Japan's Economic Aid* (London: Croom Helm, 1980), p. 23.

15. D. T. Yasutomo, *The Manner of Giving: Strategic Aid and Japanese Foreign Policy* (Lexington, Mass: Lexington Books, 1986).

16. M. Ensign, *Doing Good or Doing Well?* (New York: Columbia University Press, 1992) p. 92.

17. Figures on Japanese aid are from the annuals of the Ministry of Foreign Affairs publications. See Gaimusho, *Wagakuni no Seifu Kaihatsu Enjo*, Kokusai Kyōryoku Kyoku.

18. On aid decision-making, see Rix, *Japan's Economic Aid*, Part 11. Also see Y. Murai (ed.), *Kenshō: Nippon ODA* (Tokyo: Gakuyo Shobo, 1992) pp. 6–15.

19. Korhonen, 'The Theory of the Flying Geese Pattern of Development and its Interpretation', p. 104.

20. Figures on Japanese investment are from the annuals of the Japan External Trade Organisation (JETRO). See *Jetro Hakusho. Tōshihen*.

21. On the textile wrangle, see I. M. Destler and H. Fukui, and H. Sato, *The Textile Wrangle: Conflict in Japanese–American Relations, 1969–71* (New York: Cornell University Press, 1979).

22. Figures from *Ekonomisto*, 5 July 1994, p. 32. ASEAN excludes Brunei and Singapore, the latter being included in the NICs figures.

23. Y. Watanabe, 'Nihon to Ajia: Seizōgyō no Higashi Ajia Hatten to Kokunai Kōgyō Kiban no Henka', *Mita Gakkai Zasshi*, 87, 2 (1994) 165. Similarly, automobiles became subject to VERs in the 1980s. See T. Itō, 'US Political Pressure and Economic Liberalization in

East Asia', in J. A. Frankel and M. Kahler (eds.) *Regionalism and Rivalry: Japan and the United States in Pacific Asia* (Chicago: University of Chicago Press, 1993) pp. 396ff.

24. Watanabe, 'Nihon to Ajia', 166.
25. *Asahi Shimbun*, 7 January 1993.
26. M. Bernard and J. Ravenhill, 'New Hierarchies in East Asia: The Post-Plaza Division of Labour', Working Paper 1992/3, Department of International Relations, Research School of Pacific Studies, The Australian National University, Canberra, p. 27.
27. *Asahi Shimbun*, 9 October 1994.
28. Moon Dae Woo, 'Nishi Taiheiyō Chiiki ni okeru Kōgyōka no Hakyu', *Ajia Kenkyū*, 40, 2 (1993) 14.
29. *Asahi Shimbun*, 20 September 1994.
30. For examples, see Murai, *Kenshō: Nippon ODA*, pp. 22–3.
31. In September 1994 the Fair Trade Commission launched a sweeping investigation into bid-rigging in Overseas Development Aid, targetting Mitsubishi, Mitsui, Itōchū, and Marubeni's tenders, especially for technical assistance projects in Southeast Asia. See *Nikkei Weekly*, 12 September 1994.
32. For details on the changes in Japanese defence policy at this time, see G. D. Hook, 'The Erosion of Anti militaristic Principles in Japan', *Journal of Peace Research*, 25, 4 (1988) 381–94.
33. Y. Muroyama, *Nichibei Anpo Taisei*, vol. 2 (Tokyo: Yūikaku, 1992), p. 518.
34. US Department of Defense, *A Strategic Framework for the Asian Pacific Rim: Looking toward the 21st Century* (Washington DC: Government Printing Office, 1990), p. 12.
35. *Daily Yomiuri*, 20 March 1990.
36. Department of Defense, *A Strategic Framework for the Asian Pacific Rim: Looking toward the 21st Century*, pp. 17–8.
37. Yomiuri Shimbun, 3 November 1994. For a critical discussion, see O. Watanabe, 'Shin. Shintō no Hatajirushi to naru "Yomiuri" Kaiken Shian', *Zenei*, January 1995, 78–94.
38. S. Islam, 'Foreign Aid and Burdensharing: Is Japan Free Riding to a Coprosperity Sphere in Pacific Asia?', in Frankel and Kahler (eds.), *Regionalism and Rivalry*, p. 363. Also see D.T. Yasutomo, *Japan and the Asian Development Bank* (New York: Praeger, 1983).
39. *Asahi Shimbun*, 25 August 1994.
40. For a discussion of the personalities involved, see Korhonen, *Japan and the Pacific Free Trade Area*.
41. *Nihon Keizai Shimbum*, 24 October 1992.
42. Ambassador H. Fujii, 'Japan's Foreign Policy Towards Asia', Chatham House, London, 15 June 1994.
43. In the post-Cold-War period, the US government support this forum, despite its Cold-War preference for dealing with security issues bilaterally. See *Nihon Keizai Shimbun* (evening edition), 21 May 1993.

44. On the conflict over the Spratly Islands, see M. G. Gallagher, 'China's Illusory Threat to the South China Sea', *International Security*, 19, 1 (1994) 169–94.
45. *Nihon Keizai Shimbun*, 10 May 1994.
46. *Asahi Shimbun*, 30 August 1994.
47. *Nihon Keizai Shimbun*, 8 February 1991. Also see *Nihon Keizai Shimbun*, 17 January 1993.
48. *Nihon Keizai Shimbun*, 6 November 1991.
49. Ibid., 17 January 1993.
50. A discussion of the Ozawa Report can be found in O. Nishi, 'Nihon no Kokusai Kōken o meguru Giron: Ozawa Chōsakai Hōkoku na do ni tuite', *Shin Bō ei Ronshū*, 20, 2 (1992) 68–81. Also see I. Ozawa, *Blueprint for a New Japan: the Rethinking of a Nation* (Tokyo: Kōdansha International, 1994). On the defence group's ideas, see S. Hayashi, 'Seiji Taikokuka no Anzenhosho Seisaku', *Hogaku Semina*, November 1994, 16–21.
51. For development of the idea of Japan as a 'middle power', see Y. Sakamoto, 'The Role of Japan in the International System', in Institute for European Studies, *The International System After the Collapse of the East-West Order* (Luxembourg: Institute for European and International Studies, 1993).

7   The NICs and Competing Strategies of East Asian Regionalism

NGAI-LING SUM

Geographically speaking, the East Asia region can be said to comprise four rather loose groupings with somewhat different positions in the new global economic order. Japan stands in a group of its own as a mature economy able to project regional and global economic power. The first tier of Newly Industrial-ising Countries (NICs) – South Korea, Taiwan, Hong Kong and Singapore – comprises successful economies with dynamic export sectors. The Association of Southeast Asian Nations (ASEAN) group comprises Singapore, Thailand, Malaysia, Indonesia, the Philippines and Brunei. The first of these ASEAN member states can be seen as a first-tier NIC, the next two as second-tier. Finally, there is a (post-)socialist grouping, comprising China, North Korea and the countries of Indochina, with China and Vietnam in particular having embarked on capitalist economic growth trajectories with some success. Indeed, China is in the paradoxical position of being hailed as likely to become the world's largest economy in the first decade of the next century at the same time as its *per capita* income remains comparatively very low. It is important to note that the NIC growth phenom-enon only achieved international recognition in the 1970s and was first constructed as an OECD category in 1979. In the main, their success stories can be explained in terms of the conjunc-tural articulation of global–local specificities which included US military protection, economic aid, spillover effects from the Vietnam War, growth of Western mass consumer markets as well as the capacities of the NICs to utilise these aid and economic opportunities in productive ways.[1] The result was the rise of a group of countries which adopted a growth strategy of export-oriented industrialisation from the 1960s onwards (Hong Kong from the 1950s). By the late 1970s, their success was marked by the export of labour-intensive manufacturing products as well as a total share of world trade that had risen from 2 per cent in the 1960s to 8.5 per cent in 1990.[2]

The rise of the NICs occurred in a region widely anticipated as economically predominant in the next century – the so-called 'Pacific Century'. Responding to this imagined future, regional and extra-regional powers are now busy developing strategies to secure geoeconomic and geopolitical advantages. For example, the Clinton administration has been substantially redefining its policies towards the region since 1993. Although it is relatively easy to identify the cartographic boundaries of East Asia, there is little consensus over its economic, political or security boundaries. In this sense East Asia is an 'imagined region'[3] and its imagined boundaries are actively contested by different power actors. In Chapter 6, Hook examined Japan's attempt to mobilise regional actors around its particular interpretation of 'East Asia' and to define the interests of the member states included therein *vis-à-vis* a wider 'Asia-Pacific' region in which Japan and the US are the major contenders for hegemony in the 1990s. But, however significant Japan might be as a regional and global player, its attempts to re-present and mobilise the region in line with its own 'imagined community of interests' are by no means unique. They are part of a far wider struggle encompassing many other actors all endeavouring to 'map' and 'identify' East Asia and formulate economic and security strategies on this basis. Thus this chapter cannot restrict itself to the still evolving Japanese and American strategies towards East Asia; it must also consider the emerging strategies of other, increasingly important, regional actors towards East Asian regionalism and the NICs' status and interests within it. Of particular significance in this regard are China and ASEAN. In short, if regional strategies constitute the leitmotiv of this chapter, it is precisely because they have a constitutive role in redefining (and not simply reflecting) the competing identities and interests of NICs.

Before considering how these identities are constructed, it

is important to clarify the position of ASEAN as a regional actor. Even if one concedes that all its member states are located in East Asia, only some of its members can be counted as NICs. But Singapore, Malaysia, and Thailand are important first- and second-tier NICs and ASEAN as an organisation is a major player in the struggle over the identities and interests of NICs in the region. Indeed, its promotion of strategies such as that of the ASEAN Free Trade Area is as relevant for NICs which are not members (notably Hong Kong, Taiwan, and South Korea) as for its own members; and this can can also be seen as a major intervention in the debate over regional blocs and policy conducted by Japan, China and extra-regional actors.

Methodologically, this chapter differs from other contributions to the present volume because its subject matter has developed in a distinctive manner. Unlike European and North American regional institutions and governance regimes, which have tended to emerge from 'big bang' conferences or treaties, East Asian arrangements have been evolving in a much more incremental manner.[4] One way to address this specificity is to locate the construction of East Asian regionalism and NIC identities in a structure–strategy–agency analytical scheme.[5] Structurally, the rise of the NICs in the 1970s occurred at the beginning of the end of the Cold War and the first phase of the post-Cold-War era. This period was marked by the growing significance of Japan and Germany as economic giants and by the largely unexpected demise of the Soviet bloc – processes that changed an essentially bipolar security game into one that is multipolar. The current and emerging East Asian regional leaders, Japan and China respectively, are now competing with the US for geopolitical and geoeconomic advantages in the Asia-Pacific region. The particular strategies adopted by these three global and/or regional players invoke a wide and often contradictory range of identities and interests to the NICs. This can be readily discerned in the plethora of geoeconomic and geopolitical signifiers deployed by outside forces to identify the NICs and interpret their interests: these include the new Cold War, the New World Order, trade liberalisation, economic integration, democratisation and nationalism. These contradictory discourses have become key points of struggle in the NICs themselves as various domestic forces seek to renegotiate their identities, redefine their interests, and reposition themselves on changing geoeconomic and geopolitical terrains. These struggles not only concern foreign economic and political issues such as regional blocs and strategies of concern to regional and extra-regional players, but also have major implications at home as the domestic forces are re-aligned. Depending on the relative strength and alignment of external and internal forces, one can expect different types of political and economic regimes to be consolidated in the NICs in the current period of structural reorganisation and strategic reorientation.

At the time of writing, it is hard to discern clearly-defined and coherent strategies being pursued by NICs in the region. Possibly the closest approximation to such a strategy is that of ASEAN and Malaysia and even this is evolving. The absence of clear strategies is probably due to the ongoing and incremental nature of East Asian regional bloc formation and the relative newness of the post-Cold-War era in which this process is occurring. It was not until the mid-1980s that regional and extra-regional powers began actively to redefine and restructure the region. For example, Japan first started to invest seriously in the region as the yen began to appreciate in 1986; and it was not until 1993 that the US administration (under Clinton) showed real interest in the Asia Pacific Economic Co-operation forum (APEC) initiated in 1989 by Australia and taken further in various steps by other regional economic and political players.[6] Given this still emerging interest and continued expansion of key players in the field of East Asian regionalism, it would be premature to identify a dominant NIC strategy for the region. Indeed, until there is a clear regional consensus on the identity of the East Asian NICs as economic, political and security subjects, there is little point in attributing strategic interests to these regimes which they might pursue individually or collectively. This is why the main focus of this chapter is on identity construction within and across different NICs.

Historical evolution of East Asian regionalism[7]

In the nineteenth century, when commercial capitalism was first introduced by the British and Dutch to China, India and other parts of Southeast Asia, there was no sense of East Asia as a distinct region. The area then became known loosely as the 'Orient' or the 'Far East' and was continually configured and reconfigured by different European/Asian powers. The discourse on 'Commonwealth' created a colonial identity that mapped parts of 'East Asia', such as Singapore and Hong Kong, into the British empire. With Europe's relative exhaustion from the First World War, Japan began actively challenging the Atlantic powers in East Asia. In pursuit of geopolitical and geoeconomic advantages, Japan redefined the region by constructing the identity of the 'Greater East Asia Co-prosperity Sphere'. This mapped other parts of Asia under the ideology of 'co-prosperity' to persuade them (forcibly if necessary) to accept a subordinate position in the Japanese empire. During the Second World War, this Japanese project briefly succeeded in covering the area previously comprising European colonies, stretching from Indochina to the Dutch East Indies to Malaya. Japan's defeat in the Pacific War was followed by the independence of most of these colonies.

The US came to East Asia after the Second World War hoping to replace the Europeans permanently and with the intention (at least until 1952) of 'remaking' Japan. It also tried to re-configure the region under its hegemony in terms of the Cold-War discourses of anti Communism and 'embedded liberalism'.[8] Together, these ideologies prompted 'threat-driven' strategies based on 'fear' of an imminent US–Soviet conflict and an emphasis on the need to establish free-trade regimes. From 1949 onwards, East Asia has been subject geopolitically to an intensely competitive pattern of great-power involvement. For it was in 1949 that the Cold War came to Asia following the Chinese Communists' defeat of the Chinese nationalists, who fled to Taiwan and became the chief ally of the US. The US took the lead in terminating Japanese occupation of the region but it also engineered a conciliatory peace treaty with Japan, which the Soviets and Chinese Communists refused to sign. By 1951, the American-sponsored San Francisco Peace Treaty was signed with Taiwan rather than the People's Republic of China (PRC) as the signatory for China and with the Soviet Union excluded. This treaty also made Japan an important security ally of the US in Asia. Japan's defeat had also re-opened the question of who should rule Korea, which had been a Japanese colony for most of the twentieth century. With the US involved in Japan and the Soviet Union more concerned about China, for the sake of convenience Korea was split along the 38th parallel. Whereas the Communist regime in the North received Soviet aid and Chinese assistance, the South was backed by the US and its allies. In 1950, the North–South conflict was bound to be seen in Cold-War terms and the US demonstrated its credibility as an ally by organising support under the cover of the United Nations. It was around this time that Indochina also came to be polarised around the Cold-War axis. In contrast to Korea, however, conflict in this region was based on nationalist struggles against the French colonial regime; in particular, when France was defeated in the struggle for independence, Vietnam was divided into a Communist North and an anti-Communist South. The North's ambition to unify Vietnam under Communism soon spilled over into Cambodia and Laos. With Soviet and Chinese support for the North and US intervention in the South, the conflict soon turned into the Cold War's bloodiest encounter.

From this brief history, it can be seen that the US, in pursuing containment of the Sino–Soviet alliance, adopted a multi-pronged bilateral strategy of entering into security pacts with Taiwan, Japan, South Korea and South Vietnam. These pacts were achieved without a formal alliance, however, involving all five partners. The formation of NATO in Europe and the French defeat in Indochina pointed to the need for a more formal alliance in Asia. US sponsorship of the Mutual Defense Treaty with the Philippines and the South-East Asian Treaty Organisation (SEATO)[9] and the Soviet proposal for an Asian Collective Security System conformed to this notion of formal regional alliances within a superpower sphere of influence. These Cold-War alliances both created and divided Asia as a security community. The US and the Soviet Union used instruments such as security protection and economic aid to initiate patron–client relations with regional actors. With all its obvious structural constraints rooted in Cold-War struggles and asymmetries of power, this strategic context influenced the calculation of regional actors and led to the internalisation of two distinct identities. Thus regional actors could either align themselves with the US or Soviet poles in the Cold War or adopt a 'neutral', non-aligned position.

The client identity was established through the US security chain in the form of SEATO and the security pacts. SEATO was primarily a public-relations organisation, especially over the issue of how much its member states should get involved in Indochina. By 1975 the lack of a common objective had led to its failure. As for the bilateral pacts between the US and its client states, the security umbrella provided the latter with: (a) substantial contributions to their huge defence budgets; (b) foreign aid through the World Bank, ESCAP and the Asian Development Bank; (c) expanding economic opportunities in the US market; and (d) demand for their products related to the US investment in the Vietnam War effort. Where these conditions could be combined with endogenous growth potential within the client states themselves, they were enabled to develop into regional NICs. South Korea and Taiwan are good examples of how these client states productively exploited opportunities. As for Hong Kong, which is still a British colony at the time of writing, the Anglo–American partnership provided indirect security guarantees through British membership of NATO. This obviated the need for more direct US economic, political or military involvement. As long as the Anglo-American partnership continued to nurture the region through Commonwealth preference and US market/expenditure, Hong Kong remained an indirect part of this security community.

Other regional actors found client identities less attractive. This is especially clear in the case of those countries which responded to this great-power rivalry by combining in 1967 to form ASEAN. In so doing they hoped to emphasise their non-aligned identity outside any security alliance – an emphasis best reflected in ASEAN's 1971 proposal for a Zone of Peace, Freedom and Neutrality. In this regard, the Cold-War regional order was marked by the contradictions between ASEAN's claim to 'autonomy' and the reality of great-power involvement. With the onset of the Vietnam War and the Communist insurgency,

ASEAN came together as an 'anti-Communist' group. In fact, the Cold-War order provided a security umbrella for the ASEAN states and contributed to their domestic stability and economic growth. As a member of ASEAN, Singapore came to adopt a semi-client identity under the US until the post-Cold-War era began to emerge.[10]

Competing strategies and the construction of NIC identities

The onset of the post-Cold-War period in East Asia has transformed the security situation into a multipolar game in which the dominant and still emerging regional leaders (Japan and China respectively) have joined the established extra-regional players (US and Russia) in the competition for geopolitical and/or geoeconomic advantages. The various strategies pursued by these 'core' global or regional players presuppose different, sometimes contradictory, sometimes consistent, accounts of the identities and interests of the 'periphery' of NICs. For example, the US strategy of 'securing' a low risk 'Asia-Pacific' region capable of promoting and sustaining a 'trade liberalisation' order requires the NICs to embrace a new Cold-War as well as a market-friendly identity. As for Japan, its idea of 'East Asia' can be co-ordinated and created through the construction of a 'flying geese' pattern.[11] This would privilege Japan as the industrial leader and create a follower identity for the NICs. China is also entering the struggle for geoeconomic and socio-cultural advantages by re-calling Hong Kong and Taiwan into its economic-cultural orbit. It refers to the idea of growth triangles by proposing 'Greater China' as a subregional economic zone. Concurrently, Singapore is engaged in the building of a 'growth triangle' identity based on itself, Johor (Malaysia) and Riau (Indonesia). This identity is increasingly contested by Malaysia on the grounds that it challenges the sovereignty of the Malaysian federal government. In general, the promotion of growth-triangle identities signifies a form of subregionalism that cross-cuts broader East Asian regionalism. Let us start our exploration of alternative identities, interests and regional strategies by examining the US proposals for new Cold-War and market-friendly identities.

US construction of East Asian regionalism and NIC identities

Even in the post-Cold-War era, the redefined security agenda of the US still retains traces of the Cold-War mentality. Thus, although the Soviet military threat is now seen as much reduced, the 'threat-driven' approach survives in the form of marked fears about the stability of China as an emerging power. But there has also been a shift from 'threat-driven' concepts of military deployment to a strategy of 'securing' a low risk 'Asia-Pacific' region capable of promoting and sustaining a 'trade liberalisation' order. This approach is evident in the recent US hijacking of APEC.

US security strategy and NIC identity

The shift in the US security agenda from a 'threat-driven' concept is seen in its military withdrawal from Southeast Asia. Following its defeat in the Cold War, Russia's military presence in Asia-Pacific has diminished substantially. Earlier Soviet security alliances with Vietnam and India are now defunct. Russia no longer has any significant power projection capability in the region and its security priorities now stress pacifying border conflicts and protecting Russian ethnics.[12] The thwarting of Soviet 'threats' in Asia, especially in the Southeast Asian straits, contributed to the US decision to withdraw from its Subic Bay and Clark Field bases in the Philippines in 1992. In the current era, the key challenges to the US concern its relation to Japan and China. Since Japan still lacks military capabilities and/or the will to threaten other countries' security, the US remains the prime strategic player in their regional partnership. In this regard their relations are basically co-operative despite the trade imbalance and economic frictions. From the perspective of the NICs, a US–Japan alliance with a US rather than a Japanese military presence in the region may confine the Japanese to the role of economic rather than military leader. However, China's role is more ambivalent and even ambiguous. During the Cold War, China was seen as a 'swing factor' in the tangled web of US–Soviet conflict. But this unique role has declined in the new global configurations of power. Instead, there are certain signs and tendencies in post-Tiananmen Chinese foreign policy that are susceptible to interpretation as regional 'risks'. In the imagery of a redefined Cold-War mindset, insurance against these 'risks' is needed even in the post-Cold-War era. These risks comprise: (a) the nationalist and assertive character of Chinese strategic culture; (b) the modernisation of China's air and naval power; (c) Sino–Russian military technology linkages; (d) the Beijing–Taipei 'mini-arms' race; (e) China's claim of a 'historical border' in the South China Sea; and (f) the promotion of China's diplomatic realignments with its major Asian neighbours. All these features need exploring.

First, the rhetoric of nationalism is still part of China's vision of its role in the world in the post-Cold-War era. This can be seen in its policies towards Hong Kong and Taiwan and its response towards US arms sales to Taiwan in 1992. It is perceived to be more assertive than Japan and tends to favour strategic independence in its actions, a stance which has been rendered credible by dynamic growth in collaboration with its neighbours.[13]

Second, and not unconnected to its growth record, China has been upgrading its air and naval power since the mid-1980s. From 1989 to 1992 Chinese military spending increased some 50 per cent. In 1990, with French assistance, it upgraded two Luda-class destroyers with air-defence missiles and search radars and between 1991 and 1992 it purchased from the Russian Republic 24 high-performance SU-27 jet fighters and three IL-76TD military transport planes. Russia has also considered helping China develop Yak-141 fighters capable of short take-off and vertical landing, has sold China aircraft carriers and, according to the Russian Foreign Ministry, has even considered transferring the manufacturing technology of the SU-27 to Beijing.[14]

Third, these developments can be interpreted as indicating the emergence of a more permanent and mutually beneficial Sino–Russian military technology partnership of great concern to the US and its partners – especially Japan, which might feel it necessary to build up its defence capabilities. For, whereas the Chinese military feels the need to move from the Chinese mass army to high-tech arms and equipment and has acquired increased influence within the regime after the Tiananmen débâcle, the shrinking of Russian military needs at the end of the Cold War and its underemployed defence industries make the Russian élites eager to sell weaponry abroad.[15]

Fourth, the modernisation and build-up of advanced weaponry in China is also of great concern to another US partner in the region – Taiwan. According to Lin, Beijing has never openly said that its military exercises represent a threat to Taiwan, but they have often coincided with its official denunciations of the Taiwanese independence movement and of Taipei's effort to expand its international presence. These operations have also occurred in areas close to Taiwan. Taiwan itself has made marked progress in its defence capability, emphasising improvement in quality over expansion in quantity. Such efforts continued and probably accelerated after the Tiananmen incident. The US has maintained arms sales to Taiwan; and Taipei itself has become increasingly active in its own development of armaments. This 'mini-arms race' in the post-Tiananmen period has heightened tensions in the region and this too may have a bearing upon US strategy *vis-à-vis* China.

Fifth, China has reiterated its claim to an 'historical border' which encompasses the entire South China Sea. This claim maps an area of more than 800 000 square kilometres within its 'traditional maritime boundaries' and this has been 'illegally' delineated into the domain of the other nations including the Philippines, Malaysia, Vietnam, Indonesia and Brunei. China has alleged that these countries, which border the Spratly Islands, have drilled more than 120 oil wells inside China's boundaries. This claim can be seen as a 'risk' to regional security, especially if it is coupled with China's military build-up in recent years.

Sixth, in response to Western outrage over Tiananmen, China has been actively promoting diplomatic realignments with its major Asian neighbours – Japan, Singapore, Vietnam, South Korea and India. The promotion of closer ties with Japan and ASEAN within the region not only boosts Chinese diplomatic capital but also strengthens its position as an emerging regional leader. There are signs that China is performing such a role in the Asianisation of regional security politics. In relation to North Korea, it appears that Beijing applied some pressure to induce North Korea to accept international inspections of its nuclear plants[16] and for the two Koreas to conclude their historic agreement on mutual non-aggression in December 1991. In relation to Cambodia, China helped to settle the 12-year civil war through collaborative brokering with the ASEAN nations and the United Nations.[17]

In this context, China's pursuit of strategic independence and search for an autonomous posture is provoking other powers, such as the US, to develop an 'insurance' strategy to reduce risk. Such a strategy is intended to be a warning to potential regional leaders such as China. It involves building a network of bilateral security arrangements with various contiguous or maritime neighbours, such as Hong Kong, Korea and Taiwan. Integrating these states through US geopolitical bilateralism creates a new form of Cold-War identity for the region. This is especially clear in two respects: first, the bilateral arrangements involve security surveillance without military bases[18] and, second, the 'co-operative engagement' involves not only past US allies (the UK, Taiwan and South Korea) but also Singapore, an ASEAN member state. This new regional identity is expressed in such key strategies as: (a) supporting democratisation in Hong Kong, (b) selling arms to Taiwan and supporting the independence/ democracy movement there, (c) co-operating with South Korea and normalising relations with North Korea, and (d) signing a memorandum of understanding with Singapore which provides for the deployment of American aircraft and military personnel in Singapore.

The US perception of 'risks' in this regard is linked with the way in which it regards democratisation in Hong Kong as the preferred future for the PRC. This was evidenced in two ways. First, US policy towards Hong Kong after China resumes sovereignty in 1997 reasserts the importance of continuity in government programmes and intergovernmental agreements which involve Hong Kong. Second, it takes seriously Hong Kong's fears for itself about the implications of the US–China policy. This was apparent in Clinton's reception of Governor Chris Patten in April 1993. Shortly after arriving as Britain's representative in Hong Kong in September 1992, Patten introduced a 'democratisation' programme in his first Legislative Council speech. This aimed to restructure the state–society relation in Hong Kong and provoked strong critical reactions from the PRC. In his search for international support, he was enthusiastically backed by Clinton and the US government. Their concerted action contrived a 'democratisation' drama in Hong Kong between 1992 and 1994. They managed to conduct a low-intensity discursive 'war' (termed 'the war of words' by local journalists) against China. Strategically, if Hong Kong can be sustained as a democratic hub after 1997, it may become a political lever that can contribute to the growth of a centrifugal subregionalism in China. This tendency for subregionalism is also inherent in the establishment of a Special Economic Zone in Guangdong. Guangdong is seen as being a relatively powerful centrifugal force because of its high growth rate, which has been twice the national average.[19] The maintenance of Hong Kong as a democratic hub within a tendentially centrifugal Guangdong may thus weaken and induce caution in China.

Parallel to this Anglo–American bilateralism is the mainte-nance-renewal of the US–Taiwan alliance in order to induce still greater caution on the part of China. This is seen in continued US arms provision to Taiwan. For instance, in July 1992 President George Bush approved the lease of three Knox-class anti-submarine frigates to Taiwan for five years. Later, in the heat of the presidential campaign, he approved the sale of 150 F-16 aircraft to Taiwan.[20] In addition, US Congressmen and organisations of Taiwanese lobbyists based in the US continued to support the independence movement in Taiwan. In March 1992 Senators Pell, Kennedy and Lieberman introduced a resolution in the US Senate to the effect that the authorities in Taiwan should permit the return of all current and former citizens who are committed to 'peaceful' change and that Taiwan's future should be left to its own people to determine. Likewise, one of the Taiwanese-based organisations in the US, the Formosan Association for Public Affairs, which has close associations with the pro-independence Democratic Progressive Party, stepped up its lobbying activities in the US Congress. The maintenance of US–Taiwan bilateralism through arms sales and support for the independence movement may thus constitute part of the US 'insurance' strategy of reducing risks as well as indicating to an autonomous regional power such as China that the pursuit of strategic independence outside the US framework may not be beneficial to its long-term goals.

For South Korea (ROK), the maintenance of the US forces is not only critical to the security of Northeast Asia; it is also pertinent to the US 'insurance' strategy against China. From the later 1980s, the ROK–US relationship has been more co-operative in terms of financial burden-sharing and developing and producing advanced weapon systems. In spring 1993, joint ROK–US military training exercises were renewed. The US 'insurance' strategy regarding North Korea involves the use of surveillance and pressure over the latter's nuclear capacities to draw it into dialogue in the hope of normalising diplomatic relations. The US is also trying to prise North Korea out of its international isolation and to reduce Chinese influence by lowering trade and investment barriers. After all, a 'united' Korea under the influence of the US is preferred to a nuclear-prone North Korea supported by China.

The removal of US security bases from the Philippines has given rise to the 'power vacuum' theory espoused by Singapore. Responding to the Philippine call for greater 'burden-sharing' within ASEAN to ensure continued forward deployment of US forces, Singapore and the US signed a memorandum of understanding in November 1990 which provided for the deployment of American aircraft and military personnel in Singapore. During President Bush's visit to Singapore in January 1992, the two countries reached agreement on the relocation of a major naval logistics facility from Subic Bay to Singapore. The facility, the 'Command Task Force 73', consists of about 200 personnel and would be responsible for port calls and the resupply of US navy ships, as well as co-ordinating warship deployments in the Pacific region. Apart from the bilateral arrangements between the US and Singapore, there are also two recent tendencies within ASEAN that may be of some importance to the renegotiation of identities of some NICs, especially those within ASEAN.

While the US is constructing a new Cold-War identity through bilateralism, ASEAN members are busily renegotiating their own security identities in the direction of a more East Asian-led security forum based on multipolarity. The ASEAN nations have shown themselves willing to discuss security issues with outside 'dialogue partners' in the ASEAN Post-Ministerial Conference (PMC) and ASEAN Regional Forum (ARF) contexts.[21] In 1994, the ASEAN PMC led the decision to launch ARF by inviting 18 foreign ministers from ASEAN and their 'dialogue partners' – the US, the European Union, Japan, Australia, New Zealand, Canada and South Korea – as well their former adversaries such as Russia, China, Vietnam and Laos. It is a forum for discussing regional security issues and for potential antagonists to consult in a peaceful atmosphere. This may nurture an East Asian-led multipolarity as well as an arena in which to develop a new consultative strategy. Apart from ASEAN, South Korea has spoken in favour of a Northeast Asian security forum. In the academic sector, the Council for Security and Co-operation in the Asia-Pacific (CSCAP) was established in 1993 to provide a non-governmental dialogue and give direction and research support for ARF in the manner that PECC used to function for APEC by sponsoring seminars and reports.

In short, as this account of regional security illustrates, the US is attempting to revamp the Cold-War regional identity through its cultivation of bilateral links with the NICs. This strategy is complicated by ASEAN's attempt to create a new, more consultative self-identity through its 'preventive diplomacy'. The ARF and CSCAP have turned ASEAN into a player in the regional security network by creating opportunities to enter 'dialogue with the adversaries'. In this regard, one can argue that ASEAN is seeking to serve as regional security balancer or mediator. It has gained some support from Japan, though the positions of the NICs are still unclear.

US-sponsored APEC and NIC identity

On the economic front and in reaction to the seeming forma-tion of a 'Fortress Europe', the US geoeconomic strategy is to map Asia together with other countries in the Pacific and identify them as the 'Asia-Pacific' region. For the US, APEC shows the way. Now under close US sponsorship, APEC is committed to promoting market-friendly identities and trade-liberalisation interests in the NICs. At the November 1993 inaugural summit held in Seattle with President Bill Clinton in the chair, the leaders adopted most of the ideas of the APEC Eminent Persons Group (EPG) which recommended that priority be given to achieving free trade in Asia and advancing global trade liberalisation. Various options are under consideration: the EPG has recommended the date of 2020 to be reached by a form of 'variable geometry' under which developed countries (the US and Japan) would proceed faster towards free trade than less-industrialised countries such as Indonesia and China. The emphasis is thus on keeping collaborative agreements open to all – 'open market-led regionalism' in APEC parlance.

The formation and evolution of APEC needs to be understood against the backdrop of the post-war liberal international economic regime and its active promotion through the General Agreement on Tariffs and Trade (GATT). At least in theory, GATT members agreed to treat each other equally and reduce barriers to trade. The tariff concessions were linked to non-discrimination through the principle of most-favoured nation (MFN) treatment.[22] As is well-known, the system reached a critical juncture in the 1970s and there was a slowdown in the dismantling of trade barriers. Contracting parties in the West tried to protect their own domestic industries by weakening the competitive pressures from high-growth economies such as Japan and the NICs with their large trade surpluses with the US.[23] However, in order to avoid confronting the GATT and the international community as a whole, the protection sought by the US and western European countries tended towards bilateral solutions such as the imposition of national regulations and safety standards. These have increased since the 1970s. Relevant measures include 'Voluntary Export Restraints', 'Orderly Marketing Arrangements', 'Anti-dumping Provisions', the US 'Super 301' (unfair trade law) and abolition of the Generalised System of Preferences (GSP) status. From the US viewpoint, these measures served a dual purpose since they restrained imports from Japan and the NICs and served as bargaining chips in the attempt to open these markets.

The shift of US trade strategy from multilateralism to bilateralism – which has even amounted at times to unilateral action – illustrates the resort to more aggressive means in pursuit of protecting national markets and opening the Japanese and NIC markets for trade and investment under the banner of trade liberalisation.[24] This strategy has in effect invited Japan and the NICs to reposition themselves in the trade order. In reaction to US protectionism and the rising yen value, Japan has stepped up its trade and investment in the NICs. This has spurred growth in intra-regional trade and investment fuelled by technological synergy and currency realignments. As for the NICs in general, they have reacted by 'moving upmarket' and producing more expensive products, exporting their labour-intensive industries to neighbouring low-cost countries and exporting capital to other parts of the world. Such Japanese and NIC reactions have, to some extent, forestalled the US (neo-)protectionist strategy for correcting its trade imbalances and domestic unemployment. Up to the time of writing, US officials still argue that they are pursuing a three-pronged strategy – multilateralism under GATT, the network of bilateral relationships and 'open market-led regionalism' under APEC.

Getting involved with APEC certainly represents a new US strategy for projecting itself into 'Asia-Pacific'. To a certain extent, it serves mainly as a tool for prising open fast-growing Asian markets and for pressing Europe into further trade concessions. The Clinton administration openly endorses the APEC project and actively redefines it as an arena for trade liberalisation. It envisages its own future as 'docking on' to APEC by strengthening trans-Pacific links as NAFTA is extended. In this regard, an APEC-based liberalisation is seen as likely to sustain outward-looking US interests. This 'Asia-Pacific' con-struction is often conceptualised by academics as 'open (market-led) regionalism'.[25] In other words, it is a co-operative enterprise of national governments and its primary concerns are intra-regional trade liberalisation and support for the World Trade Organisation (WTO). But, unlike the European Community, APEC has economic rather than political objectives: it desires neither political nor monetary union and it is most emphatically and deliberately non-discriminatory towards outsiders. This essentially means an 'Asia-Pacific' free trade area with non-conditional MFN treatment accorded to non-member countries.

Despite the promotion of this market-friendly identity for APEC members with its implied interests in trade-liberalisation, the East Asian NICs and ASEAN have not fully embraced this definition of their place in the world. Although there is a broad consensus on market-friendliness, the case for trade liberalisation is more controversial. In Hong Kong and Singapore, which are already free ports, a well-entrenched alliance of international and domestic capital is able to secure a firm basis of support for their role as trade liberalisation enclaves. As for Taiwan and South Korea, they experience stronger domestic resistance to any opening of their domestic markets, especially in the automobile industry and financial sector. It was not until July 1994, for example, that the South Korean government announced some 50 sectors of the economy would be opened to FDI and even these were limited to activities such as sand quarrying and poultry slaughter.[26] In addition to these diverse attitudes, there is, however, a more general mistrust of APEC. This stems from the association of APEC with GATT. The fear is that APEC would follow in the footsteps of GATT and show the same inconsistency between a 'free trade' philosophy and protectionist and neo-mercantilist practices on the part of its Western members. There is also an apprehension that the US might use APEC as a club to force the NICs and the ASEAN countries to make more trade concessions under a new institutional setup and discursive guise. Given this aura of suspicion, APEC is seen as an attempt to institutionalise bilateralism/unilateralism, and, at its extreme, as a scheme to re-subordinate 'Asia-Pacific' to US hegemony rather than generalise prosperity.[27]

In response to this construction, ASEAN and Malaysia are proposing alternative identities and interests for themselves in the face of the 'open market-led regionalism' favoured by APEC. Up to the time of writing, two new subregional identities have emerged with one related to ASEAN and the other promulgated by the Malaysian prime minister. First, ASEAN has developed an identity parallel to that of APEC but with a stronger subregional focus. In 1992, it created the idea of its own free-trade area which covers all manufactured goods, including capital goods and processed agricultural products. The lowering of tariffs was to have been implemented over the next 15 years. However, in the ASEAN economic ministers' meeting in Chiang Mai in September 1994, the implementation period was shortened to ten years and tariffs were to be cut from 20 per cent to 0–5 per cent by 2003. In spite of the criticism that the volume of demand in the regional market is small, ASEAN aspires to create a common market for 340 million people. If ASEAN expands to include the Indochinese countries, the potential of the free-trade area will increase further. The construction of an intra-ASEAN free-trade identity may well also signal to Japan that it has the potential to be a leading partner in the region.

Second, Malaysia has promoted a counter-identity to the market-friendly image favoured by APEC. Its prime minister, Mohamed Mahathir, openly called for the establishment of an East Asian Economic Group (since accommodated in 1990 as a caucus within APEC (EAEC)) which grouped together ASEAN and Northeast Asian countries, including Japan and China, but excluded the US, Canada and Australia. He conceives of the caucus as a form of 'closed regionalism', i.e., an exclusive intra-Asian economic bloc that would counteract the EU and NAFTA. This construction can be seen as a symbol of resistance to 'outside' pressure to speed up the pace of trade liberalisation in the region as well as the harbinger of a possible yen bloc.[28] It has resulted in a Malaysia-initiated confrontation with the US and involves an open offer to Japan of a 'leadership' role in the EAEC. This confrontation has highlighted a growing dilemma facing the Japanese government and the NICs. For they are seemingly caught up in the struggle over an Asian or an American partnership, with all that this implies for their preferred self-identity. Certainly, on geopolitical grounds, the NICs are engaged in bilateral relations with the US, and, on geoeconomic grounds, they are involved in the APEC framework of 'open regionalism'. The creation of an Asian identity under EAEC offers a new imaginary alternative with which the NICs must now wrestle. At the time of writing, it is premature to conclude that the NICs are ready for an Asian identity. They still prefer to assert that an East Asian-led EAEC needs to operate under APEC's auspices.

Japan's construction of East Asian regionalism and NIC identity

At the same time as the US has been trying to redefine the identity of 'Asia-Pacific' in an APEC framework, Japan has been co-ordinating and reconstructing the region to enhance its own geoeconomic advantages. This has occurred against a backdrop of intensifying US moves to correct trade and employment problems, in particular by forcing the appreciation of the yen relative to the dollar under the Plaza Accord in 1985.[29] Saddled with uncompetitive prices in export markets, rising domestic labour costs, and fearing greater protectionism in US and European markets, Japan has in turn tried to co-ordinate and redefine the complementarities of the East Asian region on discursive and material levels through the 'flying geese' construction.

On the discursive level, this particular model of development has attained some popularity in the region. Given the diverse stages of economic development achieved, the growth model is compared to the delta-shaped formation of 'flying geese'. It represents Japan as the spearhead of the flock, the four first-tier NICs as following close behind, and the six ASEAN economies as next to have taken off. The post-socialist bloc is expected to join the flight at a later date. This 'flying geese' metaphor represents the NICs's growth trajectory in terms of a movement from traditional to modernised economic orders, with Japan as the pioneer and exemplar of the developmental pattern. This developmental trajectory envisages the late-comers replicating the experience of the countries ahead of them in the formation. Thus Japan guides the 'flock of geese' in its techno-economic 'flight to success' but each member of the flock follows under its own independent flight power, albeit via the staging points of Japan. This construction assigns a follower identity to the NICs but is more palatable than the earlier 'Greater East Asian Co-prosperity Sphere' with its stress on imperative co-ordination.

On the material level, the 'flying geese' interpretation fails to capture the complexities of technological change and how technology is actually transferred. Instead of a simple process of replication and convergence with Japanese economic structures, technological diffusion in East Asia has been partial, varies from country to country, and has remained linked throughout to a 'supply architecture' built around on-going Japanese innovation in components, machinery and materials.[30] In this sense, East Asia is increasingly dominated by the regionalisation of industrial production co-ordinated by Japan through increasing investment and trade ties with the NICs and ASEAN countries. In the period 1985 to 1993, some US$41 billion worth of Japanese

FDI found its way to the 'East Asian' economies. Unlike FDI in Europe and the US, it is largely focused on the manufacturing sector rather than services. In the NICs, according to a survey by the Toyo Keizai Shimposha, manufacturing investments amounted to 50.4 per cent of the total cases of FDI. For the EU and North America, the figures were 21.2 and 30.2 per cent respectively. Typically, FDI in the NICs tends to foster a distinct regional division of labour which is simultaneously giving rise to a new division of knowledge. None of this is consistent with the 'flying geese' model of simple, guided, but still autonomous replication.

Originally Japanese FDI was largely concentrated in Northeast Asia. Since 1986, there has been a spatial expansion of the regional production network from Northeast Asia to the NICs and ASEAN. This has been largely due to currency realignments, the threat of protection in the US and western Europe and the restructuring of the Japanese economy from an export-led to a domestic demand-oriented type of growth. The growth of Japanese FDI in the region contributes to the emergence of trade triangles in East Asia. While Japanese companies concentrate on improving foreign technology through indigenous R&D, South Korean and Taiwanese companies in similar export industries have relied on Original Equipment Manufacturing (OEM).[31] South Korea and Taiwan have high-level manufacturing bases for producing textiles and electronics components. Conversely, simple consumer electronics such as TV games and electronic watches are produced in Malaysia, China and Thailand. There is an increasing tendency for Japanese FDI to move into the service sectors of Hong Kong and Singapore. In Hong Kong, Japanese FDI has mainly gone into finance, commerce, telecommunication and technical support services – in part to take advantage of Hong Kong's ready access to, and plentiful knowledge of, China as a cheap production site. Conversely, Singapore has come to act as regional headquarters of Japanese multinationals (for example, SONY) as well as providing offshore markets for financing and hedging their FDI in the region. These patterns suggest how Japanese FDI has given rise to a new regional division of knowledge in which Japan is a base for high-tech and R&D; South Korea and Taiwan manufacture sophisticated components; Hong Kong and Singapore are important for producer services and finance; and other ASEAN countries engage in low-wage production.[32]

This new division of knowledge is co-ordinated in regional centres (such as Hong Kong and Singapore) that link production, distribution, settlement and finance. These regional centres are mediated by networks which possess the capacities to serve not only as manufacturing and distribution bases but also as suppliers of R&D and finance.[33] As well as co-ordinating intra-company logistics, they also link the regional and international flow of raw materials and inventories by providing business logistics (for example, land transportation, warehousing, marine transportation). It is through such co-ordinating services that finished goods can be delivered just-in-time and just-in-place from source to end-users in and beyond the region. In this regard, Japanese FDI in the NICs and ASEAN is not only cost-reducing but trade-enhancing. It creates regional and regional–global networks that serve to enhance the regional dependence on supply of Japanese components and machinery. Even with the relocation of final assembly in Southeast Asia, there is no demise of the domestic consumer industry in Japan nor the replication of Japan's industrial trajectory in the NICs as predicted in the 'flying geese' pattern. Furthermore, contrary to some more sophisticated versions of the 'flying geese' model, 'reverse exporting' from the NICs to Japan has largely failed to occur. Japan runs a trade surplus with each NIC and this occurs in part because Japanese subsidiaries in the NICs rely more heavily on imported machinery and components from their home country. More generally, the NICs import advanced intermediate components from Japan and assemble them as capital- and technology-intensive goods to be exported to the US and western Europe. In this sense, Japan co-ordinates a production network that links firms engaging in production, exchange and distribution in the region. Instead of the emergence of 'reverse exporting', Japan co-ordinates production and trade triangles in the region for exports to the US and western Europe.[34]

All of this suggests that the intra-regional development implied in the 'flying geese' analogy has largely failed to occur on two grounds: (a) the technological trajectories of the NICs are not linear replications of Japanese experience; and (b) rather than following Japan under their own flight power, the followers are dependent on regional flows organised under the leadership of Japan. At first sight, the regionalisation of production seems to have given rise to a complementary and synergistic intra-regional relationship between Japan and the NICs. The former concentrates on high-tech and R&D; the latter specialise in higher-valued OEM production to be exported to other regions. However, this intra-regional relationship/arrangement is more complex in so far as it is marked by competition as well as complementarity. For, while the NICs are being assigned a follower identity, their relation with Japan is actually far more complex. In conjunction with the dialectic of competition and complementarity, there is the emergence of a 'leapfrogging' identity from within the NICs, especially in South Korea. For the South Koreans, the historical legacy of oppression at the hands of Japanese imperialism is a crucial ingredient in this identity formation, though it is of a less intense nature among other NICs. However, the will to 'leapfrog' through innovation coexists with the dependency relationship with Japan in the form of regionalisation of production. Essentially, the Japan-NIC relation is characterised by a dialectic of 'leapfrogging' and dependency.[35] This dual dialectic is inherent in the development process of the region. In recent years, the typical pattern of technological development in South Korea and Taiwan has been somewhat more advanced in research capabilities than that occurring in Singapore and Hong Kong.[36] There are some well-known 'leapfrogging' cases and some firms are able to compete with their Japanese counterparts. These firms include prominent NIC multinationals in both manufacturing and service industries (for example, Hyundai, Goldstar and Samsung (South Korea), Singapore Airlines, Hong Kong Bank and Acer Computer (Taiwan)). In the electronics industry, for example, Samsung was able to produce the advanced 16-megabit memory chip to compete with advanced Japanese chips on the global market. Likewise, in the service sector, Singapore Airlines and Hong Kong Bank are also strong competitors of their Japanese counterparts in the service industries.

However, these examples are best treated as exceptions rather than the rule. Developing the capabilities to acquire and operate foreign technology does not necessarily lead, in each country, to an ability to adapt, innovate or even 'leapfrog'. The ability to foster such activities depends on various other factors, including accumulated technical expertise, a high-quality communications infrastructure and good levels of general and technological education. In this regard most firms in the NICs are dependent on their Japanese counterparts. A study of Singapore's electronics industry shows that local firms pursued a long-term, painstaking, incremental learning path rather than leaping from one vintage of technology to another. Their development involved a 'hard slog' rather than a 'leapfrog'.[37] Many of their technological advances in the electronics industry were in 'pre-electronic' fields, such as machine tooling, plastic moulding, and mechanical and precision engineering. This suggests that firms progressed incrementally in response to market growth and were heavily dependent on international suppliers and overseas experts for advanced technology. As labour costs increased, firms relocated more mature products to other parts of the region. Thus one firm opened a factory in Batam in Indonesia for labour-intensive operations and then introduced new products to the main plant. Similar cases can be found in Taiwan and Hong Kong as firms have relocated labour-intensive processes to southern China. The process enables the NICs to produce higher-value products and/or services consistent with the regionalisation of production.

With the relocation of labour-intensive processes overseas, the NICs, especially Singapore and Hong Kong, can be seen as cases of peripheral intermediation.[38] Thus, to use Wallersteinian terminology, it is more appropriate to see them as a part of a 'semi-periphery' than as belonging to the periphery. In other words, they serve as intermediaries between the 'periphery' (other ASEAN economies and the post-socialist countries) and the 'centre(s)' (Japan, the US, and the core European economies such as Germany). Such global–regional arrangements position the NICs as followers on a global rather than purely regional scale – an identity which no more goes unchallenged by new and emerging social forces within the NICs than the more localised 'flying geese' pattern. These forces may configure themselves into new social and political alignments to spearhead new strategies oriented to 'leapfrogging' possibilities. However, although there are some successful sectoral cases, one cannot ignore the current structurally-inscribed powers of Japanese capital to shape the region and to maintain certain dependent relations among actors. In this regard, one can argue that there is a dialectic at work in this aspect of 'East Asian' regionalism which is characterised by the complex articulation between uneven and combined technological development and asymmetrical complementarities among different sectors and economies. In this sense, the NIC identity is characterised by the dual consciousness of 'follower' and 'leapfrogging' images.

China's construction of East Asian subregionalism and NIC identity

In opposition to the US and Japanese projects, China has developed its own categories to inscribe certain NICs into the orbit of an East Asian subregionalism in which it can play a leading role. As an emerging regional leader, China has entered into the struggle for geoeconomic and/or socio-cultural advantages by creating the concept of 'Greater China' (or the 'China Circle'). This represents an attempt to co-ordinate and redefine the internal complementarities of evolving subregional arrangements. In particular, it maps China, especially southern China, Taiwan and Hong Kong–Macau, as a viable growth triangle and thereby assigns to these NICs an economic and nationalist identity. This imagined subregion of 'Greater China' was rendered ever more plausible from 1978 onwards as China created special economic zones and opened its coastal cities. In these zones, preferential treatments have been provided in the form of reductions in profit taxation, less restrictive foreign exchange controls and tax exemptions on the import and export of raw materials and products. Moreover, the general economic environment in these zones has been made more favourable as more economic autonomy has been granted and better infrastructure built. China first opened its manufacturing sectors but other sectors, such as finance and property, have followed more recently.

In response to this new 'open-door' policy, the rise of Western protectionism and an increase in its own domestic costs for land and labour, Hong Kong's Chinese FDI has grown rapidly.

Thus it is now by far the biggest investor in China, accounting for 60 per cent of that country's FDI. Southern China is now a major production base for its more labour-intensive products. It is estimated that almost 20 000 Hong Kong manufacturing enterprises, mostly in textiles and clothing, toys and consumer electronics, have moved to this region. Together, they employ about three million workers. Hong Kong has also diversified into sectors such as tourism and real estate. Unlike Hong Kong, the Taiwanese government in the early 1980s saw few advantages and many serious risks in trade between Taiwan and the mainland. However, the opening of China made the Chinese market increasingly attractive to Taiwanese businesses. Some urged the government to cease restrictions on trade and expressed concern that they were losing out in the rapidly growing China market to their Japanese and South Korean competitors. The Taiwanese government conceded to growing popular pressure by allowing indirect links with China, beginning with the decision in November 1987 that Taiwanese citizens would be allowed to 'visit relatives' in China. The legalisation of travel in turn sharply accelerated the growth in trade between them. In 1988, the Chinese State Council promulgated a set of 22 measures to encourage investment from Taiwan. The resulting broad trend is thus towards growing material interdependence among Hong Kong, Taiwan and China.

This interdependence is reflected in the crystallisation of a subregional division of knowledge, as well as labour, between Hong Kong, Taiwan, and Guangdong and Fujian in China. Hong Kong and Taiwan are moving up the industrial technology ladder by shifting their labour-intensive industries to low-wage regions in southern China.[39] This change has involved economic cooperation across the Formosa Strait as well as in the Pearl River Delta. Without any direct link between Taiwan and China, most of the flow of people and money targeted on Fujian province has passed through Hong Kong. The cross-Strait area has been subordinated to developments in the Pearl River Delta within the 'Greater China' bloc. This delta area (the Hong Kong–Shenzhen–Guangzhou triangle) has been fashioned by the Chinese government as an 'open district' to pioneer many innovations (for example, outprocessing and stock trading). Shenzhen offers Hong Kong/Taiwan entrepreneurs land, cheap labour and a market for labour-intensive manufactures drawn from overseas Chinese family capital. As a result of the shift of the labour-intensive processes to the Pearl River Delta, Hong Kong engages in what I term 'subcontracting management' in order to co-ordinate the subregion.

Subcontracting management involves sourcing, production, authority and distribution management. First, Hong Kong/ Taiwan producers seek Chinese partners through formal and informal contacts. On establishing contacts, they enter into agreements with private/state-owned factories in China. This may consolidate into more long-lasting ties such as joint ventures and strategic alliances. The sourcing and consolidation of such alliances need to draw on more complex services related to business consultancy, legal services on production-sharing contracts and licensing, accounting expertise on mergers, takeovers, and franchising in Hong Kong. After establishing sourcing networks, the Hong Kong/Taiwanese firms then engage in cross-border production management. Essential to this is the building and maintenance of good relations with local and/or central officials in China. This kind of institutionalised networking with state officials is important because state authorities still control enormous resources such as land, labour, capital and regulations. In addition to production and authority management in a multi-spatial production process, business services are needed for distribution management. Finished goods need to be exported and distributed to overseas markets to meet consumer demand. This involves the management of a multi-spatial export process of import/export licensing, customs liaison and arranging shipments so that goods can be delivered just-in-time and just-in-place for overseas buyers. Again, this involves a network of service-based firms in Hong Kong and China as well as the trading and customs authorities in China and elsewhere. In essence, this cross-border private-public network can be, in the ideal case, cemented by the three Ts: time, trust and truth. Certainly, it is through the production and reproduction of this strategic network that Hong Kong is crystallising its position as a gateway region[40] in providing business and financial services and Taiwan its position as the source of investment and technology.

In addition, China-affiliated companies, which are wholly or partially owned by the central, provincial and municipal/local authorities, have been established in Hong Kong. In 1991, it was estimated that China's investment in Hong Kong had reached US$10 billion. Investment has diversified from production to commerce, finance and real estate. One estimate of China International Trust and Investment Corporation, which is a multinational under the direct supervision of the State Council, amounted to an investment portfolio in Hong Kong worth over HK$34 million. In recent years, China-affiliated companies, through the services provided in Hong Kong, have become active in local and international equity markets. They are particularly active in stock-market fund-raising activities. Between 1982 and 1988 China launched a total of 39 bond issues on the international market through the financial services provided in Hong Kong. China re-entered the bond market in 1991 in increasing volume after the Tiananmen incident. In addition to bond issues, China also raises its investment funds through the sale of equities to foreigners on both domestic and international markets. In October 1992, the Chinese Securities Regulatory Commission approved the listing of nine China-affiliated companies on the Hong Kong Stock Exchange (the so-called H shares). A second batch of 22 companies have been approved for listing on foreign markets in 1994. Most are expected to be listed on the Hong Kong market and some in New York and London.[41]

These developments on the material level are reinforced by an imagined identity of 'Greater China' on the discursive level. There is an increasing amount of literature using 'Greater China' to summarise the vibrancy of economic interactions in the economically, culturally, and linguistically compatible area of Taiwan, Hong Kong, Macau and the mainland Guangdong and Fujian provinces. Most such literature forecasts an optimistic future for economic growth in this region.[42] Ethnic Chinese business people and interested Chinese intellectuals envision a 'Greater China' of a much larger territorial scope and maintain that the formation of an economic 'Greater China' of sorts is the first step towards national reunification. This form of 'pragmatic nationalism'[43] is used to redefine and co-ordinate the internal complementarity of the region in relation to China and its competitiveness in the changing global economy.

According to China, Hong Kong can be defined as a strategic gateway for Beijing to implement its policies to attract *huaqiao* (patriotic) investments into the Chinese 'motherland'. Thus the construction of identity of 'patriotic ethnic Chinese investors' links nationalism with economics rather than politics in this guise of 'pragmatic nationalism'. This discursive construction enables China to acquire Taiwanese and Hong Kong investment/ technology without having to engage directly in the thorny problem of the relation between nationalism and politics, at least in the short term. As for Taiwan, the new economic relation with China is redefined under the rubrics of 'flexible diplomacy' and 'economic reunification' in the 1990s. These enable Taiwan to join major international/regional organisations (for example, the Olympics and the Asian Development Bank) under the name of 'Chinese Taipei' and also to orchestrate unofficial contacts between Taipei and Beijing.

Nevertheless, these redefinitions of economic relationships in 'Greater China' have assigned an economic-nationalist identity to the subregion. Different agents have reacted diversely to this particular geopolitical and geoeconomic intersection. I noted above how US strategy has shifted towards an 'insurance' concept of risk reduction by building a network of bilateral alliances with Britain (Hong Kong), Taiwan, Singapore and Korea that warn China against taking precipitate action. These bilateral partnerships strengthened Britain's claim for 'democratisation' in Hong Kong as well as the Democratic Progressive Party's claim in Taiwan. This Anglo-American geopolitical strategy, as indicated earlier, is complicated by geoeconomic developments rooted in the economic dynamism of a regional bloc and discursively reinforced by an imagined identity of 'Greater China'. In this context Hong Kong is defined not so much in terms of its role as a bastion of Western democracy as its role as a strategic gateway for Beijing and Taiwan in pursuit of the policies to attract *huaqiao* investments to the 'motherland'. This geopolitical/geoeconomic intersection clearly confronts social forces, whether located within or outside this economic network, with crucial dilemmas as to what interests to pursue and how to act.

The dilemmas can be understood in terms of two sets of competing discursive formations rooted in two different imagined

identities. Thus, whereas the new Cold-War identity is reinforced
by the discourse on 'democratisation', the nationalist-economic
identity is being promoted by the rhetoric of 'pragmatic nationalism'. These contrasting discourses have prompted highly
politicised ideological struggles in the 'Greater China' bloc over
what should become the dominant identity around which this
subregion should be socially integrated. In Hong Kong, such
struggles are expressed in the opposition between Patten's
'democratisation' measures and China's 'pragmatic nationalist'
vision of the colony's future. Thus, whereas Patten treats citizen
participation as the axis around which the struggle over Hong
Kong's future is to be waged, China stresses the national unity
of the 'Chinese in China' and the pragmatic consolidation of
Hong Kong's gateway role. Likewise, in Taiwan, we find these
struggles expressed in terms of the state-sponsored project of
'reunification (with China)' and the counter-project of
'independence (from China)' favoured by the opposition Democratic Progressive Party, which is dominated by native Taiwanese.[44] In both cases, then, we find that the new Cold-War identity
of 'democratisation' is contested by subregional identities based
on the newly invented bondings of 'Greater China'. Something
similar is occurring in Singapore. Its government is activating
the Confucian heritage to promote its trade and investment
linkages with China through Hong Kong in the name of a shared
'Confucian capitalist' tradition. Singapore also promotes its vision
of replacing Hong Kong as a gateway to China after the latter
are reintegrated in July 1997.

Other constructions of East Asian subregionalism and NIC identity

At the same time, in pursuit of its geoeconomic interests, Singapore is seeking to redefine other subregional complementarities with reference to the idea of a 'growth triangle'. The
creation of such a 'growth triangle' identity maps Singapore
with Johor (Malaysia) and Batam in Riau (Indonesia). This mini-
region is popularly known as 'Sijori' and ASEAN members
sometimes refer to it as the Southern Growth Triangle. There
is now another mini-regional construction, known as the

Northern Growth Triangle, involving the northwestern coast of Malaysia (four states), southern Thailand (14 provinces) and western Indonesia (two provinces in Sumatra). These can jointly develop infrastructure, natural resources and industries. Let us concentrate on the Sijori project which is closely related to Singapore, one of the important NICs.

As early as 1979, the Indonesian Minister of Research and Technology, B. J. Habibie, had propounded a 'balloon theory' for linking the interests of Singapore with Riau. This construction likened Singapore's economy to that of a balloon which had a 'limited capacity'. Singapore's balloon would burst if it did not have a 'safety valve' to draw out some of the 'excess capacity'. For Habibie, the surrounding Riau islands, especially Batam, would be Singapore's safety valves. Their presence would allow Singapore's economic balloon to continue growing while at the same time inflating other economic balloons in the region. Habibie's proposal did not receive much attention in Singapore until the late 1980s, but Singapore has since become increasingly concerned that its economy is approaching saturation point. Indonesia's desire to see rapid industrial development in Batam led to a meeting between President Soeharto and Prime Minister Lee Kuan Yew in 1989 and in December of that year the Sijori Growth Triangle project was promulgated by the then Deputy Prime Minister of Singapore, Goh Chok Tong. In August 1990, Singapore and Indonesia signed two bilateral agreements providing the framework for joint development of the Riau province. Although Malaysia's Prime Minister Mahathir endorsed the 'growth triangle' idea, Malaysian federal support for Johor's involvement is not as enthusiastic as that given by the Indonesian central government to Riau. However, the Johor state government is a strong advocate of promoting bilateral Johor–Singapore economic linkages.

Discursively, an integrated Sijori region is promoted as more attractive to investors than its separate parts. It is suggested that Singapore's advantage lies in its managerial and professional expertise and its well-developed financial, transportation and telecommunications infrastructure. Johor and Riau can offer land and labour at lower cost than Singapore. The creation of Sijori will help Singapore to achieve economic restructuring; become a high-value-added service economy and a hub city;

promote the regionalisation and internationalisation of
Singaporean enterprises; provide nearby leisure areas; achieve
a secure water supply; and draw on enlightened self-interest to
help the economic advancement of the ASEAN region. Johor
and Riau are also said to have their own motives for co-operating with the growth triangle framework. Their policies are
explicitly aimed at twinning their investment attractions with
Singapore's to take advantage of its infrastructure. Proximity
to Singapore will enable investors in Batam and Johor to be
more efficient and competitive in production and distribution.

On the material level, the creation of Sijori enables multinationals based in Singapore to relocate their labour- and land-
intensive activities to Johor and Riau. Singapore–Johor links
had already started in the early 1980s without much fanfare.
Though Singapore was not the lead investor, there was a jump
in FDI to Johor in 1990 from Malaysian $132 million to $407
million.[45] The Singapore–Riau links only became a reality after
1989. In January 1990 Indonesia and Singapore established
industrial estates, Batamindo, in Batam with an initial investment of US$400 million. In August 1990 Indonesia and Singa-
pore signed an economic agreement to carry out a joint
development of the Riau islands, especially Batam and Bintan.
Unlike the Singapore–Johor connections, which were started
by the private sectors and the government in Johor, economic
co-operation between Riau and Singapore was only possible
because of the direct involvement of the Indonesian government. The formal agreement between Indonesia and Singapore
provides the necessary incentives for the private sectors from
both countries and from overseas to invest in Batam and the
other islands in Riau. In 1991, Singapore was the biggest foreign
investor in Batam, accounting for 44 per cent of the investments,
followed by the US (19 per cent) and Japan (7 per cent).

This suggests that Sijori is not yet a real triangle. Close economic co-operation has only taken place between Singapore and
Johor; and between Singapore and Riau. The triangle's third
side, that between Johor and Riau, is still missing. Moreover,
the 'growth triangle' identity is increasingly contested by Malaysia
and, to a lesser extent, by Indonesia. Up to the time of writing,
Malaysia is more interested in promoting the following form
of subregionalism: (a) the Northern Triangle between Penang,

Medan and Phuket; (b) the ASEAN free-trade agreement; and (c) the EAEC. The Sijori triangle is contested on three grounds. First, the Singapore–Johor co-operation is national-to (Johor) state-level in form. Constitutionally, the Johor state government cannot make autonomous decisions affecting land, religion and Malay culture without federal approval; any formal inter-state agreement must also be decided at the latter level. Thus the close link between Singapore and Johor involves conflicts over national sovereignty and Malaysian federal-state issues. Second, the rapid development of Johor is also aggravating the distributional problems linked to Malaysia's uneven development. Third, the Malaysian government is very concerned that close co-operation between Johor and Singapore has largely benefited the ethnic Chinese who dominate the economic sector in Malaysia. Kuala Lumpur is also worried about increasing land sales by Malays to Singaporeans which could well disturb the delicate ethnic balance between Malays and Chinese in Malaysian politics.[46] In short, Singapore's 'growth triangle' subregional identity is increasingly contested by Malaysia, an emerging NIC. The challenge is launched in terms of sovereignty and ethnic issues pertinent to Malaysian politics.

Conclusion

Two main sets of conclusions can be drawn from this chapter concerning the regional specificity of East Asia. The first is grounded in the fact that the development of East Asian regionalism and the NICs has an ongoing and incremental nature in comparison with its European and North American comparators. This is reflected in the importance of competing NIC identities and identity struggles in the process of regional development. The end of the Cold War marked the emergence of multipolarity in the region as the US (the main extra-regional player) was joined by Japan and China (the established and emerging regional leaders) in a competitive search for geopolitical and geoeconomic advantages in the 'East Asia' region. Given this general structural context, the strategies adopted by each of these actors are associated with different regional/subregional projects which, in turn, signify a multiplicity of regional/subregional identities for the key agents in the region.

The main identities proposed for the region(s) can be summarised as: (a) a US-orchestrated new Cold-War and market-friendly identity; (b) a Japanese-co-ordinated follower identity; (c) a China-related national-economic identity; and, on a more restricted scale, (d) a Singapore-based 'growth triangle' identity. Each of these identities employs different signifiers to re-define/map/recall some or all of the NICs into its strategic orbit. These signifiers are internalised as identity conflicts and/or strategic dilemmas which constitute a chronic identity struggle within and across the NICs. This often involves the coexistence of multiple identities rooted in the rivalry between geoeconomics and geopolitics and leading to schizophrenic economic and political projects. For example, Hong Kong is involved in an identity struggle indicated by signifiers such as democratisation and pragmatic nationalism. Singapore is torn between between 'open' and 'closed' regionalism symbolised by APEC and EAEC respectively – although it is currently more inclined towards the former. In addition, its 'growth triangle' subregional identity is increasingly contested by Malaysia in terms of its challenge to sovereignty and ethnic issues pertinent to Malaysian politics. As for Taiwan, it is engaged in the search for a democratic Taiwanese identity to counteract the pragmatic nationalism entailed in a 'Greater China'. South Korea is divided between trade liberalisation and neo-mercantilist identities and is also attracted to 'leapfrogging' over Japan to avoid continued dependency. Given these identity conflicts and struggles, social forces seek to reposition themselves in their search to build a strong social basis of support for a strategy that would advance their geoeconomic and geopolitical interests in the post-Cold-War era.

The second main set of conclusions involves the specificity of the formation of East Asian regionalism. In this regard it can be concluded that the formation of regional blocs takes the form of network-building in which business, academic and state participants co-ordinate their activities to define the region, at least in the initial stage. This can be seen in the way that the formation of APEC and ARF was driven by medium-sized or small powers in the region. Given the consensus-building impulses that drive the formation of networks under the leadership of medium-sized or small powers, it is not surprising that bloc formation in East Asia is taking the form of an incremental process in which the NICs are seeking to reposition themselves gradually.

Notes

1. For discussions of the growth of the NICs in East Asia, see S. Haggard, *Pathways from the Periphery: the Politics of Growth in the Newly-Industrializing Countries* (Ithaca: Cornell University Press, 1988); J-E. Woo, *Race to the Swift: State and Finance in Korean Industrialization* (New York: Columbia University Press, 1991); M. Castells, 'Four Asian Tigers with a Dragon Head: A Comparative Analysis of the State, Economy and Development in the Asian Pacific Rim', in R. P. Appelbaum and J. Henderson (eds.), *States and Development in the Asian Pacific Rim* (London: Sage, 1992) pp. 33–70; and N-L. Sum, *Reflections on Accumulation, Regulation, the State and Societalization: A Stylized Model of East Asian Capitalism and Integral Economic Analysis of Hong Kong*, Ph.D. thesis submitted to the Department of Sociology, Lancaster University, January 1994.
2. For a more general discussion of the NICs, see A. Chowdhury and I. Islam, *The Newly Industrializing Countries of East Asia* (London: Routledge, 1993).
3. The idea of an 'imagined region' is derived from B. Anderson, *Imagined Communities: Reflection on the Origin and Spread of Nationalism* (London: Verso, 1991).
4. See J. Clarke, 'APEC as a Semi-Solution', *Orbis: A Journal of World Affairs*, 39, 1 (1995) 81–96.
5. Jessop's strategic-relational approach attempts to transcend the structure-agency dichotomy. He regards strategies as mediating the reciprocal relations between structures and agencies. Structures can be analysed in terms of their strategic selectivity insofar as some structural forms are more suited than others for the purpose of realising particular strategies. On the other hand, strategies also occupy and thereby help to constitute a terrain of struggle in which competing agents attempt to change the present structures. The present paper seeks to locate the dialectic interface of Hong Kong as a gateway region of the 'Greater China' bloc in this schema. See B. Jessop, *State Theory* (Cambridge: Polity, 1990).
6. See R. Higgott, 'Asia-Pacific Economic Co-operation: Theoretical Opportunities and Practical Constraints', *Pacific Review*, 7, 4 (1994) 103–18.
7. In the writing of this section, the author draws heavily on the work of G. Segal, *Rethinking the Pacific* (Oxford: Clarendon Press, 1991).

8. See J. G. Ruggie, 'International Regimes, Transitions and Change: Embedded Liberalism in the Postwar Economic Order', *International Organization*, 36, 2 (1982) 379–416.

9. It comprised the US, Britain, France, Pakistan, Australia, New Zealand, Thailand and the Philippines.

10. See Castells, 'Four Asian Tigers with a Dragon Head', p. 63.

11. This concept was first proposed by the Japanese economist Akamatsu Kaname, 'Shinkoku Kogyokoku no Sangyo Hatten', *Ueda Teijiro Hakushi Kinen Ronbunshu*, 4 July 1937. An English-language summary of his argument appears in 'A Theory of Unbalanced Growth in the World Economy', *Weltwirtschaftliches Archiv*, 86, 1 (1961).

12. See C. Ziegler, 'Russia in the Asia-Pacific: A Major Power or Minor Participant?', *Asian Survey*, 34, 6 (1994) 534.

13. For China's security policy in the post-Cold-War era, see P. Goodwin, 'Force and Diplomacy: Chinese Security Policy in the Post-Cold War Era', in S. S. Kim (ed.), *China in the World: Chinese Foreign Relations in the Post-Cold War Era* (Boulder: Westview Press, 1994) pp. 171–86; and X. Yi, 'China's US Policy Conundrum in the 1990s: Balancing Autonomy and Interdependence', *Asian Survey*, 34, 8 (1994) 675–91.

14. For discussion of China's military buildup, see J. Hsiung, 'China in the Post-nuclear World', in J. Hsiung (ed.), *Asia Pacific in the New World Politics* (London: Lynne Rienner Publishers, 1993), pp. 71–92; L. Dittmer, 'China and Russia: New Beginnings', in Kim, *China in the World*, pp. 94–112; and C-P. Lin, 'Beijing and Taipei: Interactions in the Post-Tiananmen Period', *The China Quarterly*, 136 (1993) 770–804.

15. See Goodwin, 'Force and Diplomacy', pp. 178–9; and P. H. Chang and Z. Deng, 'China and Southeast Asia: Overseeing the Regional Balance', in D. J. Myers (ed.), *Regional Hegemons: Threat Perception and Strategic Response* (Boulder: Westview Press, 1991), pp. 215–7.

16. *Financial Times*, 12 June 1994.

17. See Hsiung, 'China in the Postnuclear World', p. 80.

18. *Far Eastern Economic Review*, 22 April 1993, 22.

19. See G. Segal, *China Changes Shape: Regionalism and Foreign Policy*, Adelphi Paper No. 287 (London: The International Institute for Strategic Studies, 1994), p. 38.

20. See J. Hsiung, 'Asia Pacific in Perspective: The Impact of the End of Cold War', in Hsiung (ed.), *Asia Pacific in the New World Politics*, p. 227.

21. The PMC is held annually after the ASEAN foreign ministers' meeting and has been convened since the mid-1970s.

22. In general contracting countries aim to reduce the tariffs imposed on imports from other GATT signatories. The MFN rule obliges contracting states to extend to other GATT signatories the most favourable trade treatment accorded to any individual country.

23. Geoeconomically, the rise of major East Asian growth poles prompted the OECD to create the NIC category in 1979 and this distinction in turn enabled the US and western European countries to target them for 'tougher' trade negotiations and treatments.

24. See S. Haggard and T-J. Cheng, 'The New Bilateralism: The East Asian NICs in American Foreign Economic Policy', in S. Haggard and C-I. Moon (eds.), *Pacific Dynamics: The International Politics of Industrial Change* (Boulder: Westview Press 1989), pp. 305–30.

25. For the concept of 'open regionalism', see P. Drysdale and R. Garnaut, 'The Pacific: An Application of a General Theory of Economic Integration', in C. F. Bergsten and M. Noland (eds.), *Pacific Dynamism and the International Economic System* (Washington DC: Institute for International Economics, 1993), pp. 183–224.

26. *The Times*, 5 December 1994.

27. For more sceptical views of the APEC, see G. R. Winham, 'The GATT after the Uruguay Round', in R. Higgott, R. Leaver and J. Ravenhill (eds.), *Pacific Economic Relations in the 1990s: Cooperation or Conflict?* (St. Leonards, NSW: Allen Unwin, 1993), pp. 184–200; and W. Bello and S. Cunningham, 'Trade Warfare and Regional Integration in the Pacific: The USA, Japan and the Asian NICs', *Third World Quarterly*, 15, 3 (1994) 445–58.

28. See P. J. Rimmer, 'Regional Economic Integration in Pacific Asia', *Environment and Planning*, 26, 4 (1994) 1731–59.

29. In September 1985, the ministers of finance of the Group of Five (the US, Japan, West Germany, the UK and France) agreed to the devaluation of the US dollar, especially relative to the yen and mark, to strengthen US competitiveness and reduce its cumulative current balance deficits. This was the so-called Plaza Accord. Between September 1985 and December 1987, the yen more than doubled in value against the dollar, from around ¥250:$1.00 to just over ¥120:$1.00. The New Taiwan dollar simultaneously rose around 40 per cent against the US currency; the South Korean won rose about 16 per cent; and the Singapore dollar by a much smaller amount. The Hong Kong dollar remained tied to the US dollar, resulting in an effective 50 per cent devaluation against the yen and, although less pronounced, depreciation against North Asian NIC currencies.

30. See M. Bernard and J. Ravenhill, 'Beyond Product Cycle and Flying Geese: Regionalization, Hierarchy and the Industrialization of East Asia', *World Politics*, 47, 2 (1995) 171–209.

31. See ibid., 186.

32. For details of the new division of knowledge, see C. H. Kwan, *Economic Interdependence in the Asia-Pacific Region: Towards a Yen Bloc* (London: Routledge, 1994); E. Chen, 'Foreign Direct Investment in East Asia', *Asian Development Review*, 11, 3 (1993) 24–59;

and S. Tokunaga (ed.), *Japan's Foreign Investment and Asian Economic Interdependence: Production, Trade and Financial Systems* (Tokyo: University of Tokyo Press, 1992).

33. See Tokunaga, *Japan's Foreign Investment and Asian Economic Interdependence*, p. 29; and G. Rodan, 'Reconstructing Division of Labour: Singapore's New Emphasis', in Higgott *et al.* (eds.), *Pacific Economic Relations in the 1990s*, p. 235.

34. For a discussion on 'reverse exporting', see J. Ravenhill, 'The "Japan Problem" in Pacific Trade', in Higgott *et al.* (eds.), *Pacific Economic Relations in the 1990s*, pp. 106–132.

35. It has been argued by some observers that certain developing countries may be able to 'leapfrog' older vintages of technology and thereby begin to catch up with advanced economies. According to this view, some developing countries are less hampered by investment commitments to previous generations of technology. Developing countries with adequate levels of skills and infrastructure may benefit from the 'window of opportunity' provided by a new techno-economic paradigm, especially at the early stages of diffusion when barriers to entry are relatively low and markets are in a state of upheaval. Leapfrogging is consistent with Schumpeter's notion of 'creative destruction', where radical new innovations give rise to the destruction of industries based upon old technologies.

36. Capabilities refer here to the enterprises' relative capacities to react speedily to given incentives within a given institutional setting. Incentives derive from prices and are shaped mainly by macroeconomic policy. But it is educational, industrial and technology policies which are crucial for shaping capabilities. The latter represent economic competencies which enable the identification, expansion and exploitation of the opportunity set. In this regard, capabilities can only be built and cannot be transferred or bought. For further discussion, see S. Radosevic, 'Strategic Technology Policy for Eastern Europe', *Economic Systems*, 18, 2 (1994) 87–116.

37. For an in-depth discussion of the 'hard slog' nature of Singapore's electronics industry, see M. Hobday, 'Technological Learning in Singapore: A Test Case of Leapfrogging', *Journal of Development Studies*, 30, 3 (1994) 831–58.

38. This process can be defined as the 'production of goods and services in a given country, predominantly utilizing inputs from abroad for the principal purpose of export to other countries'. For details, see H. Mirza, *Multinationals and the Growth of the Singapore Economy* (London: Croom Helm, 1986).

39. In the case of sports shoes such as Nike, most of the raw materials and skills come from Taiwan through Hong Kong to South China. Hong Kong staff deal with designs, make sure the sample and raw materials reach the factory on time, and ship the finished products out of China through Hong Kong to their destined

markets, mainly the US. For details, see Chen, 'Foreign Direct Investment in East Asia', 102.

40. A gateway region is an area located near the boundary between major geostrategic realms, often containing a nation or ethnic groups that has not yet achieved political independence. For details, see F. M. Shelley, 'Political Geography, the New World Order and the City', *Urban Geography*, 14, 6 (1993) 557–67.

41. For a detailed account of China's economic involvement in Hong Kong, see G. Shen, 'China's Investment in Hong Kong', in P-K. Choi and L-S. Ho, *The Other Hong Kong Report 1993* (Hong Kong: Chinese University Press, 1993), pp. 425–54. As for China's involvement in the world economy, see N. R. Lardy, *China in the World Economy* (Washington, DC: Institute' for International Economics, 1994).

42. This literature is mainly written in Chinese by scholars in China. See S. Fang, 'A Proposal for Establishing a Mainland–Taiwan–Hong Kong Economic Commission', *Jingji Ribao*, Beijing, 24 June (1992); and L. Fu, 'Hong Kong–Macao and Both Sides of the Taiwan Strait: A Chinese Economic Sphere', *Journal of Beijing University*, Social Science Edition, 5 (1992) 85–92.

43. For an analysis of the discursive construction of 'pragmatic nationalism' in Hong Kong, see N-L. Sum, 'More than a "War of Words": Identity Politics and the Struggle for Dominance during the Recent "Political Reform" Period in Hong Kong', *Economy and Society*, 24, 1 (1995) 68–99.

44. See C. Clark, 'Taiwan in Post-Cold War Asia Pacific', in Hsiung (ed.), *Asia Pacific in the New World Politics*, pp. 113–34; and R. N. Clough, *Reaching Across the Taiwan Strait: People-to-People Diplomacy* (Boulder: Westview Press, 1993), chapter 7.

45. See S. Y. Chia and T. Y. Lee, 'Subregional Economic Zones: A New Force in Asia-Pacific Development', in Bergsten and Noland (eds.), *Pacific Dynamism and the International Economic System*, pp. 225–72.

46. For a discussion of the contradictions within the Sijori subregional bloc, see D. F. Anwar, 'Sijori: ASEAN's Southern Growth Triangle Problems and Prospects', *The Indonesian Quarterly: ASEAN and the Asia Pacific*, 22, 1 (1994) 22–33.

8 Conclusion: The New Regionalism

ANDREW GAMBLE and ANTHONY PAYNE

In *1984* George Orwell pictured a world divided between three rival totalitarian powers – Eastasia, Oceania, and Eurasia. It was a condition of perpetual war and total mobilisation, in which two of the powers would always be fighting the third. Orwell took his names for these three powers from the three geographical centres of the struggle for territory and resources during the Second World War. Fifty years later, the same three areas feature once again in predictions that the world order is dividing territorially and is heading towards conflict. The nature of this conflict is assumed to be a zero-sum game in which each state competes to improve its relative share of territory, resources, and wealth within a global total which is fixed. In this neo-realist perspective regionalism simplifies and intensifies this conflict, by combining the most important states into more or less cohesive groups under the leadership of the dominant state in each region. The pressure on a region to become cohesive increases in relation to the success of other regions in unifying themselves. As each regional power seeks to maximise its wealth and extend its territory, the risk of economic wars rises, because in a zero-sum world each regional power calculates that conflict will yield more benefit than co-operation.

An even bleaker scenario has been put forward by Samuel Huntington. He foresees the future of world politics being determined by a clash between three civilisations – Christianity, Confucianism and Islam. These map on to the geographical areas described by Orwell, with Christian Europe and the Americas forming Oceania, battling against the rival civilisations of central and eastern Asia. These three civilisations are rooted in different ultimate values and make claims which are

247

exclusive in character, and cannot be negotiated. Since no reconciliation between them is possible, conflict once it starts is likely to be bitter and prolonged. The possibility is conjured up of a return to holy wars, of the sort which used to occur between Christianity and Islam.

In the present febrile state of world politics, however, such gloomy forebodings of economic wars and holy wars have been appearing at the same time as predictions of a future of increasing prosperity and peace, the settling of the ideological conflicts which have dominated world politics for 200 years and the universal acceptance of a common set of ideas about economic and social organisation. Intractable problems remain, but they are seen as practical rather than ideological, belonging to the sphere of technical rather than value rationality. Solutions to them have to be sought within the institutional framework of free-market capitalism and liberal democracy. That institutional framework is no longer in question because it has proved itself the only viable way of organising modern societies. On this view the clash of civilisations will not materialise because there is only one civilisation – western civilisation – which is adapted for survival. The ethics of ultimate ends contained in Confucianism, Islam, and Christianity all belong to the premodern stage of social development, and are destined to be left behind.

Even in the brave new world of a unified global civilisation capitalist states might still fight one another as they have in the past. Liberal institutionalists, however, argue that as the world economy becomes more interdependent, it becomes rational for states to prefer co-operation to conflict. States increasingly face common problems which can only be handled through agreement on new institutions and rules. This optimistic scenario predicts that as interdependence deepens so the risk of major economic or military conflict should decline. This trend is reinforced by the observation that democracies do not fight one another, so that as democratisation spreads, the less likely it becomes that conflicts between states will be settled in the future by resort to arms. These theories reject the assumption that states face a zero-sum game. Instead they assume that there is a positive sum game in which states can co-operate either through competition or through intergovernmental negotiation to increase the total output of goods and services available for distribution. Economic welfare can be improved for everyone so long as positional goods such as territory and resources do not become the focus of competition.

These scenarios are at such variance in their predictions of the future that they hardly seem to be describing the same world. Yet such conjunctions of pessimism and optimism are not new. They seem inseparable from how modernity is experienced. Polarisation of views about the future are often found at times of increasing change in the global political economy. The 20 years between 1971 and 1991 was such a period. It opened with the breakdown of the Bretton Woods international monetary system, the first major sign of the weakening of United States hegemony, and ended with the collapse of the Communist regime in the Soviet Union and the disintegration of the Soviet state. These were contradictory events for the future of the world order. The end of the Bretton Woods system brought American hegemony into question and inaugurated a time of increasing doubt about US capacities and political will to sustain the burdens of its global interests and responsibilities, while the collapse of the Soviet Union appeared to vindicate the United States post-war strategy of containment and left it without any serious military rival.

It was against this background of declining US hegemony and world economic recession that the possibility of new regionalist projects began to emerge. The turn to regionalism at the end of the 1980s coincided with the breakdown of the oldest regionalism in the global political economy, the division between the capitalist and the socialist worlds which developed after the Russian Revolution. The unity of the global political economy was restored for the first time since 1914 and the era of national protectionism and rivalry between socio-economic systems ended. This event which occurred much earlier than most observers predicted appeared as a dramatic confirmation of the trends towards globalisation in the world economy, and their ability to undermine and at times sweep away established political structures.

This tide of globalisation seems to be contradicted by the emergence of regionalist projects. Is the new regionalism simply a product of the recent decline of US hegemony which will be overtaken by the pressures towards globalisation? Or is it an essential part of globalisation? These are the key problems which have been addressed in this book. The findings will be summarised here and an assessment made of the current direction of development of the global political economy.

Regionalism is a type of state project which can be distinguished from other types of state project such as globalism. State projects generally emerge as the outcome of detailed bargaining and negotiation among domestic political actors. The concept of regionalism assumes that states and state actors are a key level of explanation in a theory of the global political economy. The calculations that state actors make of their interests and the costs and benefits of alternative courses of action are the starting point for understanding the wider context of their behaviour. This wider context is constituted by two kinds of structure – the historical residues of past social interaction and the emergent patterns of current social interaction. Together these provide both constraints and opportunities. Agents do not act within structures; rather they cannot act without reproducing structures, confirming or modifying them through the intended and unintended consequences of their calculations and actions.

Globalisation and regionalisation are not state projects but combinations of historical and emergent structures – a complex articulation of established institutions and rules and distinctive new patterns of social interaction between non-state actors. State projects like regionalism typically seek to accelerate, to modify, or occasionally to reverse the direction of social change which emergent structures like globalisation and regionalisation represent. Such structures define the limits and the possibility of agency and have continually to be reproduced through the calculations and actions of agents, including states. The strategic calculations of states is only one level of analysis for understanding the global political economy but it is a necessary one. If it is made the only level of analysis then it becomes narrow and one-sided; but equally one-sided is an analysis which conceives of globalisation as though it were a process occurring outside and beyond the system of states.

In practice, regionalism as a set of state projects intersects with globalisation. The relationship between the two has come into particularly sharp focus with the end of the Cold War. The world order now has not two but three cores – North America, the European Union and East Asia. The former core around the Soviet Union has disintegrated, allowing the three embryonic cores within the former capitalist world economy to emerge as the constituent elements of the new order. The relationships between these three cores and between the cores and their peripheries is both complex and diverse. No single pattern has become established. The main characteristics of regionalist projects in the three core regions can best be summarised under three headings: what they have in common; where they diverge; and relationships between cores and peripheries.

Common features of regionalist projects

One of the most striking characteristics common to all the regionalist projects is their commitment to open regionalism. Although fears have often been expressed that they might develop towards closed regionalism, these have not so far been realised. The idea of 'Fortress Europe' never accurately reflected the objectives of the Europeans. Many observers see the move towards regionalism at the end of the 1980s and in the 1990s as a step towards globalism rather than as an alternative to it. Open regionalism means that policy is directed towards the elimination of obstacles to trade within a region, while at the same time doing nothing to raise external tariff barriers to the rest of the world.

Regionalist projects have often raised fears that they might become exclusive and protectionist. The creation of a regional leadership and regional institutions that can express a regional political will means that the potential is always there for that to happen. But although protectionist arguments have been stronger in the 1970s and 1980s than earlier they have not set the policy programme of any party that has formed a government in one of the leading capitalist states. The nature of the argument has been rather different; not a dispute between free trade and protection, but rather between free trade and strategic trade. The strategic-traders have argued that maintaining and improving international competitiveness needs to be the central goal of economic policy. Instead of insulating the economy from foreign competition the aim is to expose it to competition while at the same time ensuring that it is able to meet it. Strategic-trade arguments deny free-trade arguments that an optimum specialisation of labour dictated by comparative advantage will arise spontaneously. States instead must act strategically to protect key sectors and ensure that they become international leaders. These ideas have long been current in political economy. An earlier formulation was the idea of the developmental state as opposed to the *laissez-faire* state.

All the current regionalist projects have been driven to some extent by a strategic-trade view. One of the benefits of greater regional co-operation has been the possibility of enabling regional companies and sectors to be successful in global markets. The emphasis is placed on training, research, investment, public procurement, and infrastructure, and the need to maintain legal and managerial control over firms. Strategic-trade assumptions have always been important in some states, but they have become more prominent recently. Free traders regard them as a diversion from the task of building a non-discriminatory open world trading system, and dispute that states are equipped to plan strategically in the way that companies attempt to do.[3]

The strategic-trade argument has been carried further by those like Michel Albert who argue that there are distinctive models of capitalism which are regionally specific.[4] The dominant Anglo-American model with its emphasis on free trade, arms-length banking, and *laissez-faire* policy regime contrasts with the Japanese and Rhenish models which emphasise strategic trade, long-term investment, corporatist and partnership modes of corporate governance and policy formation. Such models, however, are ideal types. Although there are some significant differences between the institutional patterns the differences are easily exaggerated. Strategic-trade considerations, for example, have always been important in some sectors of the US particularly in defence, while many sectors in Europe and Japan have been governed entirely by the rules of free trade.

All the recent moves towards regionalism have therefore been consistent with open regionalism. The free-trade/strategic-trade debate does not question that commitment. This commitment reflects a second factor which all the regionalist projects have in common; they originate in discussions and negotiations within the policy-making élites in the core states. There has been little popular involvement or pressure for such projects. The élites have devised them in response to changes elsewhere in the world order. The overriding need to maintain international co-operation despite the difficulties of doing so in many areas has been an important political consideration. The leading states are still committed through the G7, the IMF, the World Bank, and the World Trade Organisation to continue to manage the international system, to keep it running as smoothly as possible, and to avoid shocks and crises as best they can. The regionalist projects are not intended as rivals to this globalist project, but rather as means to help achieve it in a world where there is no longer a single state with the authority and capacity to impose its leadership. But the extent to which regionalism has now to be promoted as a means of managing world order is itself a sign of weakness and a potential source of tension.

The diversity of regionalist projects

Although regionalist projects have certain assumptions in common and have been framed within a common globalist perspective, they are also quite different from one another. This diversity reflects the different historical structures which exist within each region, as well as the uneven impact of globalisation. The emergence of a regionalist project in North America has been the single most significant development in shaping the debate on regionalism. The United States has been the dominant power within the Americas ever since the promulgation of the Monroe Doctrine. But although its dominance has been overwhelming and has tended to increase, the United States has not previously sought to establish itself as a regional hegemon. Its power has been exercised more through coercion than consent in the Americas. The political culture and political identity of Latin America and the Caribbean has for much of the twentieth century been framed in opposition to the United States. With the establishment of US global hegemony in the 1940s the Americas were incorporated within it but were still often referred to as the United States' 'backyard' which the

US reserved the right to intervene in at will if it felt its vital interests were threatened.

In economic policy large parts of the Americas had been incorporated within a dollar bloc during the 1930s, but with the establishment of the new liberal world order under US leadership after 1945 the United States became firmly committed to multilateralism and discouraged any regional arrangement. The turn in US policy at the end of the 1980s is therefore very significant, signalling the willingness of the US government to consider a framework to integrate other states within the region. Bush's Enterprise for the Americas and the successful establishment of NAFTA, and the possibility of extending it in due course to create an American Free Trade Area embracing the whole of Latin America and the Caribbean, quickly became a regionalist project of considerable ambition and scope. One of its aims was to deconstruct the old identity of Latin America, organised in opposition to the US. The new partnership was to be founded on acceptance of the basic assumptions of economic liberalism and democracy.

The shift in United States policy was partly due to the ending of the Cold War with the USSR. Communism has ceased to be a military or an ideological competitor to capitalism, and this has rendered many of the attitudes towards Latin America obsolete. Some long-standing problems, like Cuba, remain to be resolved, but no one doubts that when it is it will be done on US terms. The United States can therefore afford to take a much more relaxed view towards Latin America, in the sense that it can promote democracy in the region without fearing that it will produce security risks for the United States. It is in a much stronger position now to assert moral and ideological leadership, especially since the élites of all the Latin American countries have become increasingly keen themselves to abandon' their radical ideologies and to embrace economic liberalism, and in many cases, democracy.

A second reason for the change in US policy was directly related to US perception of its own declining ability to act as a global hegemon. The increasing conflict with Japan over the latter's 'unfair trade' and the uncertainty about future European intentions as European integration advanced, combined with awareness of the importance of the regional market to the US economy. The Mexican debt crisis in 1982 was a powerful reminder of just how interdependent the US and Mexico had become, and was one of the important steps on the path that led to the NAFTA agreement. The initiative for NAFTA originally came from Mexico, but the United States policy-making élite soon became enthusiastic. The dominance of the United States in the region then made the launch of the project relatively easy. Canada with some misgivings was forced to join in NAFTA because of the risks it might have run had it remained outside. Opposition was considerable within both Canada and the United States, particularly from labour interests and national-populist groups, fearing the loss of jobs and the weakening of regulation of transnational capital, but in both cases it was contained. The opposition forces were considerable, as the success of a maverick political figure like Ross Perot demonstrated. But the bipartisan consensus still held.

The European Union has appeared at times a very different kind of regionalist project. After 1985 the project of European integration acquired a new momentum. The signing of the Single European Act in 1986, the move to Qualified Majority Voting as the decision rule for many policy areas, and the revival of the plans for economic and monetary union, made the European Community the focus of international attention. Before 1985 few saw the European Community as a potential leader of the world order. But after 1985 a new political will began to emerge. The successful launch of the programme to complete the Single Market by 1992 led to the negotiations for the Treaty of European Union signed at Maastricht in 1991. The possibility of the European Union moving to a single currency and a European Central Bank and beyond that to political union was considered a serious possibility.

Between 1985 and 1992 the European Union appeared to be moving towards the creation of a new unified political core. At present Europe lacks such a core. There is no single state which dominates in the way that the United States dominates its region. The federalist impulse behind the European project points towards the creation of a new state, a United States of Europe. Since a formal agreement of the ancient nation states of Europe to abandon their separate sovereignties and create a new European state was never likely, the federalists hoped to advance towards their goal through encouraging economic integration. Economic interdependence it was argued would create its own momentum for political union, by creating groups with an interest in promoting the emergence of supranational institutions to co-ordinate and develop the economic market. The co-ordination of low-level technical functions would both create the need for further co-ordination and convince élites of the value of extending such co-operation to other spheres to deal with central policy issues.

European integration has never advanced smoothly in a linear fashion. Its progress has at best been cyclical. Periods of stagnation have been succeeded by periods of movement such as that between 1985–92 when new goals are set and new structures created. Nevertheless despite the evident deepening and widening of the original European Community that has taken place in the last 40 years there is still lively debate as to whether a genuine political union will ever emerge to complement the economic union. The debate has focused particularly on whether the goal set in the Maastricht Treaty of achieving a single European currency is realistic. The establishment of such a currency and the institutions necessarily associated with it such as a European Central Bank would be clear evidence of the emergence of a supranational political dimension, and would require a similar evolution in the mechanisms for formulating policy at the European level.[5]

Europe remains divided over its future direction, a debate which is reflected in the continuing dispute between French and British views of how Europe should develop. In economic policy this is an argument about whether Europe should adopt a strategic- or a free-trade policy. The French and British views are not uniform; there are significant dissenters from the central government line within each country. The French referendum to approve the Maastricht Treaty in 1993 was won only narrowly, despite the strong support of the French government and the bulk of the political élite for the Treaty. In Britain popular hostility to the Maastricht Treaty and to further moves towards European integration was pronounced, but a significant element of the political élite, represented in all political parties, was in favour of further pooling of sovereignty through intergovernmental negotiation.

The situation in Europe is further complicated by the continuing unwillingness of Germany, although now the preponderant economic power, to assert itself politically. This fact itself was a product of the Cold War and the division of Germany. Now that the country is reunited this reluctance of Germany to assert itself is likely to diminish. If the project of European integration is to regain momentum again, German support will be critical. But future German leaderships will have other options available, including expansion of economic and political influence towards the East. The continued willingness of Germany to participate in the European project will be tested. The sacrifice of the mark and the Bundesbank in the cause of European union are strongly opposed at present by German public opinion, and although the underlying rationale for further integration remains strong, the steps by which a unified political core for the European Union might emerge are now unclear.

The third regionalist project, in East Asia, is the least well-defined, and the least advanced. In the Americas there is no dispute over the state which is capable of becoming the regional hegemon. In Europe there is no prospect at present of a single regional hegemon emerging. Capacity and resources are divided relatively evenly between Germany, France, and Britain. But the combination of these states in the EU has the potential of creating a very powerful regional hegemon. In East Asia however the region is the least well-defined of the three. Multiple identities exist. There are two potential regional hegemons in Japan and China, as well as involvement in the region by two other great powers, the United States and Russia. The region is still divided ideologically and there are major unresolved security issues. The state currently best equipped to launch a regionalist project, Japan, is characterised by weakness in decision making and an unwillingness to assert itself politically. As in other regions a considerable amount of regionalisation has taken place centred on the interaction of other states in the region with the dynamism of the leading economy. East Asia, however, is a region without a single centre from which a regionalist project could emerge. Japan has so far shunned the promptings of Malaysia to take a much more active leadership role in the region through the East Asia Economic

Caucus (EAEC). Instead it has given priority to Asia Pacific Economic Co-operation (APEC) which because it also involves the United States is a guarantee against the development of any closed regionalism project in East Asia. Out of APEC a free-trade agreement might eventually emerge, but its main role at the moment appears to be to head off other kinds of regionalist project. Given Japan's involvement with global trade there is little possibility that Japan will seek unilaterally to develop a regionalist project which in any way excludes Europe or the United States. But the Japanese have naturally become concerned about the development of regionalist projects in the other two cores of the world economy. If Japan were to espouse a more explicit regionalist project in the future it would be in response to further developments in the regionalist projects in the Americas and in Europe.

Cores and peripheries

As already indicated, regionalisation refers to those processes which deepen the integration of particular regional economic spaces. There are many ways of measuring it but particularly important are flows of trade, investment, aid and people. Regionalisation can develop prior to any cultural or political unification, and may be the spur to such unification (as the neo-functionalist theory of European integration predicts); or it may occur within a territory that has already achieved political union. Regionalisation like globalisation, however, is normally uneven in its impact. Certain places and sites will be integrated while others are marginalised. Unless the regionalist project embraced by the core explicitly addresses the issue of inequality and uneven development, the process of deepening integration is also likely to be a process of increasing polarisation.

The structural weight of the cores in all three regions has created asymmetrical relations. The cores act as powerful magnets which drag other states into their orbit, and with the collapse of alternative models of development this trend has become ever more pronounced. The increasing incorporation of Mexico within the US economy is one illustration; so too is

the network of relationships which have been built up in East
Asia through aid, investment and exports by Japanese companies. The result is an economic structure in which an increasing amount of Japanese production is located in other parts
of East Asia, but the technology remains Japanese and the business strategy is firmly controlled from Japan. Countries are eager
to interact with the core because they perceive it as a means
to increase their own rate of growth and wider social development, however unequal the relationship with the core may seem.
There is no evidence that regionalisation moves different parts
of a region closer together. The same phenomenon of cumulative uneven development long evident in national economies
is also true, often more so at the regional level, because of the
difficulty of organising even the modest redistributionist measures
which are often found at the national level. Many regionalist
projects, including NAFTA and APEC, have no institutional
mechanisms for redistribution.

The position is most stark in the case of eastern and central
Europe. The core that is still in the process of formation as
the European Union is itself internally divided, with a sharp
regional split between the richest regions in Germany, France,
and the Benelux countries and some of the southern and western
regions. But this divide is dwarfed by the scale of that between
the European Union and the impoverished territories to the
east, all of which have suffered (from a very low base) a sharp
fall in output, employment, and investment. These countries
are being rapidly penetrated by European Union capital, particularly German capital, but they are also at the same time
seeking entry to the European Union as full members. If this
were permitted the problem of convergence of economies
measured by inflation rates, interest rates, exchange rates, and
public debt would become completely intractable. Within the
existing EU it is already threatening to sabotage moves towards
a single currency.

What happens in this situation is that the core reduces the
countries of the periphery to satellite status, at least in economic terms. Aid is provided but at the price of the imposition
of adjustment programmes and stabilisation packages on countries whose economic performance is poor. The question is
whether the impact of this kind of regionalism on the periphery

is sustainable, given the huge adjustments that are often involved, and the austerity programmes which they entail. The cost of the package needed to lay the foundations for long-term economic growth in east and central Europe is equivalent to a new Marshall Aid Plan. What has been offered so far falls far short. But with the end of the Cold War there is no longer any ideological or security incentive to provide aid on this scale, and the preoccupations of local electorates in the regional cores makes it extremely difficult to provide even if a political leadership emerged which was prepared to give it priority. The result is an uneasy stand-off. The potential regional hegemons in all three areas are mainly preoccupied with relatively small parts of their regions and show few signs of endeavouring to construct a more permanent and inclusive framework within which to assert their leadership and address some of the more deep-seated problems in their regions.

Hegemony and world order

The present stage of world order after the end of the Cold War displays no simple pattern. The United States is no longer hegemonic over the capitalist economy in the manner that it achieved in the 1940s, 1950s, and 1960s. But in some fields, particularly the military and the cultural, its dominance is greater in the 1990s than it has ever been. The collapse of Communism and the disintegration of alternative development strategies in the Third World has reunited the global political economy around the ideological principles of the United States. But the United States now lacks both the capacity and the political will to relaunch itself as the global hegemon. To do so would require a huge commitment of resources to develop disadvantaged regions of the world economy – particularly in east and central Europe, Latin America, Africa, and south Asia. No such commitment is likely to be made by the United States. All the political pressure in its deadlocked political system is moving it in the other direction, towards disengagement.

A curious situation has arisen. Capitalism has triumphed and almost everywhere the opposition to it has collapsed. But in the moment of its triumph the political capacities to make its triumph permanent are inadequate for the task. The new global order based on the principles of free-market capitalism and liberal democracy is likely to prove unable to extend the benefits of prosperity and economic development to all the states that now seek it. Capitalism and democracy have never enjoyed greater legitimacy as organising principles than they possess at the end of the twentieth century. But legitimacy does not simply depend on the claims of the powerful; it also depends on the active consent of the powerless. If the governance of the world order fails to address the many acute problems which the global political economy is creating, then a new radical challenge to capitalist civilisation may arise.

Regionalism is in part a response to this situation. If a global hegemony organised around one state is no longer possible, might not a number of regional hegemonies be more successful? The United States, the European Union, and Japan might use the undoubted economic dominance they enjoy in their regions to establish a political and security framework and a set of economic institutions which promote prosperity and development through trade, investment and aid. If such regionalist projects embrace open regionalism they would still be compatible with the pursuit of policies at the global level through the G7 to stabilise the world economy and maintain economic growth.

The intentions of the regionalist projects, however, are much more limited than this. What is often described wrongly as the regional hegemony of Japan and the United States is based more on dominance and traditional asymmetries of power, than on true moral and political leadership. The key aspect of hegemony which makes it a rather rare as well as very powerful political relationship is the incorporation of subordinate groups through the granting of special privileges and benefits. Usually this involves not simply the acceptance of a common set of ideological principles but the construction of a new identity in which both leader and subordinate share. US global hegemony was founded on the development of just such a new identity, that of the 'West'. In East Asia the emergence of a settled identity seems problematic in the short term at least, while in the Americas the long historical suspicion of the United States may make the consolidation of the new liberal democratic identity difficult. The best prospect would appear to be in Europe, although even here there is a conflict between using the new political identity of 'Europe' as a basis for unifying a new 'core' or for creating a wider political association embracing the states of east and central Europe as well as the Balkans, Turkey and north Africa. Despite the rhetoric, the dispute between Britain and France is really an argument over how the core should be organised. While this remains unresolved the European Union is in a very weak position to develop as a regional hegemon.

If there is no longer any prospect of a global hegemony re-emerging based on a single state, and if regional hegemonies are also proving slow to emerge, and may indeed never emerge, what kind of world order will be feasible in the future? Two further scenarios for the future of world order are worth considering. Both move beyond the simplistic scenarios discussed earlier. The first is a cyclical view of the development of world order. It suggests that each world order, even the most powerful, only has a limited span. Eventually the organising principles on which it rests become exhausted and decay, and give rise to new challenges. Karl Polanyi, for example, argued that the triumph of the doctrines of free market-economics in the nineteenth century eventually produced a reaction, and the reimposition of social regulation on market activities. The rise of collectivism in the twentieth century followed. But what Polanyi did not foresee was that collectivism in the varying forms of Fordism, Keynesianism, welfarism, and state socialism would in turn prove to be short-lived, and that at the end of the twentieth century all forms of collectivist doctrines would be in retreat, and economic liberalism would once again be in the ascendancy.

One response is to argue in turn that the revival of economic liberalism will prove to be no more permanent than collectivism before it. In time resistance will form in response to the damage which unrestricted markets inflict on human communities and to the need to manage common problems, the externalities and asymmetries which are inherent in market processes, but which often cannot be solved by market processes themselves. On this view as globalisation intensifies and the control of states weakens, the present world order will descend into a state of anarchy, which will not lack order in the sense of patterned behaviour, but in which uncertainty will sharply increase. A point will be reached where the harmful effects of an unregulated global economy, particularly on the environment and on the distribution of resources, will bring a reaction and the institution of a world government. Then history might really end, because the dynamism of so much of the history of the modern period which has lain in the competition between states would disappear. The interdependence of the global political economy created by the interaction of capitalist and state competition would be formally recognised through the creation of the appropriate global institutions to govern it. In short, preservation of the human species would require the subordination of the principles of free-market individualism to those of social regulation and community.[6]

This view effectively reinstates the dialectic of history, providing for one more stage beyond Fukuyama. It receives some support from the logic of interdependence stressed by the liberal institutionalists, which also points to the possibility of a new era of regulation at a global level, following the undermining of the sovereignty of nation-states. The new regionalism is an essential step towards this.

Belief in the approach of a new era of regulation and global government is rooted in a classic view of world order and the stages of its development. It assumes that the cyclical pattern of the past will be repeated again. But what may be happening is rather the birth of a qualitatively new stage in the development of the world order, which renders redundant many of the categories we have used in the past for understanding its history and its future prospects. The idea that world history is always moving to a stage which is in some sense 'higher' than the previous one, more complex, more integrated, more comprehensive, is hard to abandon. But what we may be witnessing is the emergence of a global political economy whose basic structures will no longer change or develop very much. Its governance will be characterised neither by a world government nor by a system of powerful nation-states. Instead it will be suggestive of what some have called the new medievalism. The need for new forms of governance for the global political economy continues to expand as interdependence increases. These might be provided by new kinds of networks rather than states, but the provision will still involve political negotiation and decision. Instead of political authority being defined through sovereignty and territoriality there will be a complex pattern of crosscutting identities and authorities. In this mosaic local agencies, national agencies, regional agencies, and global agencies will all have a part to play.

Such a world order would be extremely complex, and conflicts would be common. Quite radical changes and shifts could be expected. It would be a world order of considerable flexibility. There would be no hegemon, and no requirement for one. Some steering functions for the world economy might be taken on by the G7, or possibly the G3 if the European Union succeeds in forging a coherent political will. But there would be no attempt to provide an overall political capacity at the global level to deal with problems. Many of these would be dealt with in other ways, for example by transnational corporate networks. In such a world regionalism would have a role, as one level of governance, as a means for states to manage certain common problems which were identified as being handled best at a regional level. In this vision successful regionalisms would add to the overlapping authorities and identities which made up the world order. They would not signal the beginning of a return to the state of nature and the war of all against all.

Notes

1. S. P. Huntington, 'The Clash of Civilizations?', *Foreign Affairs*, 72, 3 (1993) 22–49.
2. F. Fukuyama, *The End of History and the Last Man* (London: Hamish Hamilton, 1992)
3. P. Krugman, *Peddling Prosperity* (New York: Norton, 1994)
4. M. Albert, *Capitalism against Capitalism* (London: Whurr, 1993)
5. A. Gamble, 'Economic Recession and Political Disenchantment', *West European Politics*, 18, 3 (1995) 158–74.
6. G. Arrighi, *The Long Twentieth Century* (London: Verso, 1994).
7. The term was originally used by H. Bull, *The Anarchical Society* (London: Macmillan, 1977). For contemporary use, see R. W. Cox, 'Structural Issues of Global Governance: Implications for Europe', in S. Gill (ed.), *Gramsci, Historical Materialism, and International Relations* (Cambridge: CUP, 1994).

Index

265